Schönberg
and
Kandinsky

Contemporary Music Studies

A series of books edited by Peter Nelson and Nigel Osborne, University of Edinburgh, UK

Schönberg
and
Kandinsky

An Historic Encounter

Edited by
Konrad Boehmer
Royal Conservatory, The Hague, The Netherlands

 harwood academic publishers
Australia • Canada • China • France • Germany • India
Japan • Luxembourg • Malaysia • The Netherlands • Russia
Singapore • Switzerland • Thailand • United Kingdom

Amsteldijk 166
1st Floor
1079 LH Amsterdam
The Netherlands

British Library Cataloguing in Publication Data
Schönberg and Kandinsky: an historic encounter. -
  (Contemporary music studies)
  1. Schönberg, Arnold, 1874–1951 - Congresses   2. Kandinsky,
  Wassily, 1866–1944 - Congresses   3. Art and music - Congresses
  I. Boehmer, Konrad
  700.9'22

  ISBN 90-5702-047-5

Front and back cover illustrations:
Die glückliche Hand, © A. Schönberg c/o Beeldrecht Amstelveen
Composition VI, 1912, © W. Kandinsky c/o Beeldrecht Amstelveen

Contents

Contents

Introduction to the Series

The rapid expansion and diversification of contemporary music is explored in this international series of books for contemporary musicians. Leading experts and practitioners present composition today in all aspects—its techniques, aesthetics and technology, and its relationships with other disciplines and currents of thought—as well as using the series to communicate actual musical materials.

The series also features monographs on significant twentieth-century composers not extensively documented in the existing literature.

Nigel Osborne

Preface

One of the main paradoxes of 20th-century art is that which opposes invention and composition. Whether it be Italian Futurism, the 'automatic writing' of French Surrealism, the international Dada-movement on the eve of World War I, or Action Painting, Fluxus, Pop Art and Chance Composition after World War II, they all put forward psychological, aesthetic or ideological reasons to explain their rejection of the principle of *composition* which most of them considered old-fashioned, or belonging to the 'bourgeois' era. The emphasis most of these currents put on new artistic material as such leads us to question to what extent modern art is identical with its material, no longer able to develop its own narrative structures and aesthetic norms. It might seem to a superficial observer that the afore-mentioned avant-garde art forms are the main initiatives of the fundamental transformation which all art has undergone in our century. This selective view forgets that there have been other very important currents of aesthetic renewal, which have had more differen-tiated opinions concerning the relation between material innovation and composition. It was their firm conviction that any artistic material is not just a given fact but is the *result* of compositional processes. Thus any true renewal of the artistic material should be motivated by new ideas about language and form.

The historic encounter around 1911 between the composer Arnold Schönberg and the painter Wassily Kandinsky occurred at a moment when the first wild revolts against traditional art, Dada and Futurism, had just manifested themselves. Independently of those – sometimes spectacular – activities, both Schönberg and Kandinsky had already come to the conclusion that the material and the compositional methods they had relied on in the past were exhausted and did not satisfy the development of their artistic ideas. Both artists had already submitted their modes of production to a critical analysis which resulted in Schön-berg's 'Theory of Harmony' and Kandinsky's 'Concerning the Spiritual in Art', both of 1911 – indeed the two artists had already been putting their self-criticism into practice for some time. In Schönberg's case this led to breaking with tonality; Kandinsky effected the transition to 'abstract' painting. Their mutual contact had not only considerable consequences for the further development of the two artists themselves, but also a profound impact on the evolution of music and painting in general.

When in January 1993 the Royal Conservatory in The Hague organised a symposium on Schönberg and Kandinsky, it did so for practical and artistic reasons. The symposium was part of a larger series of events celebrating the inauguration of the new premises of the Institute of Sonology and the Department of Sound and Image. As both institutions deal with problems of 'synesthetic' phenomena in modern art and collaborate closely together, they decided to concentrate on the contact between Schönberg and Kandinsky and the revolutionary consequences it had for modern music and painting. The lecturers are specialists in their respective fields, but amongst a (fortunately) increasing number of Fellows dealing with the work of the composer or the painter we chose those who had a special affinity with both of them. It was not our purpose to organise a 'synesthetic' symposium which could have led to a kind of 'symphonic poem'. What we intended, rather, was a survey on the *specific* problems inherent to the work and experiments of both artists, to create a better understanding for their common roots and motivations. Synestheticism is not a simple mix between pictorial and musical elements, although the modern culture industry (in its 'avant-garde' or 'trash' manifestations) tries to suggest the persuasive power of such a superficial approach. Though mixing up sound, image, rhythms and words seems to be *the* formula of our present world, we were convinced that it should be our task to choose a *structural model* from recent history to prove that *real* artistic renewal lies not on the surface but in the essence.

My special thanks go to Frans Evers, who organised the entire gigantic ante-show, and to my colleague Dick Raaijmakers who translated the idea of Schönberg's music theatre *Die glückliche Hand* into a fascinating new piece: *Die glückliche Hand – Geöffnet* (a de-composition of the historical work, creating a dialectical opposition *and* synthesis of Schönberg's 'synesthetic' dreams). My thanks go to Henk Guittart, who realised a marvellous project and performance of Schönberg's *Pierrot Lunaire*, and to Frans de Ruiter, Director of the Royal Conservatory, who made it all possible and delivered the necessary bottles of Spanish champagne. My special thanks go to Mr Anton Scheuer who still keeps us busy, leading us towards new adventures and new perspectives of artistic productivity.

Konrad Boehmer

Introduction

The Schönberg–Kandinsky Symposium

In the second week of January 1993 The Hague was the setting of an international symposium about the relationship between the composer Arnold Schönberg and the visual artist Wassily Kandinsky. The symposium was held to celebrate some newly formed alliances between a number of different art institutes: the Municipal Museum of The Hague (Haags Gemeentemuseum), the Royal Conservatory, the Institute of Sonology, the Royal Academy of Fine Arts and the Interfaculty of Image and Sound.

A recurrent theme in the evolution of modern art is the interest of some generations of artists in developing forms of art in which music, theatre, the visual arts and language are brought together to create new intermediary effects. The challenge to develop new approaches for multimedia creativity has been accelerated by modern CD-ROM technology, but at present there is a fundamental lack of knowledge of intermediary creative effects caused by the different languages of over-specialised professionals. Unfortunately, Kandinsky's criticism of the 19th-century cultural over-specialisation has not lost anything of its validity. In contrast, professional differentiation is still the main stream of professional development, and is especially manifest in scientific endeavor, which has become even more specialistic than ever before. Despite some hopeful expectations aroused by the generalistic tendencies of information science and cognitive science, we are still far from understanding complex intermediary relationships. Therefore it is important to be aware of the early attempts of artists who wished to relate and combine different forms of art.

A century and a half ago, Wagner introduced the concept of the *Gesamtkunstwerk* in his attempt to create all-embracing perceptual effects, which resulted in an unprecedented enhancement of experienced intensity, based on a parallelism of music, movement, drama, choreography and stage design. Reflecting on Wagner's concept, Kandinsky proposed in 1911 an alternative approach based on composed juxtaposition and opposition of expressive means. In his view, the 'Monumental Theatre' should consist of contrasting Wagner's effect of doubling with an effect of abstraction, a temporal isolation of the inner voice of the music, the movement, the visual stage effects, and the text. 'Indeed, people thought: two is greater than one, and sought to strengthen every effect by means of repetition. As regards the inner effect, however, the reverse may be true, and often one is greater than two. Mathematically, $1 + 1 = 2$. Spiritually $1 - 1$ can $= 2$.' Kandinsky shared with Schönberg the need to show the existence of an unconscious reality, or, as Schönberg called it when writing *Die glückliche Hand*, an imagined 'extreme unreality'. Because of the turmoil resulting from the First World War, Kandinsky was not able to get his theatrical experiments staged and Schönberg had to wait many years for his première, though he was disappointed by the result. Despite the impossibility of realising and extending their experiments, it is still exciting to study the thoughts and proposals of these geniuses, especially when one considers the later genesis and rise of the 'open' art form in the '50s and '60s.

The initial proposal to focus on the theme of interdisciplinarity in the arts by organising a symposium on the relationship between Schönberg and Kandinsky was made by Hans Locher, the present director of the Haags Gemeentemuseum, together with the prominent Schönberg expert, Henk Guittart, when they were discussing the possibility of performing Schönberg's *Pierrot Lunaire* in front of Kandinsky's painting *Bild mit weisser Form* in the Museum. At the same time the Conservatory was planning one of the first Interfaculty projects, a new production of Schönberg's music theatre piece *Die glückliche Hand*, on the occasion of the opening of fifteen new studios which had been built by the Royal Conservatory to create new space for the Departments of Music Registration, Sonology, and Image and Sound. The last ten years have witnessed a substantial expansion, within the Conservatory, of the degree programs and of the teaching facilities of music-related media. The first electronic studio for composition students in the Royal Conservatory had already been opened in 1966 by Dick Raaijmakers and Jan Boerman. At the beginning of the eighties a new training course was added in the field of sound technology: Music Registration. In 1986 the Institute of Sonology was moved from the University of Utrecht to the Royal Conservatory. In 1989 the Royal Conservatory merged with the Royal Academy of Fine Arts. Using this organisational concentration of different art disciplines I developed a new program, offered by the newly formed Interfaculty of Image and Sound, for students who wanted to study interdisciplinary art forms. The Haags Gemeentemuseum played an important role in the development of this program. In 1988, after years of research and discussion, the music department of the Museum opened its first exhibition

''Electric Music: Three Years of Acquisition of Electric Musical Instruments'', followed shortly after by ''Anti Qua Musica'', an exhibition about the 'open' musical instrument, proposed and realised by Raaijmakers. Since that time the Museum has owned the first (and probably the world's most important) collection of electric musical instruments, including Mauricio Kagel's Zwei-Mann-Orchester. Inspired by the history of the electronic composition studio of the Royal Conservatory, with its cultivation of serial techniques, open forms and action-oriented attitude, in 1990 a communal project was launched: the Aula Lectures. The idea was to offer new courses and formats (like the multidisciplinary course ''The Language of Image and Sound'') in the Aula (Hall) of the Haags Gemeentemuseum, in which students from different arts courses could be brought together: music students, fine art students, art history students, musicology students and students from the new departments for media arts.

With support of the Los Angeles-based Schönberg Institute a Symposium program was developed, consisting of lectures, workshops and performances. The papers which were presented in the Symposium are printed in the present volume. They show different aspects of the spirit of avant-garde which started in the period 1910–13, when Schönberg as well as Kandinsky formulated their far-reaching views on the ways in which music and painting should develop, and discussed their common interest in new theatrical forms of presentation. As a preparation for the Symposium, two workshops were organised in December 1992 for students who were interested in the historical analysis of the performance practice of *Pierrot Lunaire* and *Die glückliche Hand*.

The *Pierrot Lunaire* workshop focussed on the analysis of a wide range of historical presentation experiments: scenic, semi-scenic, concert, cinematic, etc. This workshop was given by Henk Guittart, Marianne Pousseur, Hans Jansen and Hans Locher, and culminated on the first day of the Symposium in a performance of the piece in the Kandinsky Hall of the Gemeentemuseum, where the music was played against the background of the *Bild mit weisser Form* and surrounded by other paintings by Kandinsky, which fostered a new encounter with the spirits of Schönberg and Kandinsky such as had never been experienced before.

The workshop on *Die glückliche Hand*, which had been prepared by a collective of teachers of the Royal Conservatory directed by Raaijmakers, concentrated on the dramatic central role of the light-crescendo, and on Schönberg's early wish to present the work as a film, supported by the use of an electric organ of the Aeolian Company, one of the first mechanical player pianos. In 1924 and in 1930 the piece was performed in ways

Schönberg had not liked at all. His efforts to compose 'with all theatrical means' had to result in an 'extreme unreality' – a result which, in his lifetime, was never accomplished. In the few post-war performances, often only the music was performed; or, when a theatrical performance was staged, the essential *Licht- und Sturmcrescendo* was entirely neglected. In the workshop it was found that Schönberg had taken great care in composing the crescendo, which he based on a spiral development of the color circle, starting with one cycle of the dark colors (reddish, brown, dirty green, blue-grey, violet, dark red) and culminating in a second cycle of bright colors (blood-red, orange, 'yelling' yellow, bright yellow). The movement of light was paralleled by a shift of orchestral coloration from string- to brass-instruments, combined with the increasing intensity of the noises of a wind machine.

To do justice to the complexities of Schönberg's approach to theatre ('making music with the media of the stage') it was decided that the performance would start with a prelude, consisting of a reconstruction of the expressionistic and often rather emotional style of drama of the early years of the 20th century, accompanied by music recorded by the Columbia Symphony Orchestra and Chorus under the direction of Robert Craft. After this prelude, the piece was 'opened': musical fragments and scenic elements were recomposed, using electronic studio techniques: computer and tape synthesis; slide-, video- and filmprojections; high voltage lighting objects; prisms, open flames, etc. These elements were linked together as much as possible, using morphing techniques, in which one type of form or style was transformed into another form or style. These changes were considered as 'crescendos', connecting the authentic expressionist style of drama with the modern approach of object theatre, linking the 'sound culture' of Robert Craft with the sound culture of electronic composition as exemplified by Jan Boerman, and relating asynchronous stage events with precise moments of synchronised movements and rests. The applied method of opening the piece by a recomposition of its elements created the possibility of integrating Kandinsky's important new insights into stage composition which he had published as an introduction to the stage work *Der gelbe Klang* in the almanac *Der blaue Reiter* (1912). Thus the piece which was presented during the Symposium in the Schönberg Hall of the Royal Conservatory was finally called *Die glückliche Hand – Geöffnet*. In it, Kandinsky's principle of contrast, or juxtaposition, was combined with an extension of Schönberg's principle of the light-sound crescendo 'with all the media of the theatre'. Thanks to the unconventional presentations of *Pierrot Lunaire* and *Die glückliche Hand – Geöffnet* during the symposium, a one-dimensional retrospective view on

Schönberg and Kandinsky was avoided. It was shown that, even today, totally new and unexpected extrapolations can be made in which the modernist spirit is revitalised.

The important role of new technologies in the contemporary experiments in music theatre and multimedia was anticipated by Schönberg and Kandinsky, since they both had stressed the necessity of using electrical light-color compositions in their stage experiments. To honor the early experimenters with electric light, a number of pioneers of light art were invited to participate in the Symposium and to give demonstrations of their early experiments with the electric media. On the opening night these artists presented their historic contributions under the title "The Academy of Light", an event sponsored by the Municipality of The Hague. The name for this event was borrowed from László Moholy-Nagy, who in 1946 proposed the formation of an Institute of Light where artists could study light technology as an artistic tool. Christian Sidenius, "Lumia" artist in the tradition of Thomas Wilfred, could not attend on account of ill health. So a videotape with examples of "Lumia" light projections was running while the audience took their seats in the Aula of the Gemeentemuseum. The evening was opened by Christa van Santen who presented the first Academy of Light Awards to Lev Theremin, Elfriede Fischinger, Gustav Metzger, Bulat Galeyev and William Moritz.

96-year-old Lev Theremin then gave a speech about his work in electronic communication, sound synthesis and the projection of light-music. Despite his weak voice, he was able to share this special blend of revolutionary enthusiasm and industrious sophistication, which is so typical of the Russian pioneers, with the highly attentive audience. His performance acquired a historical dimension when he mounted the stage to perform on the Theremin. In 1921 he himself had invented this instrument – the world's first completely electronic musical instrument – which has only recently been added to the collection of the music department of the Gemeentemuseum. Only since 1989 had Theremin, who generally was believed to have died in Stalin's concentration camps, been allowed to visit places outside the USSR. After the Bourges Festival in France, he visited the centennial of Stanford University in the USA in 1991. Theremin's performance at the Schönberg–Kandinsky Symposium was his last public appearance. On the 3rd of November 1993 Lev Sergeyevich Theremin died in Moscow aged 97. The music he had played on the Theremin was identified by Konrad Boehmer as being the peace tune of the Komsomol, the youth organisation of the former Soviet Union.

After Theremin's performance, Bulat Galeyev, another prominent example of Russian spiritual techno-syncretism, projected and discussed video fragments of artistic and technological achievements made by the members of his group "Prometheus", named after Skriabin's symphony in which he introduced a light-organ, "Luce", into the symphony orchestra. In 1962 Galeyev had founded a studio of music-kinetic art in Kazan, the capital of the Tatar Republic. "Prometheus" has been engaged in a variety of large-scale public projects, including laser art concerts and 'son et lumière'; and All-Union Conferences on Light and Music were organised between 1967 and 1986. After Galeyev's introduction, Gustav Metzger gave a spectacular performance of parts of his work in which auto-destructive principles are used to create sound and light effects. Metzger, who applied these effects in the concerts of different pop groups like The Move, Cream and The Who in the 1960s in London, showed the auto-creativity of auto-destruction. It is hard to communicate the feeling of suspense engendered by his performance. The disappearance of a piece of nylon, caused by the heat of the lamp of the slide-projector, created a time-event in which, after a slow transformation of the structure, the moment of flux – the very sudden change of material structure into pure light – is astounding to watch.

The last demonstration of historic light experiments of "The Academy of Light" was given by Elfriede Fischinger and William Moritz. The instrument they played was the "Lumigraph", an apparatus built by Oskar Fischinger in the years after he had concluded his career as a film-maker and had embarked on the final stage of his life as a painter. The screen of the instrument (borrowed from the Deutsches Filmmuseum Frankfurt am Main) is made of an elastic material which allows the player to form relief patterns by moving the fingers of both hands and by pressing in the cloth. Lamps, mounted on the frame of the screen, throw beams of light on the relief and make it possible to play a ballet of lighted dots and shadow color-stripes, reacting freely to any type of music which is played together with it. The "Lumigraph" offers the possibility of a very sensitive and humorous application of the idea of the light-organ. This instrument embodies the spirit of physical and spiritual relativism which is so often lacking in purely mechanical combinations of color and music, of 'son et lumière'. Until now, the importance of the pioneer work in film animation achieved by Oskar Fischinger, in which musical movement, movement of color and form, and choreographical movement are combined and united in an unprecedentedly elegant way, has been seriously underestimated.

In the workshops of the Schönberg–Kandinsky Symposium, an amalgamation of the creative process of producing art, music and theatre, and of the intellectual process of analysis and historical reflection was attained. It is regrettable that this volume can only offer the papers which were presented at the Symposium. It is impossible to represent in a book the special flavor of the social atmosphere which resulted from the international, inter-institutional and interdisciplinary meeting and exchange. Happily, the texts by J. B. M. Janssen, Klaus Kropfinger, Jelena Hahl-Koch, Bulat Galeyev, Irina L. Vanechkina, Albrecht Dümling, Reinhold Brinkmann, Konrad Boehmer, Job IJzerman and Laurens van der Heijden offer the reader an opportunity to appreciate the timbre of the inner voices of the scholars who participated in the lecture program. This volume, it is hoped, reflects the light directed by them on some important aspects of the works of Arnold Schönberg and Wassily Kandinsky and their historic artistic relationship.

Frans Evers

The Construction of *Painting with White Form* by Wassily Kandinsky

J. B. M. JANSSEN

Since 1975 *Painting with White Form* has been part of the collections of the Haags Gemeentemuseum (Municipal Museum, The Hague). In that year, it entered, together with the painting *Ein Zentrum* of 1922, the collections of Modern Art as a long term loan, in exchange for two early paintings by Piet Mondriaan, the painter that is represented in such an excellent way here in The Hague.

Painting with White Form is a very strange painting. It has, to me at least, a real haunting quality. The after-image of the painting remains in one's thoughts in an ambiguous way: it appears as a purely dramatic abstraction and at the same time it figures as a quite normal representation. It may be possible to compare the picture to a person that desperately wants to behave in a normal way, without being able to conceal the fact that although his actions make sense, none of these actions might be described as conventional.

This quality of the image is somehow rooted in the persistent way it wants to give all the properties it has at once to the onlooker. Firstly, there is a movement of pulsating colors, tumbling forms and rude lines. This movement spins around a very dense center. It loosens its tension somewhat and its energy gives way as it moves centrifugally towards the borders of the image. There is also – and at the same time, it seems (I do not know what version of the image I do want to give priority in describing the perception of the work, because everything seems to happen at once), a rather strange image of hills and skies, of horizons and firmaments, of struggling and mutually opposing protagonists. Finally there is the image that consists of all sorts of different techniques and styles, forged to unity and bringing them together in one single image: we can distinguish broad and bold brushstrokes, elegantly flowing painterly areas, bristly passages, dashing paint, but also very conventional highlighting, next to aggressive scratching, neat and graphic drawing, sudden blots and exploding areas, all this without any apparent system or order.

Now all or most of this occurs in any painting that has some basic quality. But the strange difference is, that in *Painting with White Form* everything seems to be happening all at once, in any case in such a way that it seems very hard if a all, to distinguish between all the levels of perception that I distinguished in my short enumeration. In the literature on *Painting with White Form*, the different authors are somewhat hampered in their description of the work by all this 'hard to distinguish levels of perception'. Will Grohmann chops the work up into three vertical areas, and he does so in complete agreement with Kandinsky who stated that most of his paintings could be described in three parts, like a triptych: the center with the tumbling forms, the right with a very bold drawing and floating colors, and the left with a big, leaning form.

In the footsteps of Grohmann, there are also authors that divide the work into six areas. The three areas that were seen by Grohmann, each of which on its turn could be divided into two: one above and one below. This made visible a back and a front, a conventional 'near the frame' and a 'further away' as in a normal landscape built up along the lines of normal perspective. There is, however, also much to be said in favour of splitting up the image into a indefinite number of loose fragments: all the parts and details of the image are being kept separate in this way, and the overlapping of elements finds a main cause in the crowding, due to the stable and firm border that surrounds the image and binds everything together. Because in the end it must be said that *Painting with White Form* appears as a stable unity.

All these experiences make *Painting with White Form* to be a quite chaotic painting, in any case more chaotic than most of the paintings to be seen in the permanent collection on show in this museum. In the very end it seems that chaos itself is the principle theme and object of this very expressive work of art. Kandinsky himself stated in "Concerning the Spiritual in Art" about this chaotic type of unity, that it was simply a matter of construction. He writes: "The harmony of the new art demands a more subtle construction..., something that appeals less to the eye and more to the soul. This 'concealed construction' may arise from an apparantly fortuitous selection of forms on the canvas. Their external lack of cohesion is their internal harmony."

Now it happens that the concepts of "chaos" and "construction" form the central theme in most of the letters that Kandinsky and Schönberg exchanged between January 1911 and early 1914. Kandinsky, in his first letter, explains to Schönberg that the manner in which most artists try to search for the 'new Harmony' by way of a geometrical strategy is not his way of thinking. His own idea of construction is quite different. It is not to be found by way of geometry, but only by anti-geometrical, anti-logical means. The only possible way is the choice for discord: "Dissonanz statt Consonanz" is the motto of the new art.

What I want to do now, is not to find out what the purpose of this strategy of dissonance was exactly, and why Kandinsky preferred the one over the other. What I want to know is the exact functioning of this aspect of construction in view of *Painting with White Form*. In the center of the image appear rather big and pointed forms, that hide behind one another. The forms seem to swell out from the amount of different colors, with which they are loaded. We can distinguish a blue/green form, a rose/red/white form, a brown/white form, a ochre/green form, and black and dark blue, without any apparent system. They stand out against a poisonous green hill, that marks off a background of dark bordeaux red, in which a meandering line is to be seen, that "finishes" the image towards the frame. This background, together with the flickering, meandering line has something of an upcoming thunder-storm. Seen in this way, the forms below might be read as a landscape.

In this case the image shows the representation of some reality. Grohmann makes clear that what we see here is the landscape around Murnau, where Kandinsky and Gabriele Münter owned a little house. Waston Long instead sees a disguised reference to the "tumbling tower-motive" that Kandinsky used frequently in the years between 1909 and 1914. Further there is this remarkable "phasing" of the color-application: Peg Weis relates this "phasing" to the theory of color-crystallization by Anton Azbè, one of Kandinky's teachers. This theory favors the vibrating effect caused by the application of different colors in layers next to each other. Peg Weis also refers to the techniques of the woodcut, that Kandinsky made his own and developed and was so fond of since 1906. This technique forces the artist to give up any sense of perspective, to weigh form and line as equal partners in the game of making, and to value positive as well as negative form.

In *Studie zur Berglandschaft mit Dorf* of 1908, one can see why Ringbom was the first to acknowledge the importance of the series of landscapes that Kandinsky made around Murnau between 1908 and 1913. In this and other landscapes he adapted the possibilities of the woodcut in converting an image to the medium of painting. In the adaption from one technique to the other, he transformed his own painting into a very individual style. In two studies, one in watercolor and the other in oil (which is shown here), Kandinsky developed the imagery of this central part of *Painting with White Form*.

If one looks at *Study for Painting with White Form* from Detroit, it is possible to read the image in terms of simple representation. One can

Figure 1 Kandinsky, *Painting with White Form*
© W. Kandinsky c/o Beeldrecht Amsterdam

clearly distinguish the hills of the near distance, the sky above, the rain-
bow, or perhaps better, a waterfall breaking halfway in its course on some
obstacle, a house with a chimney, and pointed trees behind the house.
What is excluded from this ordinary reading are the flame-like elements
in the foreground. Also missing is a reading of the circle-segments in
front of the house. Both of these elements will play an important role in
the further transformations of *Painting with White Form* before it will take
its definite form. The main difference with ordinary representation is the
crowding of the flattened, single-colored elements and the resulting den-
sity of the forms that make up the image. Further, one has to get used to
some remarkable features in the picture: the strange, unreliable elonga-
tion of for example the hillside to the left, the geometrization of natural
features and the spattered skies above.

When one searches through the work of Kandinsky produced between 1910 and 1914, one finds several examples of such distortions. There is the *Romantische Landschaft* of 1911 where the elongated hills are initially to be seen as a first instance of the geometrization of natural features and the flattening of forms through the single-coloring of shapes.

To the left of the center of *Painting with White Form*, the image shows a strangely floating, a morphous, white shape. It is highlighted and the color is tightly fitting into the jacket of its contour. Thus the form appears as a volume, something that cannot be said of most of the other forms in *Painting with White Form*. More than likely this is the form that is alluded to in the title. It is floating in the air, statically and quietly. Judging from the white areas in the middle of the yellow form, it seems to have been released by the yellow form, or for that matter, emanated from this form. In connection to this observation it should be noted that Kandinsky describes the color white, in "Concerning the Spiritual in Art", as harmonious and quiet, full of expectations for the future. In the same context, yellow, in contrast to blue, could be conceived of as warm color, with bodily, excentric movement towards the spectator. An admixture of blue, as is the case in our painting, introduces a sickly and unreal quality to the yellow. All this can be read into the painting.

But one can also interpret *Painting with White Form* as a quite realistic image, a representation the way Rose-Carol Washton Long conceives of the painting. She deduces from photographs of spiritistic apparitions, published by the Russian scientist A. Aksakov, that the white form, together with the yellow form, must be interpreted as an apparition of a ghost that dangerously hovers with his raised arm towards the landscape in the center. The only problem I have with this interpretation, is that it takes a line of argument in which the image must be conceived of as a normal case of representation. And it was exactly this sort of outward appearance that Kandinsky wanted to get rid of, in the name of the higher goal of expression of the inner need, the "Innere Notwendigkeit" that stood at the core of his art.

A more grave objection to Washton Long's interpretation is that already in the first studies for our painting, Kandinsky conceived of the white form as distinct, static and as having volume and mass. This cannot be said of the yellow form, that is linked up with all the other flat or broken forms that fill the picture. The distinctness, as well as the static, floating massiveness of the white form, links it to the black form in the famous analysis of *Dame in Moskau* of 1912 in the collection of the Lenbachhaus in Munich, resulting in the special device that Ringbom calls "parallel action". The figuration in this image is contrasting with abstract forms and colors that stand presumably for thoughts and emotions. Ringbom links the blue colour around the lady, according to theosophical belief, to the 'health aura' which is strengthened by the sun. A nasty black shape is trying to eclipse the sun on the horizon. It seems the black spot is going to threaten the lady badly. Next to the lady is a rose-red emanation, indicating to Ringbom the presence of love and goodwill. It seems that Kandinsky in this picture expressly contrasted the thoughtforms with the physical forms by way of experiment, to find out about the possibilities of this device.

In *Painting with White Form*, as in other paintings from the same time, Kandinsky is using independent forms to introduce spiritual content at the expense of representational form. The coloring of the form is of considerable importance. In a text published under the title "Mein Werdegang", written in mid 1913 as an introduction for a show in Cologne, Kandinsky recalls the extremely hot summer of 1911, with all its physical stress. The intense light in Munich influenced him heavily: "Plötzlich kam mir die Natur Weiß vor. Das Weiß (das große Schweigen–voll Möglichkeiten) zeigte sich an allen Stellen und verbreitete sich sichtbar. An dieses Gefühl habe ich mich später erinnert, als ich eine besondere Rolle und Pflege des Weiß auf meinen Bildern beobachtete. Seitdem weiß ich, welche ungeahnten Möglichkeiten diese Urfarbe in sich birgt." One is tempted to conclude that in *Painting with White Form* as well, the white form has the possibility to color a situation with its immanent 'Hauptklang' as Kandinsky calls it.

To the right, there is an equally prominent form visible, flat and blue/black, toothed along the upper side as if it was a comet, shooting out of a bordeaux-red sky into the pale green area that provides the border between the central area and the area to the right. This shape is aggressive and introduces movement in the painting and acts therefore in complete contrast to the white form.

The conception of the blue-black form was not intended from the start as a contrast to the white form. In the Detroit oil sketch for our painting it is lacking completely. In a further study in pen and ink from a private collection in New York, we can see the form in statu nascendi, as trees and architectural forms, being drawn in one color. They tend to collude somehow. This collusion becomes evident in the last study, a watercolor in the collection of the Museum of Modern Art in New York. Here we can see the fusion of forms that do not have any relationship beforehand. Outside this center the image is less hectic and crowded. To the right there is a waving line that acts as the horizon for a landscape made up of red, violet, orange ochre, yellow and finally a dirty white. On top of this plane there is superimposed a rude drawing, that accompanies a set of colormarkings in red/brown, green, orange/red, yellow and white. Above all, it is the white plane that anchors this part of the image and that brings breadth in line and color.

In the first study for *Painting with White Form* this side of the painting was not foreseen. It only pops up in the second drawing in pen and ink. This may account for the difference in style of this part of the painting in comparison to the central and the left part. Especially the confusing mass of short lines and floating colors, in such discordance to the rest of the painting, is remarkable.

It is a very good example of how Kandinsky uses free floating colors as a means to attain the goal of eliminating materialistic representation. Kandinsky chose this strategy in accordance with anthroposophic theory which stated that only in the material world, color binds itself to objects and to forms. Washton Long interprets the lines and colors as horses, engaged in battle. Rudenstine relates the configuration to the limp towers that acted so centrally in Kandinsky's art that he chose to use the image as the cover illustration for "Über das Geistige in der Kunst". In *Painting with White Form* the image is disintegrating completely and ends up as a confusing mass of straight and curved lines and blots of yellow, ochre and blue. In this way Kandinsky transforms the original motive into a strictly formal structure, as described by himself in a text about the painting *Kleine Freuden* of 1913, now in the collection of the Guggenheim Museum in New York. Here he describes the city on top of the mountain as "ein Durcheinander von Linien und Farben" of the plane below.

In the air above the disintegrated city there hovers a swarm of sharp, short strokes and blots. Judging from *Kleine Freuden*, this swarm might be interpreted as an explosion of light and energy, emanating from the edge of the picture, as is so often the case in Kandinsky's work from these years. Comparison to the pen/ink study learns that the source for this instant, might have been the testing of the pen with which the study was going to be made.

To the left of our painting, there is more calm and tranquillity than everywhere else. The forms are big and easy to read, it seems. The yellow form dominates, together with a darkly green/blue background. Halfway through the yellow form we can distinguish a green cloud, sprouting from the backbone of the yellow and marked off from the background by a piping of white paint. From this green cloud, there explodes towards the upper edge of the painting, a fan of ochre. To the right of this fan, a notched, grey form is visible, which appears like the slim sister of the black comet in the center. From the green cloud, there appear three white lines, hanging down towards the left edge of the painting where they meet some lost lines and color blots that introduce a primitive form of perspective in the painting, a "before" and a "behind" that creates the illusion of space. All these elements belonged in the beginning of the development of the painting to one, undivided image of a landscape. Therefore we have here a perfect example of the disintegrating force of the division of elements and motives. This division might have been caused by two peculiarities. In the first place, the decision to transform the lower part of what I call "the waterfall" into three lines, might have been informed by the continuous presence of the three ochre lines in the middle area of the painting. In the second place, the decision to transform the "breaking water" of the waterfall into the independent green cloud might have been informed by the enormous pains Kandinsky took in designing the central motive for another painting that haunted him at the time of the making of *Painting with White Form*. This is *Painting with White Border* of 1913, also in the collection of the Guggenheim. Kandinsky describes the white piping as "the accidental sound of an inner simmering". As a motive it is possible to trace it back to the image of St. George. This same inner simmering recurs in *Painting with White Form* as the contour of exactly the same form. With the pen and ink studies for *Painting with White Border* in mind, one is easily inclined to conclude that Kandinsky here changes completely his starting-point and transforms the meaning of a form from – what I call "breaking water", but what can certainly be not interpreted as a riding horseman – into the central motive of his art.

This hypothesis is supported by what happens in the central lower part of the image. Here the same forms occur, three in line with an ochre piping, formalized into the tense curves that characterize the horse-rider. The three curves get company in the form of the ochre stripes that might be read as lances and in the white meandering border that might be read as horses. The conclusion is tempting that as an image, *Painting with White Form* works simultaneously on different levels of representational strategy. As a construction, paintings like *Painting with White Form* are sort of machines that are able to transform representations, themes and motives in a continuous process of assimilation. The methods used in this process of assimilation are abbreviation of forms and motives, extension of forms and motives, resolution of forms and motives, fusion of forms and motives and, finally, disintegration of forms and motives. The effect all this has is the continuous mingling of form and content and the heavily relying on the concepts of contingency and association in the formation of the image.

Latent Structural Power versus the Dissolution of Artistic Material in the Works of Kandinsky and Schönberg

KLAUS KROPFINGER

"Gegensätze und Widersprüche – das ist unsere Harmonie"[1] (Kandinsky 1911)

I

On January 18, 1911 Kandinsky first wrote to Arnold Schönberg. The impulse for his letter came from a concert the painter had attended on January 2, 1911 accompanied by Franz Marc, Alexei Jawlensky, Marianne Werefkin, and others, in which the program included performances of Schönberg's *String Quartets* in D (op. 7), in F-sharp (op. 10) (1907/08), five songs from op. 2 and op. 6, and the *Piano Pieces* op. 11 (1909).[2] To the composer, Kandinsky wrote:

> "In your works, you have realized what I, albeit in uncertain form, have so greatly longed for in music. The independent progress through their own destinies, the independent life of the individual voices in your compositions, is exactly what I am trying to find in my paintings. At the moment there is a great tendency in painting to discover the 'new' harmony by constructive means, whereby the rhythmic is built on an almost geometric form. My own instinct and striving can support these tendencies only half-way. Construction is what has been so woefully lacking in the painting of recent times, and it is good that it is now being sought. But I think differently about the type of construction. I am certain that our own modern harmony is not to be found in the 'geometric' way, but rather in the anti-geometric, anti-logical way. And this way is that of 'dissonances in art['], in painting, therefore, just as much as in music. And 'today's' dissonance in painting and music is merely the consonance of 'tomorrow'"[3]

Schönberg and Kandinsky apparently saw each other for the first time on September 14, 1911;[4] in reality, however, they had already met mentally, that is, on artistic grounds, at the beginning of the year. It is highly significant that Kandinsky, after having heard Schönberg's astounding new compositions, wrote a letter to the composer almost immediately in which he reflected on fundamental aspects of the artistic process, not in terms of music *or* painting, but of music *and* painting. His reaction indicates the degree to which artistic evocation and reflection among artists at the threshold of abstraction, were no more than two sides of the same coin. It also demonstrates in Kandinsky a readiness to grasp and perceive the pivotal importance of the music of Schönberg, who at this time and for decades to come would struggle for acceptance. Last but not least, the painter's letter stands as an 'essay' in reception theory insofar as it points to the importance of an artist's readiness for aesthetic and intellectual communication and exchange.[5] Kandinsky's own reflections are matched by those of friends such as Franz Marc, who – no less impressed by Schönberg than Kandinsky – wrote on January 14 of the same year to August Macke:

> *"Can you imagine a music in which tonality (that is, the adherence to any key) is completely suspended? I was constantly reminded of Kandinsky's large composition, which also permits no trace of tonality...and also of Kandinsky's 'jumping spots' in hearing this music, which allows each tone sounded to stand on its own (a kind of white canvas between the spots of color!) Schönberg proceeds from the principle that the concepts of consonance and dissonance do not exist at all. A so-called dissonance is only a more remote consonance – an idea which now occupies me constantly while painting...."[6]*

II

The idea of dissonance being nothing more than 'remote consonance' was prefigured by a poster for the January concert in which short excerpts from the chapter on 'Parallel Octaves and Fifths' in Schönberg's *Theory of Harmony* were presented graphically.[7] These theoretical excerpts, which were appropriated by the concert promoter to render something like a catchy headline, were soon taken up as watchwords for the avant-garde of painters in the ambit of Kandinsky. He immediately reacted by obtaining, translating, and publishing the text as part of the catalogue of an exhibition of Russian artists organized by Vladimir Aleksejeff Izdebskij at Odessa, Kiev, and St. Petersburg in 1910–1911.[8] And, it is precisely this interpretation of dissonance that played an important role in Kandinsky's own treatise *On the Spititual in Art*, which appeared in 1911. Here he refers explicitly to the excerpt from Schönberg's *Theory of Harmony*.

> *"The Viennese composer Arnold Schönberg, with his total renunciation of accepted beauty, regarding as sacred every means that serves the purpose of self-expression, goes his lonely way unrecognized, even today, by all but a few enthusiasts. This 'publicity seeker', 'charlatan', and 'bungler' says in his* Theory of Harmony. *'Every chord, every progression is possible. And yet I feel already today that even here there are certain conditions that govern whether I choose this or that dissonance'."[9]*

Both artists confessed that their writings at this stage of development were merely first steps. As Kandinsky puts it:

> *"The characteristics of our harmony today make it self-evident that in our own time it is less possible than ever to establish a ready-made theory, to construct set procedures of pictorial harmonization."*[10]

Kandinsky's remarks resonate in those of Schönberg, who emphasized at the end of his *Theory of Harmony* that:

> *"However much I may theorize in this book – for the most part, in order to refute false theory –, I am compelled to expand narrow and confining conceptions to include the facts ... But not to set up new eternal laws ...."*[11]

He goes on to write:

> *"Hence, I can just as well abstain from giving an aesthetic evaluation of these new harmonies ....."*[12]

In concluding, Schönberg indicates 'tone-color melodies' as the ultimate achievement of this development:

> *"Tone-color melodies! How acute the senses that would be able to perceive them! How high the development of spirit that could find pleasure in such subtle things! In such a domain, who dares ask for theory!"*[13]

III

The shared reluctance of the two artists to theorize definitively – a reluctance absolutely in keeping with artistic development in their milieu – corresponds with the particular way in which they dealt with the aesthetic problems of music and painting. They focused on investigations and reflections Kandinsky describes as the "weighing-up of the inner value of one's material."[14]

In musicology today, there seems to exist a certain – if not a strong – tendency to refrain from use of the term 'material' in the sense that it is introduced and elaborated by Theodor W. Adorno.[15] Clearly we must be aware of the problems inherent in the stringency of historical tendencies according to Adorno's conception, and in his understanding of 'dialectics' in material, which could be directed – as Ernst Krenek perceived – against aristic 'freedom'. These problems would erupt into an epistolary dispute between Adorno and Krenek during the autumn of 1932.[16] However, we should not forget the foreshadowing of a possible shift in Adorno's position when, some three decades later, he wrote in *Vers une musique informelle* that "the material itself is changed by composition. From every coherent one it steps forth fresh and as if new."[17] Neither is it clear to what extent the next passage in Adorno's text, where he writes that "The secret of composition is the strength which transforms the material in a process of proceeding adequacy...."[18] in fact refers to the question of the reduction of 'free will' that so preoccupied Krenek. In Adorno's *Philosophy of New Music* itself, however, it is precisely the dialectics of 'material' that opens the way to a more adequate understanding of the relation between historicity and creative freedom. It seems that even in Adorno's conception, the stringency of material was, finally, relative to the historical configuration.[19] And, it is the example of Schönberg's renunciation of material that eventually undermines the rigidity of the idea.[20] Given its limitation, the essence of Adorno's understanding of 'material' is nonetheless valid, for while

> "musical material has usually been conceived as an inventory of physical resources...,
> Adorno, in contrast, conceived of musical material as sedimented history. Following a
> thought that he first presented in his early lecture 'The Idea of Natural History', he
> described this sedimentation as occurring in such a way that the more the material
> appears as nature, as second nature, the more intensively historical it is. As he wrote
> [in his Philosophy of New Music], the elements of music 'bear historical necessity
> within themselves the more perfectly, the less they are immediately readable as historical
> characters...'."[21/22]

Adorno's stringent definition of artistic material has its roots in Schönberg's free 'atonality'; but Kandinsky's aristic approach has its own affinity to Adorno's notion of material in art.[23] This may be valid above all because both artists' consciousness of material is rooted in a kind of teleological thinking that heightened their sense of strictly progressive traits in artistic material. For both of them, this became the powerful impetus to 'materialize' the progression in the 'new' avant-garde work of art.

According to Kandinsky "...every art bears within it the seed of the future and awakens the strings of the soul...Art is the seer of the future and is a leader....This embarkation on an almost forgotten path of prophetic revelations took place almost simultaneously in the various other arts."[24] Schönberg stresses that "the laws native to the genius...are the laws of future generations."[25] This methodical striving to apply to the artistic material a conception of progressive development, is of larger importance for the understanding and interpretation of their artistic theoretical texts. According to Panofsky, "what an artist has said about his own works must always be interpreted in the light of the works themselves;"[26] reflections on material – when driven to the point of its practical application in a work of art – necessarily cover both aspects. It is clear that the texts of Kandinsky's *On the Spiritual in Art* and Schönberg's *Theory of Harmony*, together with their letters and relevant statements, can be understood as self-interpretative theoretical texts, supporting and supplementing the artists' own writings concerning individual works;[27] but even more important, these 'texts' enlarge our understanding of each of the artists' creative stature and oeuvre *as a whole*.[28]

The interplay of reflection and practice in terms of artistic material may also demonstrate that artistic intentions, encompassing the whole horizon of the artist's mind, are relevant for the understanding of the art work. The focus on the 'whole horizon' is especially important for Schönberg and Kandinsky, who each charge their material with expression, rooted in an 'internal necessity' that is the core of human existence, in order to pave the way to the future.[29] This is an argument that opposes the rigid concept of "intentional fallacy" according to which "the design or intention of the author is neither available nor desirable as a standard for judging the success of a work of literary art"[30] – a hotly-debated paradigm which in the meantime has been applied to the visual arts as well as music.[31] It is clear that what artists consciously or unconsciously experience and intend does not 'contain' the work of art;[32] but this does not nullify the relevance of the artist's ideas, commentaries, and sketches as means of approaching a process of analysis and understanding in which the *dialogue* between written/outlined texts and the work of art plays a role.

Adorno has also applied his definition of artistic material to the elements of painting. In his *Aesthetic Theory*, he writes that

> "*Material . . . is the stuff the artist controls and manipulates: words, colors, sounds . . . Material, then, is all . . . that he must make a decision about, and that includes forms as well, for forms too can become materials . . . The state of the material largely also determines innovative expansion into unknown areas. The concept of material is for instance crucial if we want to distinguish between a composer operating with sounds that belong to tonality and its derivatives, and another composer who radically eliminates them. This distinction is a material one. Along the same lines, representational versus abstract, perspectival versus nonperspectival, and a host of other conceptual pairs are all distinctions made at the level of materials.*"[33]

Adorno surmised that in this sense, the term 'material' might not have entered the artist's mind earlier than the 1920s.[34] However both

Schönberg's *Theory of Harmony* and Kandinsky's *On the Spiritual in Art* bear witness to the fact that the aspect of material, bearing historical and consequently also mental or spiritual implications, had already arisen in both their thinking and writing before this time. On the one hand, Schönberg writes that "The material of music is the tone."[35] This comes up in the chapter on 'Consonance and Dissonance', that is, as regards the necessity to prove the relativity of dissonance within the range of natural laws governing overtones. On the other hand, he distinguishes between "natural laws," which "admit no exception," and the "laws of art," which "consist mainly of exceptions."[36] This rests on his more fundamental assertion that art, "in its most advanced state,[37] ... is exclusively concerned with the representation of inner nature."[38] The artist expresses himself, "according to the laws of *his* nature."[39] The real artist, doing "only what is necessary for him to do,"[40] strives "toward the future," in that he believes "in the new," which he thinks "is that *Good* and that *Beauty* toward which we strive with our innermost being."[41]

Schönberg theorizes a historical development that deviates from the laws which have been fixed as 'natural'; following this, he declares those sounds and harmonic progressions – those dissonances – which up to then had been considered 'ugly', 'exceptions' to be excluded, or 'problems' to be resolved, to be on the contrary fundamental and 'normal'. This striving for the new, however, has as its corollary those elements of material that become obsolete. Schönberg argues in terms of a double strategy, whereby 'nature' and 'history' function, so to speak, like communicating channels.[42] He weighs the historically developed phenomena of material in music against the final aim of his endeavors: their justification 'in accord' with both nature and history. In a striking example of his view of an historic development that brings about not only progress but also the erosion of material, Schönberg presents the diminished seventh chord:

"Wherever one wanted to express pain, excitement, anger, or some other stronger feeling – there we find, almost exclusively, the dimished seventh chord. So it is in the music of Bach, Haydn, Mozart, Beethoven, Weber, etc. Even in Wagner's early works it plays the same role. But soon the role was played out. This uncommon, restless, undependable guest, here today, gone tomorrow, settled down, became a citizen, a retired philistine. The chord had lost the appeal of novelty, hence, it had lost its sharpness, but also its luster. It had nothing more to say to a new era. Thus, it fell from the higher sphere of art music to the lower of music for entertainment. . . . It became banal and effeminate. . . . Other chords took its place . . . These were the augmented triad, certain altered chords, and some sonorities that, having already been introduced in the music of Mozart or Beethoven by virtue of suspension or passing tones, appeared in that of Wagner as independent

chords.... Yet, these too were soon worn out, soon lost their charm; and that explains why so quickly after Wagner, whose harmonies seemed unbelievably bold to his contemporaries, new paths were sought: The diminished seventh chord provoked this movement, which cannot stop before it has fulfilled the will of nature...so that we can then turn away from the external model and more and more toward the internal, toward the one within us."[43]

The correspondence of these passages with Adorno's arguments is obvious. In *Reaction and Progress* Adorno emphasizes that

"As has often been noticed, the proportion of overtones, for example, which could be used as the strongest element of tension in the diminished seventh chord, given the state of the material during Beethoven's time, at a later state of the material becomes an innocent consonance, and with Reger, it is devalued to the extent that it becomes an unqualified means of modulation."[44]

That the historical state of material also determines the artistic consciousness of Kandinsky is demonstrated by many details in *On the Spiritual in Art*. In accordance with the title, the "weighing-up of the inner value of one's material" suggests an evaluation of the material's historically developed and sedimented qualities. The 'inner sounding' of colors and forms, their structural and latent relational values, are taken as the measure of artistic quality and applied to the development of material in painting – as occurs in the paintings of Delacroix, Cézanne, Monet, Signac, Matisse, Hodler, Segantini, and Picasso,[45] as well as those of of Manet, Van Gogh, and Gauguin.[46] Kandinsky's scrutiny of artistic material is demonstrated by his reflections on the qualities of pictorial material in comparison with those of musical material. Musicians used sounds and combinations of sounds in ways that painting up to that time could only dream of. It was Kandinsky's main concern that painting might be able to derive a language from its own pictorial means, comparable to that which was possible for music:

"An artist who sees that the imitation of natural appearances, however artistic, is not for him – the kind of creative artist who wants to, and has to, express his own inner world – sees with envy how naturally and easily such goals can be attained in music, the least material of the arts today. Understandably, he may turn toward it and try to find the same means in his own art. Hence the current search for rhythm in painting, for mathematical, abstract construction, the value placed today upon the repetition of color tones, the way colors are set in motion, etc."[47]

In a letter of December 18, 1911, published here for the first time,[48] Schönberg writes to Kandinsky:

"I have just read your book [On the Spiritual in the Art] *from cover to cover, and I will read it once more. I find it pleasing to an extraordinary degree, because we agree on nearly all of the main issues..."*[49]

We may assume that it was precisely Kandinsky's special focus on artistic material that gained Schönberg's approval, in particular because Kandinsky stressed the catalytic function of material in music in his notion of weighing the inner value of one's material in painting.

IV

In his effort to investigate the material's "inner sound,"[50] which causes a "vibration from the soul,"[51] Kandinsky went beyond his forerunner's achievements to gauge his own subjective experiences with colors, forms, and relations of colors and colored forms[52] – always keeping his acute experience of music sharply in focus. Kandinsky's knowledge of literature on the topic,[53] as well as his efforts at introspection, are pointed out in the artist's letter to Gabriele Münter of 1915, where he writes

"First I will make different color tests: I will study the dark – deep blue, deep violet, deep dirty green, etc. Often I see the colors before my eyes. Sometimes I imitate with my lips the deep sounds of the trumpet – then I see various deep mixtures which the word is incapable of conceiving and which the palette can only feebly reproduce."[54]

This statement sheds light on his earlier statements in *On the Spiritual in Art*, in particular regarding synesthesia.[55] It shows that Kandinsky was not only synesthetically gifted,[56] but that he experimented with his given capacities. Thus, his remarks on the evocation of movement, tension, and time with colors like yellow and blue[57] show that material in painting includes a whole range of perceptual and spiritual valences. Experiences like these may also have functioned as 'relays' between abstract and objectively allusive pictorial elements, in that their psychological or expressive impact is at once connected with abstract and still figurative elements and shapes.

To train a focus on the issue of material in Kandinsky's *On the Spiritual in Art*, we turn to the second part of the text, starting with 'Effects of Color'. The following aspects are of principal importance:

1   Weighing of the expressive forces of colors: aside from the physical, there is, above all, the psychological effect of colors;

2   Investigation of the potential structural qualities of colors,[58] such as contrasting configurations,[59] and the eccentric and concentric motion of colors;[60]

3   Weighing the 'inner content' of forms;[61]

4   Weighing the relationships between color and form,[62] and the expressive qualities of colored forms;[63]

5   Investigation of the potential structural qualities of forms;[64]

6   Investigation of the potential structural qualities of color plus form, and of colored forms;

7   Investigation of the structural possibilities and 'laws' of *composition* in painting.[65]

Kandinsky emphasized pairs of contrasting colors, declaring yellow and blue to represent the qualities of warm and cold, "as the most important polar opposition among the spectral colors,"[66] followed by black and white,[67] red and green,[68] orange and violet,[69] while red – mediating between extremes – is split in its warm and cold variants.[70] It is well known that Kandinsky's contrast of yellow and blue was related to Goethe's color theory,[71] especially his 'plus-minus' polarity. But Kandinsky was also familiar with Philipp Otto Runge's reflections on color.[72] In his research into the nature of expressive and structural qualities of material, contrasts are of focal import, not least because they require fine distinction and mediation. This is also the case for forms. "Form itself...has its own inner sound;"[73] the fact that there exists a great variety of combinations of color and form as well as of relations between different forms of color, allows for the elaboration of the "principle of contrast"[74] as Kandinsky expressively formulated it.

Kandinsky's 'principle of contrast' was not merely an artistic one in the sense of art for its own sake – a notion he explicitly rejected later on. This is made clear by one of the pivotal passages in *On the Spiritual in Art*, in which he relates art to its historical constellation:

> *"From what has just been said about the effects of color, and from the fact that we live in a time full of questions and premonitions and omens – hence full of contradiction [consider too the divisions of the triangle] – we can easily conclude that harmonization on the basis of simple colors is precisely the least suitable for our own time. It is perhaps with envy, or with a sad feeling of sympathy, that we listen to the works of Mozart. They create a welcome pause amidst the storms of our inner life, a vision of consolation and hope, but we hear them like sounds of another, vanished, and essentially unfamiliar age. Clashing discords, loss of equilibrium, 'principles' overthrown, unexpected drumbeats, great questionings, apparently purposeless strivings, stress and longing (apparently torn apart), chains and fetters broken (which had united many), opposites and contradictions – this is our harmony."*[75]

Artistic material, in Kandinsky's view, not only resonated with 'inner vibration': This inner vibration itself reverberated with tensions and clashes of highly disparate dimensions and origins in the external world. This view is supported by his chapters II on 'Movement', III on 'Spiritual Turning Point', and IV on 'The Pyramid'. They characterize the absurdities of life and the cultural context from which the urgency of genuine art derives.[76]

In his Bauhaus lectures, Kandinsky clearly presented this interconnection between art and life. According to his conception, politics and economy on the one hand, and the spiritual realm on the other, are related to each other like low and high tides. Thus:

> *"Art has two qualities:*
> 1. reflection *of the present time – i.e.: to gain knowledge of the present time by analysis of art;*
> 2. building up *of the future – i.e.: to portend things to come*
>   *beyond our time*   *That is the way one can*
>   *where do both directions come from?*   *recognize past, present time*
>   *from the past*   *and future by art."*[77]

It is this comprehensive sensitivity of the artist that also characterizes Schönberg. In an aphorism of 1909, he had declared art to be the outcry of those who experience, envisage, and tackle the fate of mankind as their own:

> *"Art is despairing cry of those who experience the destiny of mankind as their own. Who not do acquiesce to it, but who stand out against it. Who do not stupidly work the machine's 'dark powers', but who throw themselves into the wheel[s] in order to conceive the construction. Who do not avert their eyes in order to shield themselves against emotions; but who open them wide, in order to tackle what must be tackled. Who, however, often close their eyes in order to become aware of what the senses cannot convey, in order to intuit what only delusively happens in the external world. And internally, within them is the motion of the world; only the repercussion reaches outward: the work of art."*[78]

The work of art, being the product of internal necessity – the innermost impulse of artistic expression and articulation[79] – and the refraction of phenomena belonging to the internal and external worlds,[80] is configured and balanced by a 'sense of form' of which Schönberg is also conscious throughout his *Theory of Harmony*.[81] In a way comparable to Kandinsky,[82] Schönberg distinguishes the 'sense of form' historically.[83] It can be understood as the notion that supersedes all observations, remarks, and reflections on the single musical element's valence of structural relationships.

These touch upon the "balanced relation of motives of harmony,"[84] as they encompass (among other phenomena) the "sense of quality for the right harmonic progression,"[85] "relations of balance between individual chords and in chord progressions,"[86] the choice of dissonances,[87] the "weighing of root progressions,"[88] the "well-proportioned" close of a composition,[89] the constructive valence of modulation,[90] the structural function of harmonic "regions,"[91] the relationship of construction and ornament,[92] the balanced, consistent placing of vagrant chords,[93] the relationship of theme and harmonics in "suspended tonality,"[94] the structural relationship of "chords with six or more tones,"[95] the balancing and coherence of "tone-color melodies."[96] The stages in the progression from the 'weighing- up ... of material' to the 'frontier of tonality' in Schönberg's *Theory of Harmony*[97] demonstrate that it was the emancipation of dissonance – the loosening of the boundaries of harmony, structure, and form – that enhanced the composer's sensitivity to the evaluation and balancing of the elements of material in music, and opened the way to new modes of configuration. The parallel with Kandinsky's efforts in *On the Spiritual in Art* – this pleading for emancipation of colors and forms – is apparent.[98]

V

The problems of material were galvanized by one artist's sensitivity for the art of the other. The other art functioned as a catalyst for each artist's creative orientation, intensifying the challenges of new construction:

> *"This is why the concept of construction, stimulating the convergence of the arts, gains importance the more directly artists are confronted with the pure material in which they are working, unobstructed by the intermediary layer of an object or an idiom ... "[99]*

Not by chance had Franz Marc – according to his letter to August Macke – noticed in Schönberg's compositions tendencies parallel to those in Kandinsky's paintings. It is not clear which painting in particular Marc had in mind, but in speaking explicitly of "Kandinsky's composition" he may have referred to *Composition II* or *Composition III* – both painted in 1910,[100] and both destroyed during World War II. Whereas *Composition III* is today only known through a black and white reproduction,[101] we can imagine *Composition II* in its final stage, not only through black and white illustrations but also in a final study in the collection of the Guggenheim Museum.[102] (Figs. 1 and 2) Angelica Rudenstine is correct in judging the

Figure 1 *Composition II*, sketch, 1909–10. Oil on canvas (97.5 × 131.2 cm). Photo: Courtesy of the Guggenheim Museum, New York. © W. Kandinsky c/o Beeldrecht Amsterdam

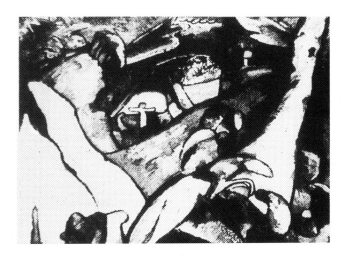

Figure 2 *Composition II*, 1910. Oil on canvas (200 × 275 cm). Destroyed.
© W. Kandinsky c/o Beeldrecht Amsterdam

two versions to be extremely close; only two obvious differences distinguish one from the other. In the final painting, the four figures huddled in the lower left corner have become one amorphous shape, and the central white vertical form extends all the way to the top edge of the canvas rather than stopping short of it.[103]

Was this the picture Marc had in mind when he spoke about Kandinsky's 'jumping spots'? The definitive answer to this question remains open to discussion. Such matters of identification are secondary to the overall impression Kandinsky's pictures made (and still make) on the spectator, an impression that was (and is) so fundamental that Marc's description ignores individual features in order to concentrate on purely structural matters. Kandinsky himself had experienced such an impression when 'accidentally' confronted with one of his own pictures:

> *"Much later, after my arrival in Munich, I was enchanted on one occasion by an unexpected spectacle that confronted me in my studio. It was the hour when dusk draws in. I returned home with my painting box having finished a study, still dreamy and absorbed in the work I had completed, and suddenly saw an indescribably beautiful picture, pervaded by an inner glow. At first, I stopped short and then quickly approached this mysterious picture, on which I could discern only forms and colors and whose content was incomprehensible. At once, I discovered the key to the puzzle: it was a picture I had painted, standing on its side against the wall. The next day, I tried to re-create my impression of the picture from the previous evening by daylight. I only half succeeded, however; even on its side, I constantly recognized objects, and the fine bloom of dusk was missing. Now I could see clearly that objects harmed my pictures."[104]*

The sudden experience of total abstraction – caused by a 'trompe-l'oeil' effect not within but beyond nature – struck the artist like a bolt of lightning. When Kandinsky and his friends heard a piece like Schönberg's op. 11, nr. 1 in the concert of September 2, this fascination, now caused by music, may have had a similar effect.[105] The experience of painting and music indeed may have coincided.

The genuinely artistic repercussion of the Schönberg concert is Kandinsky's painting *Impression 3*. (Fig. 3) For listeners of today, not only accustomed to the works of Schönberg and his circle, but also familiar with the development of modern music since 1950, a composition like op. 11, nr. 1 sounds 'classical'. The analysis of Schönberg's composition makes clear[106] that it consists of strongly contrasting zones of song form and dissolution zones. But aside from these signs of formal dissociation, there are powerful structural traits within these segments of form that correspond to the impressions described by the painters. This is especially significant for the dissolution zones structured by abruptly juxtaposed sound gestures, the disruption underlined by dynamics, registral placement, articulation, and – at least partially – by interruptive rests.[107] The result is a structure that can be described metaphorically as consisting of splashes and spots – as in the testimony of Marc, which corresponds with the structure of Kandinsky's paintings of that time,[108] but especially Kandinsky's *Impression 3*.[109]

Impression 3 is an example of Kandinsky's own distinction of the three genres in his oeuvre – "Impression," "Improvisation," "Composition" – though his categories are perhaps not in themselves sufficiently precise. 'Impressions' are those pictures that follow "the direct impression of external nature."[110] But *Impression 3* transgresses the painter's own definition. Only the event that inspired the picture and determined its external frame, that is, Schönberg's concert of September 2, recalls external nature. The true content is the impact of the expressive power of the music, which evoked in the artist inner vibrations, and permeated and transformed the relics of figural imagery through pictorial means that are derived solely from structural forces. This view is supported by the increasing degree of abstraction as we move from the artist's sketch to the finished painting.[111]

By pictorial structure, I mean the evocation of strong tension that is expressed in the relationship between two intersecting but differently organized diagonals: Oval spots of color and black contours (auditory) directed from the lower left corner toward the large black form (grand

Figure 3 *Impression 3 (Concert)*, 1911. Oil on canvas (77.5 × 100 cm). Photo: Courtesy of the Sammlungen in der Städtischen Galerie im Lenbachhaus, Munich, Gabriele Münter-Stiftung.
© W. Kandinsky c/o Beeldrecht Amsterdam

piano) in the upper right comprise one diagonal; the other consists of a broad yellow trapezoid extending from the lower right corner toward the middle (where it intersects the diagonal beginning in the lower left corner), together with the adjacent, smaller trapezoidal black shape of the grand piano.[112] The contrasting diagonals are accompanied by variously shaped and colored forms in the upper left corner; but they are balanced by two upright white 'columns' in the upper half of the picture. Overlapping the black form on the right and a red form to the left, these white verticals also 'rhythmize' the picture. They form a kind of 'structural counterpoint', organizing and enhancing the impression of 'leaping spots'.

If we 'read' the structure of intersecting diagonals according to Kandinsky's observations and remarks on colors, it becomes obvious that the large yellow trapezoid releases the most active color; it stimulates and permeates as it moves over the entire canvas. At the same time, it intensifies the strength of "all other colors," which, against black "as the most toneless color ... sound stronger and more precise."[113] Yellow in relation to black here gains a special catalyzing function that enhances the infrastructure of diagonals and color spots. It is clear that white, forming a strong contrast to black[114] and at the same time intensifying the effect of yellow, plays its own role in this configuration.[115] But it is the contrast of yellow and blue[116] that guides the second diagonal, not least by the fact that both colors function in "eccentric [and]/or concentric motion."[117]

VI

With this kind of analysis, I do not intend to propose any direct comparison between individual works of painting and music. Such comparisons – even limiting our focus to works by Kandinsky and Schönberg – are, strictly speaking, not possible.[118] They may at best be attempted for the purpose of hypothetical discussion. Kandinsky's own oft-quoted dictum "I do not want to paint music"[119] reinforces this point. The argument that "music, painting, poetry, or texts are not related to one another harmoniously, but rather are characterized by the lack of such structural analogies as a method of the mutual enlightenment of the arts would try to find" does not resolve the problem, nor does the all-embracing notion of "pure perception."[120] Here, the level of abstraction is too low – the focus inadequate. The specific materials of an artistic medium, when reduced to structural and configurative essentials, elicit states of aggregation that are comparable with those of other media, and at the same time pose problems of structural configuration and compositional balance that suggest correspondences. The erosion of elements, structures, and forms affects the patterns that manifest themselves as the fundamental categories of time and space in any artistic medium. The result is the mutual approx-imation[121] practiced by Kandinsky and Schönberg, but more importantly, attested by their strong interest in a synthesis of the arts.[122]

If we take as a point of departure not the comparison of works but rather distinctions of artistic material, structure, and form, we can also try to explain why Kandinsky in *On the Spiritual in Art* dealt much more explicitly and extensively with fundamental aspects of structure and form – especially with the phenomena of contrast and structure of contrasts – than did Schönberg in his *Theory of Harmony*. In his reflections on com-position, Schönberg was subject to the historically evolved and system-atically ordained complex of harmony as well as its erosion through compositional tendencies. He had to delve deeper into aspects of musical material that were in a sense 'theoretically petrified', while Kandinsky, in trying to purge his works of their figurative content, found it necessary to tackle the whole spectrum of pictorial material in connection with object, form, and structure. As we have seen, however, throughout his *Theory of Harmony*, Schönberg was well aware of the structural qualities of material and of balanced formal configurations. He clearly exceeded the range of common reflections in his 'theories of harmony'. With Schönberg's new compositional perspective and the erosion of tonality, hitherto inconcei-vable or undervalued aspects of material came into focus. That Schönberg was cognizant of additional problems pertaining to the material is indi-cated by a passage in the last chapter of his *Theory of Harmony*.

> "In a musical sound [Klang] three characteristics are recognized: its pitch, color [tim-bre], and volume. Up to now it has been measured in only one of the three dimensions in which it operates, the one we call 'pitch'. Attempts at measurement in the other dimenions have scarcely been undertaken to date; organization of their results into a system has not yet been attempted at all. The evaluation of tone color [Klangfarbe], the second dimension of tone is thus in a still much less cultivated, much less organized state than is the aesthetic evaluation of these latter harmonies [i.e., chords with six and more tones]. Nevertheless, we go right on boldly connecting the sounds with one another, contrasting them with one another, simply by feeling; and it has never yet occurred to anyone to require of a theory that it should determine laws by which one may do that sort of thing."[123]

While Kandinsky was 'envious' of the long-standing and highly devel-oped laws of counterpoint and harmony in music, Schönberg may have had a similar reaction when reading about the efforts to systematize experiences of color and their relevance to problems of structure – matters on which Kandinsky reflected in *On the Spiritual in Art*. Significantly enough, his later concept for a music department at an American university includes a proposal for the differentiation and description of contrasts: It is not by chance that the notion of differentiation and description of contrasts plays an important role in Schönberg's *Fundamentals of Musical Composition.*[124]

We must not forget that Schönberg's own activity as a painter – beginning in 1907, four years before he became acquainted with Kandinsky and his art – points to his striving for expanded, correlative, and collateral means of artistic expression[125] through color. His paintings as well as his musical compositions testify to a desire to penetrate the internal necessity, a longing for expression intensified to the extreme,[126] a need to utter that human outcry mentioned earlier.[127] It is exactly the "emotional complex beneath the imprint of form"[128] in Schönberg's pictures that causes us to hear his music according to the structural law of expressive volition, beyond the range of patterns, as if torn by inner contrasts. This is especially true of his 'visions'. With these, the usual pattern of presentation is broken. Only the core of expression remains in the form of 'gazes' and 'gazing colors'. These gazes also permeate Schönberg's *Erwartung*, interacting with oscillating musical eruptions. In *Die glückliche Hand*, music and its contrapuntal elements of light and color function to refract the inner tensions of – and thus carry – the configurations of the stage.[129] One can say that light and colors project the musical configurations into space, especially in the *III. Bild*, where music is transformed into a new quality. The inverse relation becomes apparent in Kandinsky's *Der gelbe Klang*. Here, music transforms configurations of colors, light, and form into moving pictures: Time, inherent in Kandinsky's paintings, unfolds with the music.[130].

Schönberg's investigation of harmonic qualities challenges the whole question of material in music. His *Theory of Harmony* is open not only to the "emancipation of dissonances,"[131] but also to a new calibration of the motif and independent voices,[132] colors of sound,[133] formal relations and patterns. The erosion and dissolution of harmonics, theme, motive, rhythm, meter, dynamics, continuosly shaped time, and formal patterns, however, have their corollaries in painting. As seen in the suspension of pictorial perspective, increasingly abstract configurations of colors and shapes, the distortion of objects, their apparent disappearance, and their abrupt reappearance as mere traces or residue of the figural image, the drifting apart of lines, the loosening and finally the total suspension of orthogonals, the weakening and eventually the release of gravity.[134] Significant comparisons may be made, for example, between Schönberg's song form and dissolution zone (op. 11/1), and Kandinsky's relics of the figure and those pictorial zones he calls "inner boiling within a diffuse form" – as in his description of *Painting with White Border*.[135] This language suggests the melting heat of abstraction that has the power to dissolve figures and patterns. And, as orthogonals and gravity lose their basic pictorial function of orientation, so the 'gravitation of stringent musical time' is decomposed. The telescopic character of continuously flowing time is lost, and with it the traditional elements, relationships, and structures of balanced succession.

VII

The new possibilities of material, structure, and artistic configuration constituted an artistic and historical challenge that could drive artists crazy. Kandinsky's reaction may be glimpsed in *Reminiscences*, where he writes

> *"A terrifying abyss of all kinds of questions, a wealth of responsibilities stretched before me. And most important of all: What is to replace the missing object? The danger of ornament revealed itself clearly to me, the dead semblance of stylized forms I found merely repugnant."*[136]

Looking back in 1932. Anton Webern expressed a similar concern:

> *"The vanishing of tonality was overdue. This, of course, was a hot fight, inhibitions of the most terrible kind were to overcome, an anxiety: Is this really possible?"*[137]

The 'abyss' that terrified Kandinsky, the impediments and uncertainties of heart and brain that embarrassed Schönberg and his circle when they finally overcame tonality, all of this had repercussions for the material, but beyond that, they were to become part of the compositional task itself. Kandinsky's "clashing discords, loss of equilibrium, principles' overthrown...great questionings...opposites, and contradictions..."[138] stood for more than the reverberation in the artist's mind of the conflict between external and internal world. They represented the situation and conflict at the threshold of a new art. 'Chaos', so often invoked and bemoaned by contemporary critics, had to be revealed, and, at the same time, artistically mastered through the methodical structuring of contrasts, the generating and then mediating of tensions, as in Kandinsky's 'harmony'.

The manifold nature of contrasts, however, caused problems other than those facing the artist. For the spectator, it raised troubling questions: How to find points of orientation? How to interpret the 'relics' of objects in Kandinsky's paintings? How to find corresponding structural traces in a composition like Schönberg's *Erwartung* that can guide the listener through a composition that seems to be totally a-thematic? And what is the role of the text in Schönberg's compositions of free atonality? Kandinsky felt like he was between Scylla and Charybdis: he was determined to banish corporeal forms, which he felt 'blurred' his paintings; but in making the break with the 'object', he drifted toward another great danger: "The completely abstract, wholly emancipated use of color in 'geometrical' form (ornament)."[139] How to avoid the pitfall of mere ornamental design?[140]

Ornament was either incomprehensible or incapable of combining structure and artistic message in a stringent form. But if not ornament, what could replace the object in painting?[141] The solution came from music: Composition! Long before he came to realize his ultimate artistic intentions, Kandinsky had ranked the idea of 'composition' ahead of all others.[142] Now, to paint a composition meant to equal music, to create a configuration of colors, lines, and forms of color that would be structurally self-sustaining and incomparably expressive.[143] The world of objects, however, could not be made to disappear on command. Kandinsky had to approach abstraction systematically, by eroding the layers of figural form. It is his distinction among impression,[144] improvisation,[145] and composition that can be understood as a categorization of the fundamental steps along the path to the new goal of abstraction. At the same time, these categories point to his increasing cognizance of material. Kandinsky's explanations of composition proceed along the following lines:

> "The expression of feelings that have been forming within me in a similar way [as in 'Improvisations'] (but over a very long period of time), which, after the first preliminary sketches, I have slowly and almost pedantically examined and worked out. This kind of picture I call a 'Composition'. Here, reason, the conscious, the deliberate, and the purposeful play a preponderant role. Except that I always decide in favor of feeling rather than calculation."[146]

When Kandinsky describes the act of transforming 'the expression of feeling' through 'reason, the conscious, the deliberate, and the purposeful' explicitly for purposes of composition, we may understand it as a kind of dialogue in the course of – and for the sake of – artistic creation, a process of simultaneously weighing and controlling the forces at play in the achievement of compositional balance. This comes close to Schönberg's position in his *Theory of Harmony*:

> "Invention, but not calculation! One may compose by taking thought, but one must not deliberately observe how one is thinking."[147]

The importance of consciousness for composition lies in the fact that Kandinsky's true aim was a "complex type of composition."[148] From this point of view, it becomes clear that he first distinguished between "simple composition" – *qua* "melodic"[149] – and "complex composition"[150] at the time of writing *On the Spiritual in Art* (that is, around 1909).[151] In his subsequent development of these concepts, however, "complex composition" – that is, "symphonic composition" – became more and more synonymous with "[genuine] composition."[152] Kandinsky's ardent desire for the structural, his tenacious engagement with the problems of structure in composition, is proven by the great number of sketches he produced for this type of painting. His propensity for structural condensation is evinced in the sketch for *Composition VI*, where he jots down only structural outlines (Figs. 4, 5). Of equally great interest are drawings where he weighs single forms and their mutual relations, as he does in the sketches for *Composition IV*, where the figural shapes on the right and the vertically oriented lines are balanced (Figs. 6, 7, 8). But the most significant demonstration of his ability to temper creativity with critical reflection is witnessed in the "more than thirty related studies"[153] for *Composition VII*, among which the expanding color studies are exemplary.

Each of these color 'studies' is a highly individual, structurally condensed, and intensified compositional configuration of its own. Because of the enormous variety of elements, colors, forms and structures that

Figure 4 *Composition VI*, 1913. Oil on canvas (195 × 300 cm). Photo: Courtesy of the Hermitage, St. Petersburg. © W. Kandinsky c/o Beeldrecht Amsterdam

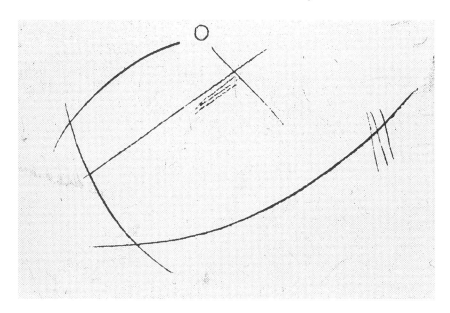

Figure 5   "Outlines of Composition VI", 1913. Mine de plomb et crayon gras (19 × 26.9 cm). Photo: Courtesy of the Collection du Musée National d'Art Moderne, Paris. © W. Kandinsky c/o Beeldrecht Amsterdam

Figure 6   *Composition IV*, 1911. Oil on canvas (159.5 × 250.5 cm). Photo: Courtesy of the Kunstsammlung Nordrhein-Westfalen, Düsseldorf. © W. Kandinsky c/o Beeldrecht Amsterdam

Figure 7   First Drawing for "Composition IV", 1911. Black lead, Charcoal crayon, India ink (10.2 × 20 cm). Photo: Courtesy of the Collections du Musée National d'Art Moderne, Paris. © W. Kandinsky c/o Beeldrecht Amsterdam

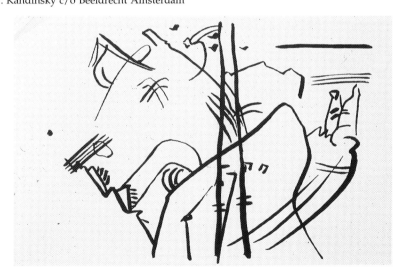

Figure 8   Drawing for "Composition IV", 1911. Black lead, India ink (24.9 × 30.5 cm). Photo: Courtesy of the Collections du Musée National d'Art Moderne, Paris. © W. Kandinsky c/o Beeldrecht Amsterdam

make up the pictures, it is of course extremely difficult – and on this occasion, for practical reasons, impossible – to discuss the salient features of each individual study. Here, it will be more productive to focus on global features, using particularly illustrative examples to demonstrate a few points.

Kandinsky's *Sketch 1* (Fig. 9) – which was already in the possession of Paul Klee as early as 1925[154] – is perhaps the most astounding. Huge waves of color and colored forms overflow the picture plane in an enormous eruption, like 'magma' washing away the scarcely detectable traces of human existence, and symbolizing fall and destruction in the extreme.[155] *Sketch 1* is determined by extremes of contrast among colors bound to large forms, such as red and yellow, black and white; pairings of intensive and calm colors such as red and green and of warm and cold colors like red/yellow and blue/green; and, contrasts among these large forms and small, colored elements, ensembles of elements, and pure lines. These relations are orchestrated in an enormous diagonal shape that surges across the whole canvas (*"Hüllkurve"*), moving from the lower left sector of the picture upwards to the right.

Despite its eruptive appearance, most of the painting's discrete forms are clear and graphically distinct. Its apparently eschatological aura[156] the

Figure 9   Sketch 1 for "Composition VII", 1913. Oil on canvas (78 × 100 cm). (Until 1992: Collection Felix Klee, Bern. Present location unknown. Cf. Sotheby's: Sketch 1 for Composition VII, London 1992.) © W. Kandinsky c/o Beeldrecht Amsterdam

fusion in this image of the "great destruction" and the "hymn of new creation,"[157] are demonstrated by a preparatory drawing[158] (Fig. 10) on which appear Russian annotations that have been deciphered and recently published by Jelena Hahl.[159] In spite of a clear relation between this drawing and *Sketch 1*, certain elements such as those at the left side connected with the inscription "Fugue" are not otherwise found in Kandinsky's works before *Sketch 2*. Another drawing[160] (Fig. 11) that stands between *Sketch 1* and *Sketch 2* brings to the fore a determinant but 'hidden' structural moment in the painting: the diagonal crossing of huge layers of forms. This becomes more clearly visible in *Sketch 2* (Fig. 14) and *Sketch 3* (Fig. 15), and above all, in the painting's final version (Fig. 17). The preparatory and analytical drawings exemplify what Kandinsky says about 'hidden construction':

> *"This hidden construction can consist of forms apparently scattered at random upon the canvas, which – again, apparently – have no relationship one to another the external absence of any such relationship here constitutes its internal presence. What externally has been loosened has internally been fused into a single unity. And this remains for both elements – i.e., for both linear and painterly form. Precisely here lies the future theory of harmony for painting [Harmonielehre der Malerei]."[161]*

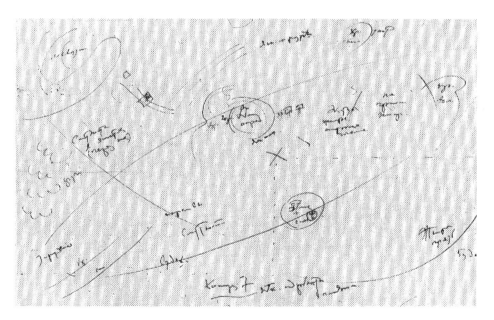

Figure 10   Drawing for "Composition VII", 1913. India ink and pen (21.0 × 33.1 cm). Photo: Courtesy of the Sammlungen in der Städtischen Galerie im Lenbachhaus, Munich, Gabriele Münter-Stiftung. © W. Kandinsky c/o Beeldrecht Amsterdam

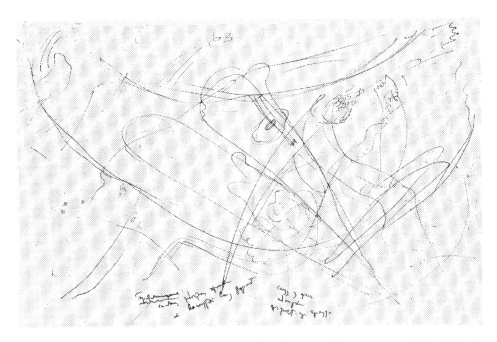

Figure 11   Drawing for "Composition VII", 1913. India ink, mounted on grey paper (21.0 × 33.0 cm). Photo: Courtesy of the Sammlungen in der Städtischen Galerie im Lenbachhaus, Munich, Gabriele Münter-Stiftung. © W. Kandinsky c/o Beeldrecht Amsterdam

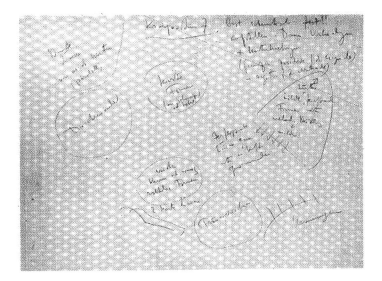

Figure 12   Preparatory drawing for "Composition VII", 1913. Pencil (23.8 × 30.4 cm). Photo: Courtesy of the Sammlungen in der Städtischen Galerie im Lenbachhaus, Munich, Gabriele Münter-Stiftung. © W. Kandinsky c/o Beeldrecht Amsterdam

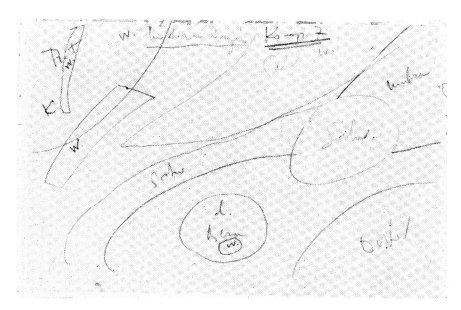

Figure 13 Preparatory drawing for "Composition VII", 1913. Pencil (11.8 × 17.3 cm). Photo: Courtesy of the Sammlungen in der Städtischen Galerie im Lenbachhaus, Munich, Gabriele Münter-Stiftung. © W. Kandinsky c/o Beeldrecht Amsterdam

Clearly connected with *Sketch 1* are two more drawings in pencil (Figs. 12, 13). While the first one only signals characteristics of form,[162] the other one indicates connections between the main colors and shaped areas.[163] It too belongs clearly to *Sketch 1*, as can be seen by the wedge-shaped yellow area above the middle, or the curved black diagonal, which crosses the picture at a subterranean level like a yawning chasm.[164]

The visual manifestation of 'catastrophe' has significally changed in *Sketch 1* (Fig. 14): Warm colors like yellow and red have been reduced and/or modified in favour of green, blue, and mixed colors. Colored lines and shapes in the lower left, but also certain 'windows' opening onto the depth of space have given way to blurred color forms and white structures similar to those Kandinsky called on another occasion "inner boiling (within a diffuse form)."[165] Here, the precision of individual forms has been drastically reduced, the facture is different, and the structure has begun to 'foam' as if from fermentation. Development – time! – suffuses the canvas, its forms, and structures, affecting every pictorial element down to its fundamental material quality. To a certain degree, the development from *Sketch 1* to *Sketch 2* is characteristic of what Kandinsky has called the step from the 'external impression' to the 'inner sound' in connection with *Composition VI*.[166] A sign of this difference in approach

Figure 14   Sketch 2 for "Composition VII", 1913. Oil on canvas (100 × 140 cm). Photo: Courtesy of the Sammlungen in der Städtischen Galerie im Lenbachhaus, Munich, Gabriele Münter-Stiftung. © W. Kandinsky c/o Beeldrecht Amsterdam

can be detected in the absence of the 'pictograph' of the reclining couple, which is visible in the lower left corner of *Sketch 1* as red and blue lines. In further abbreviated form, this motif seems to recur in the final version.

With *Sketch 3* (Fig. 15), the pendulum swings back toward more clear-cut structures and forms. The 'boiling' of colors and forms is reduced but not eliminated altogether. It is combined with purposeful intensification of structural and formal stringency. The powerful left-right diagonal of *Sketch I* is thus confirmed. This becomes increasingly evident if we take into account an additional drawing in India ink (Fig. 16), an 'analytical drawing' according to the artist's label:

"Roughest structure of Composition 7 *(Analysis of the last sketch) November 1913."*[167]

When compared with *Sketch 1*, this sketch reveals the 'crystallization' of 'hidden construction' – and of the structure as a whole – in the final version of *Composition VII* (Fig. 17), with a great accumulation of layers intersecting, permeating, and superimposing themselves upon one another. These layers crowd around and build up the center, at the same time igniting a whirling diagonal tension toward the upper right corner. One element of this concentric structure is a huge upright form

Figure 15 Sketch 3 for "Composition VII", 1913. Oil on canvas (89.5 × 125 cm). Photo: Courtesy of the Sammlungen in der Städtischen Galerie im Lenbachhaus, Munich, Gabriele Münter-Stiftung. © W. Kandinsky c/o Beeldrecht Amsterdam

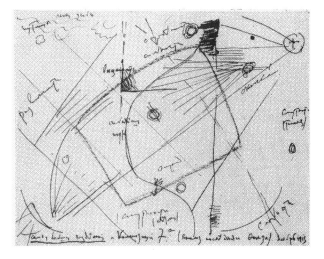

Figure 16 "Analytical drawing" for "Composition VII", 1913. India ink, red crayon (21.0 × 27.5 cm). Photo: Courtesy of the Sammlungen in der Städtischen Galerie im Lenbachhaus, Munich, Gabriele Münter-Stiftung. © W. Kandinsky c/o Beeldrecht Amsterdam

Figure 17   *Composition VII*, 1913. Oil on canvas (200 × 300 cm). Photo: Courtesy of the Tretiakov Gallery, Moscow. © W. Kandinsky c/o Beeldrecht Amsterdam

that is partially intersected by a rhomboid shape, which itself indicates the overlapping of diagonals; but other diagonal layers directed toward the left are also indicated. Gabriele Münter's four photographs of the genesis of the final version – now available *in toto* – are especially illuminating for studying this layered structure of intersecting wedge-like shapes.[168] These huge forms play against more concise forms in cool colors and white forms that permeate and deepen the entire picture. The vast scope of its view, its 'cosmic' character, is thus dramatically magnified. At the same time, however, Kandinsky enriches the number of signs that activate associations with the figurative world of painting. While the early annotated drawing (see Fig. 10) shows Genesis *(Entstehung)* in the lower left corner, boat/ship *(Boot/Schiff)* to the right of Genesis, and abyss *(Abgrund)* in the lower right corner,[169] in the final painting, Kandinsky realizes a pictorial sign for the boat that is lacking in all three sketches. At the same time as he resurrects this vestige of the figural, he alludes to the cosmic by permitting a glimpse into a distant region between earth and sky through an opening in the upper left corner.

These traces of the objective world indeed raise questions about the meaning of such figurative details; but they are obviously of functional importance to the composition. They must be studied with an eye to the

fact that the format of the final painting expands and extends the diagonals.[170] Here, from a structural point of view, the diagonal in the upper
right corner has gained dominance over the composition, an effect that is
enhanced by the fact that it originates with the 'image' of the boat in the
lower left corner. The window onto a distant view in the upper left
corner, on the other hand, corresponds with the 'abyss' in the lower
right, an element already present in the preparatory drawing. Both details
strengthen the force of the somewhat obscured diagonal directed toward
the upper left corner. But what are we to make of their figural appearance? What about their relation to the layering structure of the picture as
a whole?

VIII

Kandinsky's sketches testify to his highly developed sense for the equi-
ponderant control of structural and formal elements. As evidence of the
means of his pictorial practice, they validate his theoretical "weighing-up
of the inner value of one's material." His sensitivity to structural inter-
connections irradiates both nature and objective imagery. Not later than
1910 he had already stressed that:

> *"In painting, just as in all art, it is insufficient simply to render the appearance of nature,
> its external reality, for it contains too much that is accidental. What is 'necessary' (just as
> it is necessary that man should have a heart) is that beneath a greater or lesser degree of
> 'reality' should lie, apparent or concealed, a firm, permanent structure: the structure of
> those parts that are independent, that relate to one another, and that united within the
> picture, constitute the structure of the whole."[171]*

'Permanent structure', emphasized in Kandinsky's fifth *Letter from Munich*
(1910), is nothing but 'hidden construction', unifying figurative and
abstract painting within a wide historic horizon. It comprises exactly
those elements and layers of the picture that form a coherent substratum
underlying the phenomena of the 'objective' world. It is their configuration which forms 'the whole'. All of Schönberg's creative thought and
theorizing seems to be based on this conviction, which is characteristic of
his all-embracing analytical and creative insights. In his *Theory of Harmony*, he has expressed his belief:

> *"...that in the harmony we ultramodernists create will ultimately be found the same
> laws that obtained in the older harmony, only correspondingly broader, more generally
> conceived."[172]*

Schönberg's explicit remarks about permanent laws of harmony are implicit in his statements on the 'inner nature of the idea and its movement' with respect to choral music and also in his tentative analytical remarks on the ultramodernist *Aesthetic Evaluation of Chords with Six and more Tones*. Here, an encompassing concept of musical logic, of musical idea, hovers between or behind the lines ("in the air") that in effect prefigures his extensive later writing on this topic.[173] It is a vision of historically constant structural logic that manifests itself as central to composition just when it seems to have vanished, as in Kandinsky's works of around 1910.

The latent structural power of small groups of tones that subliminally organize the elements of his so-called athematic compositions can be detected even in the eruptive gestures of *Erwartung*.[174] The difficulty in discerning them lies in the fact that these aggregations of notes are handled extremely freely in terms of their combination, operations of transposition, inversion, and retrogression, the organization of registers, and even the modification of intervals – all of these understood to be 'proto-procedures' of Schönberg's twelve-tone technique. These small points of structural crystallization are more clearly recognizable in Schönberg's second early 'operatic' work *Die glückliche Hand*. Combinations like (major) third + (minor) second/(major) seventh, or (minor) second + (minor) seventh/(minor) ninth form webs or networks of structural relations.[175] However the notion of latent structural power becomes even more discernable in some of the *George Songs* – not only in nr. 14,[176] but also – to a greater or lesser degree – in nrs. 1, 3, 5, 6, 8, 9, 11. Such veiled structural relations as these compositions exhibit are not the product of intuition. There exist sketches for nr. 14 of the *George Songs*, sketches indicating that in fact, the composer consciously shaped the beginning with great skill.[177]

In his familiar theoretical contribution to the *Blue Rider* entitled *The Relationship to the Text*, which we now know that Schönberg announced to Kandinsky in a letter of January 15, 1912,[178] Schönberg reveals that when setting texts to music he very often composed:

> "...*inspired by the sound of the first words of the text...straight through to the end without troubling myself in the slightest about the continuation of the poetic events.*"[179]

The probing sketches for the beginning of *George Song* nr. 14, however, make clear that he had first to find a decisive structural and expressive idea that could give shape to the compositional whole according to its generative musical powers. Here, again, then, the conception of hidden structural power becomes apparent – this time in musical terms.

When compared with Kandinsky, the number of Schönberg's sketches is – as far as the works before 1914 are concerned – limited. Very often Schönberg composed from the beginning to the end at one stroke.[180] Obviously this is related to the fact that, according to his own account, he often drafted whole works in his head. This 'mental-work', however, occurred in stages. In his answer to a questionnaire prepared by Julius Bahle (1931), Schönberg mentions three stages that precede the written elaboration. That they are not represented by sketches may be because the early creative stages resist becoming visible musical signs. The progression is described schematically by Schönberg as:

(I)   the "unnameable mental image of sounding and moving space, of a form with characteristic relationships, of moving masses whose shape is unnameable and not amenable to comparison;"
(II) becomes "musical *through-fantasizing* along emotional lines;"
(III) and reaches the highly tentative stage of "a large or small number of themes . . . often proving unusable," while the "real themes . . . often appear only during a second working phase (if one may call it that)."[181]

Schönberg's comments regarding the setting of poems to music are also relevant to his instrumental compositions: It is very often the primary 'musical need' that 'draws' Schönberg "to the words,"[182] a fact that corresponds with his discussion in *The Relationship to the Text* regarding the inward correspondence of music and word, rooted in a basic musical 'sound' which permeates and determines the 'homogeneous composition'.[183] It would seem that the fundamental abstractness of music conceals the first steps of musical composition as "invisible sketches,"[184] while in painting, what is conceptualized may become visible at an earlier stage.

It is precisely the workings of the creative imagination, made visible in sketches, that reveal the narrowing of painting toward music. *Sketch 1* for *Composition VII* may come close – in terms of painting – to what Schönberg calls the "expression of some basic fact concealed behind the whole," which "could equally be represented in a different material: in words, rhymes, sounds, but also in colors, forms, and marble."[185] This, however, was only possible according to the principles of abstraction, which seeks to reveal the inner necessity as a striving toward the genuine – the spiritual – expression of material in painting. In Kandinsky's case this propensity is related to his particular make-up as an artist. He was a synesthete possessed of an eidetic memory.[186] He wrote that, having been saturated with external impressions, over the years, the:

> *"...capacity for engrossing myself in the inner life of art (and, therefore, of my soul as well) increased to such an extent that I often passed by external events without noticing them, something which could not have occured previously."*[187]

It seems that Kandinsky's distinctions of 'impression', 'improvisation,' and 'composition' stem directly from these two operations of his mind setting in motion a dialectic relationship between the impressions he absorbed from the external world, on the one hand, and his internal pictorial imaginings, on the other. Here we have to remind ourselves that the production of mimetic imagery is, to a considerable degree, due to the mind's tendency to predetermine sensory perception:

> *"What we read into...accidental shapes [of clouds or so] depends on our capacity to recognize in them things or images we find stored in our minds."*[188]

In Kandinsky's case, the mind operates the other way round: Instead of 'imagining' faces, animals, etc., when looking at clouds,[189] he rather increasingly projected onto the visual phenomena of the external world abstract configurations of colors and forms that derived from his expanding reservoir of non-figurative imagery. So, his three 'categories' of painting, as well as his 'sketches' and analytical drawings, stand as signs of a 'dialectic' process that demanded earlier and more extensive preparatory and analytical work than was the case with Schönberg's musical compositions.

This view does not reduce artistic problems to psychoanalytical terms. It is an approach to understanding Kandinsky's creative reception of a constellation of phenomena that was potentially open to his keen detection and response,[190] and which at the same time confronted him with inherent and imminent problems. The latter are exemplified by the way in which Kandinsky, in his striving for abstraction, became preoccupied with the question of ornament. His path toward abstraction was paved with milestones, so to speak, that had already been encountered and passed by in the history of ornament. Focusing on the pre-eminence of non-representational structural and formal relations,[191] he sought to avoid the scorn leveled against mere formalism. Though he would problematize ornament,[192] he nevertheless disagreed with the subordination of ornament to 'naturalistic' art. To elevate the quality of abstract configuration according to the idea of inner necessity – which Theodor Vischer had also pleaded for – Kandinsky had to accentuate the inner force of abstract elements – as had Van de Velde[193] and Endell[194] – at the expense of the figurative image. He ruptured the filiation between naturalistic and abstract form,[195] while at the same time preserving a thread of continuity that linked the two – not unlike Lipps's perspective[196] – in a process of abstraction that led to the systematic detachment from reality.

The rift between figurative and genuinely abstract imagery is catalysed in Kandinsky's research. The question of how to understand the residual traces of objects in his paintings can be solved neither by 'reading' these as 'hermetically' iconographic,[197] nor by ignoring their presence in favor of an undialectical approach to abstract composition.[198] The problem might be approached, however, in terms of Kandinsky's 'Great Realism,'

> *"That 'artistic' element which has here been reduced to a minimum [and which therefore] must be recognized as the most powerfully affective abstract element."[199]*

In this case, the traced figurative elements are not understandable as signs of a strict iconographic meaning; rather they represent what can be called 'auratic iconography'. These 'fragments' signal the coming of Walter Benjamin's 'aura', "the singular spectacle of remoteness, the nearer it seems to be."[200] With the use of pictorial elements that are abstract in nature, and which by their reverberation from within a project into a remote and mysterious realm, things that seem to belong to the realm of physical proximity or common significance, Iconographic content itself becomes increasingly impenetrable.[201] Rendering the beholder's soul sensitive to the eschatological 'scale', they 'tune' him according to the 'inner sound' of abstract configurations and to contrasts, which – by fusing subjective synesthetic qualities into structural relationships within a stringent scale or matrix – become more readily legible.[202] To 'read' these pictures, finally, means to abandon iconographic decipherment and to indulge in 'hidden construction', that is, to re-enact the whole range of compositional techniques in Kandinsky's paintings, the building of relationships among material elements, and the assignation of expressive meaning.

Kandinsky's desire to purify material and construction of the figural reference to objective reality, with its denotative and connotative capacities, while at the same time guarding against the anathema of mere ornamentalism, has a parallel in Schönberg's struggle against program music, his desire to articulate the relationship of his music to the text, and his opposition to ornament. Abandoning program music, he first emphasized "the construction of extremely large forms."[203] But the phenomenon of atonality demanded the increasing concentration of compositional elements, which in effect would swallow up ornament. Eventually the rigors of compositional structure led to extreme results: very short pieces, and condensed expression through purely musical means;[204] purification of expression focused on the core of music, 'inner necessity' – which became the code word for a correspondence of all the arts. Thus, in Schönberg's *George Songs*, music 'knows' its own integral 'inner sound' even in relation to the text. It becomes auratic in that, by emphasizing remoteness, it expresses in its very structure what is beyond the mere meaning of words but nevertheless palpably close to us.

Around these veiled structures the composition crystallizes. The versatility of tone cells, as demonstrated by *Erwartung* and *Die glückliche Hand*, prefigures the twelve-tone technique, as Kandinsky's aggregated layers of intersecting and permeating diagonals, of hovering and circulating networks of lines and colored forms would finally become structurally ordered and decisive. Kandinsky was mentally prepared for contact with the guiding principles of Surprematism and Constructivism. He was ready to tackle the challenges of such catalytic artistic confrontation. The same can be said for Schönberg. Metaphorically, one could say that Kandinsky's paintings between 1910 and 1914 gained an increasingly emblematic function for the artistic milieu in which he and Schönberg moved. This is summed up by the notion of 'composition' consisting of the three classic elements of an emblem: 'icon', 'motto', and 'epigram'[205] elaborated in the configuration 'construction' (icon), 'internal necessity' (motto), and *On the Spiritual in Art* (epigram).

This pattern expresses the fact that Kandinsky's fundamental aim is construction – the artistically conclusive and evocative structural configuration, incited by internal necessity. Construction, however, carries within itself the necessity of process – not only implying the element of time, but in particular the historical time needed to realize construction in its most perfect form, that is, through abstraction. Abstraction is both deconstructive and constructive. Its power to erode the object also engenders the lines of power that establish the new abstract pictorial order. The result was conflict. Even before the erosion of figural form became apparent, painting was increasingly fraught with great fluctuations of tension and direction, opposing diagonals and excentric and concentric forces, struggles between form and edge, and the densification of webs of color, form, and line. These virtually overtook the surface of the painting. The materials of abstraction, as it were, and the waning figurative elements fought each other on the field of the canvas. This becomes strikingly apparent with the Murnau paintings of after 1909, where the objects are attacked by oppositional – but also structurally supportive – diagonal and swirling compositional forces. However, as the power lines of abstraction gained superiority, and the relics of the objective world were engulfed by abstraction, the more this confrontation between the material and the figural was transmuted into a matter of purely structural relations. Here 'latent construction', already inherent in Kandinsky's earlier stages of development, reached a new plateau: it gained an expressive power all its own, and takes on a new structural identity. This is demonstrated above all by the great *Compositions V, VI, VII*, but also by *Compositions II, IV*, and a picture like *Painting with the White Border*, where the probing and at the same time analytical sketches demonstrate that construction is the concealed but nevertheless governing power.[206]

This transmutation of the conflicts between objective imagery and material form into structural terms coincides with the emergence of apocalyptic themes, a coincidence that calls for some discussion.[207] What triggered notions of the apocalyptic in Kandinsky's thought?[208] His special emphasis on composition in painting, going far beyond other painters' understanding of the word, cannot be overstressed. Resting his theoretical conceptions on the importance of composition, Kandinsky must have found his own question "What is to replace the object in painting?" especially urgent. We may therefore assume an interplay of the internal and external factors that stimulated his creative imagination, guided by his striving for composition in terms of pure, that is, spiritually charged material in music, which caused – or at least evoked – the apocalyptic, auratic 'tenor' of many of his paintings. This is especially true of compositions dating from after 1910. Finally it was the inner, spiritual quality of composition – symphonic composition – that informed Kandinsky's wide-ranging and many-layered (if sporadic) interest in theosophy, anthroposophy,[209] occultism, Sufism,[210] and the work of Joachim of Fiore.[211] Kandinsky was inspired by the notion of an intrinsic spirituality of art. To his dictum

> *"I do not want to paint music.*
> *I do not want to paint states of mind."*[212]

he could have added:

> *"I do not want to paint religious or occult feelings and beliefs."*

Kandinsky was convinced of the artwork's similitude to cosmic forces and phenomena. Whether or not he was influenced prior to 1914 by

Steiner, his interest in the cosmos was persistant, as is demonstrated by his later lectures at the Bauhaus, in which he commented on matters such as the enormity of the dimensions of the universe.[213] In this regard, too, Schönberg was close by. The last movement of his *Second String Quartet*, transgressing the limitations of obsolete patterns, indeed dives into the ethereal atmosphere of distant planets and strives toward the pinnacle of artistic freedom, thus already marking the way to a new structural configuration. This is the way toward – and beyond – Schönberg's *Jakobsleiter*, where atonal elements coalesce structurally around abbreviated units of musical 'idea'. And it provides the validation for the foreboding construction of *Erwartung* and *Die glückliche Hand*.

Both artists had a vision of what Kandinsky, following Fiore, called the coming "spiritual time."[214] Not by chance was Kandinsky possessed of his multi-band antenna for spiritual messages; not by chance was Schönberg intensely interested in Balzac's *Seraphita* or inclined to theosophical ideas. Theirs was a spirituality of art, mediated by art, and enacted for the sake of the human being. They exemplify not only what Panofsky described as, the striving – in times of artistic revolution – for the unknown entwined with a longing for spiritual legitimation:[215] both artists also stand for art as an eminent creative event carrying a spiritual message. In Kandinsky's words, which are as valid for Schönberg's compositions as for the painter's own works:

> *"Painting is like a thundering collision of different worlds that are destined in and through conflict to create that new world called the work. Technically, every work of art comes into being in the same way as the cosmos – by means of catastrophes, which ultimately create out of the cacophony of the various instruments that symphony we call the music of the spheres. The creation of the work of art is the creation of the world."[216]*

NOTES

1. It is purely coincidental that the same passage from Kandinky's *On the Spiritual in Art*, "Gegensätze und Widersprüche – das ist unsere Harmonie" which I use as the introductory quote, also appears in the text by Johannes Langner for the catalogue *Kandinsky in München* (München 1982), p. 107–132. Though this coincidence is accidental, it nevertheless has significance: Langner tries to unveil the figurative relics in Kandinsky's paintings; I focus on the strength of non-figurative internal structure[s] behind Kandinsky's abstraction which eventually absorb these fading figurative elements.

   I am greatly indebted to the Getty Center for the History of Art and the Humanities for supporting my research in every possible way, for making materials in the Library and Resource Collections available to me, and especially for granting me permission to publish two unedited letters written by Schönberg to Kandinsky.

I want to thank also Nuria Nono-Schönberg and the Schönberg family for granting me permission to publish the two letters by Schönberg.

Last, but not least I would like to thank Helga von Kügelgen for having read my paper with a critical eye, and Denise Bratton for sharpening its presentation in English.

2   This concert is usually dated 1 January, 1911 – see Stuckenschmidt *Schönberg. Leben – Umwelt – Werk* (Zürich/Freiburg 1974), p. 131, *Arnold Schoenberg – Wassily Kandinsky. Letters, Pictures and Documents*, ed. Jelena Hahl-Koch, trans. John Crawford (London and Boston) 1984, p. 173. However, Nuria Nono-Schönberg's book on Arnold Schönberg introduces a document that clearly establishes another date. A concert program announcing Schönberg's *String Quartets* op. 7 and op. 10, *Five Songs* (from op. 2 and op. 6) and the *Piano pieces* op. 11, clearly indicates that this event took place on January 2, 1911. It was the first concert in which these Schönberg compositions were presented in Munich. A handwritten note by Schönberg dated "5. August 1934" and referring to this concert is also quoted in Marion Bauer's *Twentieth Century Music*, p. 211, (Nuria Nono-Schönberg (ed.): *Arnold Schönberg 1874–1951. Lebensgeschichte in Beschreibungen* [Klagenfurt 1992], p. 82).

3. *Arnold Schoenberg – Wassily Kandinsky. Letters* (see n. 2) p. 21.

4. Schönberg must have fulfilled his announcement of September 11 that he would visit Kandinsky and Münter "instead [of Wednesday, the 13th] Thursday the 14th for certain". On September 18 Kandinsky writes: "Your visit gave us all great pleasure." (See *Arnold Schoenberg – Wassily Kandinsky. Letters* [n. 2], p. 30 sq.) On 23 September, Kandinsky expected a second visit from Schönberg (W. Kandinsky – Franz Marc. Briefwechsel, ed. Klaus Lankheit, München/Zürich 1983), p. 60.

5. A symbol of this communication is the exchange of both artist's writings that came out in 1911/12. The text of the slightly modified quotation from the fourth movement of Schönberg's *Second String Quartet*, taken for his dedication to Kandinsky should be read the following way: "Ich löse mich au*ch* in Tönen – endlich...", not "Ich löse mich au*s* in Tönen", as transcribed in *Arnold Schoenberg 1874–1951* (see n. 2, p. 83).

6. August Macke – Franz Marc. Briefwechsel, ed. by Wolfgang Macke (Köln 1964), p. 40 sq. This translation follows: *Arnold Schoenberg – Wassily Kandinsky. Letters, Pictures and Documents* (see n. 2), p. 136.

7. The quotations on the poster (see *Arnold Schoenberg – Wassily Kandinsky. Letters* [note 2], p. 24) can be related to the text of the first edition of Schönberg's *Harmonielehre* [HL, 1911] as follow:

    "In einem Sinne soll man nie unzeitgemäß sein – nach rückwärts." In this version – slightly altered – only in *Die Musik* X/2 [1910/11], p. 101. In the *Harmonielehre* the formulation is more sparkling with Schönbergian humour: "Unzeitgemäß darf man nur auf die Art sein, daß man voraneilt, aber nicht, indem man nachhumpelt;" (HL 1911, p. 78 – Engl. ed. [see n. 11], p. 67.)

    "Dissonanzen sind nur graduell verschieden von den Konsonanzen; sie sind nichts anderes als entfernter liegende Konsonanzen." (HL 1911, p. 76; Engl. ed. [see n. 11], p. 66.)

    "Wir sind [ja] heute schon so weit, zwischen Konsonanzen und Dissonanzen keinen Unterschied mehr zu machen. Oder höchstens den, daß wir Konsonanzen weniger gern verwenden." (HL 1911, p. 81; Engl. ed. [see n. 11], p. 70.)

    "Ich glaube, man wird in der Harmonie [Harmonik] von uns Allermodernsten schließlich [und endlich] dieselben Gesetze erkennen können, wie in der Harmonie [Harmonik] der Alten. Nur entsprechend ausgeweitet, allgemeiner gefaßt." (HL 1911, p. 82; English. ed. [see n. 11], p. 70 – In his *Theory of Harmony* Schönberg writes "Harmonik" instead of "Harmony".)

"Unsere Lehre führt dahin, auch Hervorbringungen Jüngerer, die das Ohr der Aelteren verpönt, als notwendige Ergebnisse der Schönheitsentwicklung anzusehen. Niemals aber sollte man wünschen, Dinge zu schreiben, deren Verantwortung man nur mit dem Einsatz einer vollen Persönlichkeit zu übernehmen vermag. Dinge, die Künstler fast widerwillig im Zwange ihrer Entwicklung geschrieben haben, aber nicht aus dem hemmungsarmen Mutwillen formunsicherer Voraussetzungslosigkeit." (Slightly different from: HL 1911, p. 82 sq. and the extract in *Die Musik* [p. 105]; Engl. ed. [see n. 11], p. 71.)

8. *Arnold Schoenberg – Wassily Kandinsky. Letters* [etc.], (s. n. 3), p. 210 [n. 2].
9. Wassily Kandinsky: *Complete Writings*, edited by Kenneth Lindsay and Peter Vergo, Vol. I (London 1982), p. 149; German edition: Kandinsky: *Über das Geistige in der Kunst*, mit einer Einführung von Max Bill (Bern–Bümplitz 5/1956), p. 49.
10. W. Kandinsky: *Complete Writings* Vol. I (see n. 9), p. 196.
11. Arnold Schönberg: *Theory of Harmony*, based on the third edition of 1922, translated by Roy E. Carter (Berkeley / Los Angeles 1978), p. 11 sq.
12. Arnold Schönberg: *Theory of Harmony* (see n. 11), p. 417.
13. Arnold Schönberg: *Theory of Harmony* (see n. 11), p. 422.
14. Wassily Kandinsky: *Complete Writings*, Vol. I (see n. 9), p. 177. This position of Kandinsky never changed. So, in the scripts for his Bauhaus lectures in Dessau ("I. sem. Sommer 1931) he emphasizes: "analysis = external and internal material, i.e. synthesis in analysis body and soul substance and strength." Or: (I. Semester 1930–8–9–30): "Material – inner strength = tensions – given facts, that stand outside / of time (my experiences in Ravenna) / Changes of time or the given surrounding, or of the basis of time – sociological or economic conditions – are the contributing *external* forces". (Cf. Getty Center, Resource Collections, folders 850910–1 and 850910–7.) (Unless otherwise noted or noticeable, this and all subsequent translations are my own, polished by Denise Bratton.)
15. See, for example, Peter Cahn: "Zu einigen Aspekten des Materialdenkens in der Musik des 20. Jahrhunderts", in *Hindemith – Jahrbuch*, 1980/IX (Mainz, London, New York, Tokyo, 1982), p. 193–205. It is not possible here to focus on the development of Adorno's ideas on "material" in music between 1929 ("On Twelve Tone technique") and about 1956/69 (*Aesthetic Theory*"). The term "material" as Adorno used it is apparently almost totally excluded from the history of art. However, Brisch's nuanced analysis of Kandinsky's paintings touches on aspects of material that correspond with Adorno's sense of the term (cf. Klaus Brisch: *Wassily Kandinsky (1866–1944). Untersuchungen zur Entstehung der gegenstandslosen Malerei an seinem Werk von 1900–1921*, Ph.D. (Bonn 1955), [unpublished typescript], p. 90 sqq., passim.
16. Cf. *Theodor W. Adorno und Ernst Krenek: Briefwechsel*, ed. Wolfgang Rogge (Frankfurt am Main 1974), especially pp. 30–32 and 38 sq. Take into consideration, however, the sentence: "These instructions that the material issues to the composer constitute themselves as immanent reciprocity, and inasmuch as he obeys them, he alters them." ['In immanenter Wechselwirkung konstituieren sich die Anweisungen, die das Material an den Komponisten ergehen läßt, und die dieser verändert, indem er sie befolgt."] (Th. W. Adorno: *Philosophie der neuen Musik* (Frankfurt am Main), 1958, p. 38, and *Gesammelte Schriften* Vol. 12 (Frankfurt am Main 2/1990), p. 40; English translation: *The Philosophy of Modern Music*, trans. Anne Mitchell and Wesley Blomster, New York 1973, p. 36) See also "Ernst Krenek und Theodor W. Adorno. Arbeitsprobleme des Komponisten. Gespräch über Musik und soziale Situation", in Adorno: in *Gesammelte Schriften* Vol. 19, Musikalische Schriften Vol. 6 (Frankfurt am Main 1984), p. 433–439. One of the strong arguments against Adorno's rigidly applied term "material" is also made by Busoni's encompassing consciousness of compositional material.

17. "Ist aber das Material nichts Statisches, heißt materialgerecht verfahren mehr als die handwerkliche Bescheidung, die gegebene Möglichkeiten geschickt ausschöpft, so impliziert das auch, daß das Material seinerseits durch die Komposition verändert wird. Aus jeder gelungenen, in die es einging, tritt es als Neues frisch hervor." In "Vers une musique informelle" (1961), in *Gesammelte Schriften*, Vol. 16 (Frankfurt am Main 1978), p. 504 sq. See also Adorno's dictum: "I do not want to argue against the subjective part in dialectics, but only its [the subjects] »autarchy« which exactly would suspend dialectics." ["...ich will nicht den subjektiven Anteil an Dialektik bestreiten, sondern bloß dessen »Autarkie«, die gerade die Dialektik aufheben müßte."] (*Theodor W. Adorno und Ernst Krenek: Briefwechsel* [see n. 16], p. 38.)

18. "Das Geheimnis der Komposition ist die Kraft, welche das Material im Prozeß fortschreitender Adäquanz umformt." ("Vers une musique informelle" [see n. 17], p. 505.)

19. This is exactly the point on which Dahlhaus focuses, in order to resolve the historical petrification of a term grounded in historicity (Carl Dahlhaus: "Adornos Begriff des musikalischen Materials", in *Zur Terminologie der Musik des 20. Jahrhunderts*, ed. H. H. Eggebrecht [Stuttgart 1974], p. 9–21).

20. Cf. *Philosophie der neuen Musik* (see n. 16), p. 112 sqq.

21. Hullot Kentor is referring to Th. W. Adorno's "Die Idee der Naturgeschichte" in Adorno: *Gesammelte Schriften* Vol. I, (Frankfurt am Main 1973), p. 345–365 which he translated in *Telos. A Quarterly Journal of Critical Thought*, 60, Summer 1984, p. 111–124.

22. Quotation from Robert Hullot-Kentor: "Popular Music and Adorno's 'The Aging of New Music' ", in *Telos* (see n. 21), 77 (Fall 1988), p. 86 sq.; Th. W. Adorno: *Philosophie der neuen Musik* (see n. 16), Vol. 12, p. 38 sq. English translation: *The Philosophy of Modern Music*, [see n. 16] p. 32.

23. Adorno's recently published fragments on Beethoven show clearly that the teleological implications are central to his understanding of what he declares to be the "demands" of artistic material. As for Beethoven's realization of stringent compositional processuality, Adorno says: "What has been called the obbligato style was already evident in rudimentary form during the seventeenth century, and contains within itself teleologically the demand of the totally organized, analogical to philosophy: systematized composition." ("Das, was man den obligaten Stil genannt hat, der rudimentär bereits im siebzehnten Jahrhundert sich abzeichnet, enthält teleologisch in sich die Forderung gänzlich durchgebildeter, nach Analogie zur Philosophie: systematischer Komposition". Theodor W. Adorno: *Beethoven, Philosophie der Musik. Fragmente und Texte*, ed. Rolf Tiedemann, Suhrkamp [Frankfurt am Main 1993], p. 77.) Adorno's focus on teleological stringency – also as far as earlier epochs are concerned – is emphasized when he says: If Berlioz wanted to outdo Beethoven, then Berlioz probably was teleologically immanent in the latter. (Wenn Berlioz Beethoven übertrumpfen wollte, so war diesem wahrscheinlich Berlioz teleologisch *immanent*. Ibid., p. 88.)

24. Kandinsky: "Whither the 'New' Art?", in *Complete Writings*, Vol. I (see n. 9), p. 100. See also Kandinsky's statement in a manuscript that remains unpublished: Art is the prophet of things to come.... Thus, art is a prophetic being, which, as an increasingly independent body, serves the spirit through freedom. (Die Kunst ist der Prophet des Kommenden.... So ist die Kunst ein prophetisches Wesen, welches als selbständiger Körper weiter wächst und durch Freiheit dem Geiste dient. Jelena Hahl-Koch, *Kandinsky* (München 1993), p. 151.)

25. Arnold Schönberg: *Theory of Harmony* (see n. 11), p. 325. However, neither Kandinsky nor Schönberg ever would have ventured to portend through art things to come in the political, or social realms. Their artistic convictions indeed concerned the spiritual world first and foremost, not that of material facts and events. This is stated

explicitly by Kandinsky. In response to Michael Sadler's question whether a certain "non-representational picture...demonstrated that he had already foreseen the war", he said: "Not this war. I had no premonition of that. But I knew that a terrible struggle was going on in the spiritual sphere, and that made me paint the picture." (Francis Haskell: *History and its Images* [New Haven – London 1993], p. 425.) If we take into account, however, that the tremendous tensions and upheavals of the twentieth Century had not only material but also considerable spiritual dimensions, and will even have consequences beyond our times, then Kandinsky's foresight was – in a wider sense – absolutely stringent.

26. Erwin Panofsky: "Art as a Humanistic Discipline", in: *Meaning in the Visual Arts,* Doubleday Anchor Books (New York 1955), p. 9.

27. Kandinsky's self-interpretative texts have been analyzed by Felix Thürlemann: *Kandinsky über Kandinsky. Der Künstler als Interpret eigener Werke* (Bern 1986), p. 25 sqq., 37 sqq. and passim.

28. For the different kinds of texts, see Felix Thürlemann (see n. 27), p. 29 sqq.

29. Kandinsky's "internal necessity" can be understood as a "subjective fixation [dictum]" ("eine subjektive Setzung"). (Peter Anselm Riedl: *Kandinsky,* [Hamburg 1989], p. 76.) Nonetheless, according to Kandinsky's own understanding of trans-subjective validity (*On the Spiritual* and *On the Question of Form*) its intent is far from aesthetic expurgation. The core of the dictum's meaning – that the truth-value of art originates in the internal immediacy of artistic volition and is not induced externally – is not limited to one's own art and the art of a particular epoch. The emphasis on the "internal" necessarily points up certain spiritual implications, as can be seen from Lessing's dictum: "Virtue has 'internal necessity', even if there would not be another life." (Jacob und Wilhelm Grimm: *Deutsches Wörterbuch,* Vol. 13, Reprint [München 1984], col. 960.) The fact that "internal necessity" is freighted with many layered and manifold meaning is its fortuity as well as its burden. The term's relativity comes to the fore more clearly in the context of debates surrounding it. Werner Hofmann stresses that "internal necessity" is also used by Hegel, Feuerbach and the "rationalist Burckhardt" (in "Kunst jenseits der geschlossenen Systeme", in Werner Hofmann: *Gesammelte Aufsätze* [Frankfurt am Main 1979], p. 287). Felix Thürlemann interestingly connects "internal necessity" with Alois Riegl's idea of "artistic volition" (cf. Thürlemann: *Kandinsky über Kandinsky* [see n. 27], p. 158 sqq., 213, note 145), as does David Morgan in "The Idea of Abstraction in German Theories of Ornament from Kant to Kandinsky" (*The Journal of Aesthetic and Art Criticism,* 50 [1992], p. 239). Anneliese Sinn relates it to Schopenhauer, Nietzsche and Bergson in *Kandinsky's Theory of Inner Necessity* (Chicago 1966). Many other authors have commented on the concept of "internal necessity"; cf. Kenneth Clement Eriksen Lindsay: *An Examination of the Fundamental Theories of Wassily Kandinsky,* Ph.D. (University of Wisconsin 1951) (unpublished), p. 56, n. 32; Sixten Ringbom: *The Sounding Cosmos. A Study in the Spiritualism of Kandinsky and the Genesis of Abstract Art Painting* (Åbo 1970), p. 109 ff. especially p. 110, n. 2; Rose-Carol Waston Long: *Kandinsky. The Development of an Abstract Style* (Oxford, 1980), p. 169, n. 43; Armin Zweite: "Kandinsky zwischen Tradition und Innovation", in *Kandinsky und München, Begegnungen und Wandlungen 1896–1914,* ed. A. Zweite (München 1982), p. 172 sq.

30. This passage from an article entitled 'Intention' was quoted by the authors at the beginning of their more extensive text "The Intentional Fallacy" [1946], reprinted in *On Literary Intention, Critical Essays selected and introduced by David Newton-de Molina* (Edinburgh, 1976), p. 1–13.

31. See Max Black: "Was stellen Bilder dar?", in: E. H. Gombrich / J. Hochberg / M. Black: *Kunst, Wahrnehmung, Wirklichkeit* (Frankfurt am Main 1977), 152 f., n. 40, and E. D. Hirsch: *Validity in Interpretation* (New Haven 1967), p. 11. See furthermore: S. H. Olsen: "Authorial Intention", in *The British Journal of Aesthetics,* 13 (1973), p. 219–231;

B. Lang: "The Intentional Fallacy Revisited", ibid., 14 (1974), p. 306–314; S. Davies: "The Aesthetic Relevance of Authors' and Painters' Intentions", in: *Journal of Aesthetic and Art Criticism*, 41 (1982), p. 65–76 and finally: Felix Thürlemann (see n. 27), p. 24 sq. As for this problem in Musicology see Klaus Kropfinger: Beethoven – Im Zeichen des Janus: Op. 130 ± 133. Op. 133 – Der widerwillig gefaßte Entschluß. Op. 134 – Der spät gefaßte Entschluß, in K. Kropfinger: Über Musik im Bilde. Schriften zu Analyse, Ästhetik und Rezeption in Musik und Bildender Kunst, vol. 1, ed. by Bodo Bischoff et al., Verlag Dohr. Köln 1995, p. 285.

32. Cf. Th. W. Adorno: "Kriterien der Neuen Musik", in *Nervenpunkte der Neuen Musik* (Hamburg 1969), p. 106; in *Gesammelte Schriften*, Vol. 16 (Frankfurt am Main), p. 195.

33. Th. W. Adorno: *Ästhetische Theorie* in *Gesammelte Schriften*, Vol. 7 (Frankfurt am Main 1970), p. 222; English translation as Theodor Adorno: *Aesthetic Theory*. Translated by C. Lenhardt (London/New York 1984), printed as paperback 1986, p. 213. Cf. the review by Bob Hullot-Kentor: "Adorno's *Aesthetic Theory*: The Translation", in: *Telos* (see n. 21), 65, Fall 1985, p. 143–147 and the translator Christian Lenhardt's reply, p. 147–152.

34. This is a supposition advanced rather tentatively by Adorno. The English translation, however, changes the meaning of the original sentence "Der Materialbegriff dürfte in den zwanziger Jahren bewußt geworden sein..." to a rather high degree: "The concept of material took on a serious technical connotation in the 1920s." (cf. *Aesthetic Theory* [see n. 33], p. 222 (German ed.), p. 213 (English ed.). Already in 1920 Hermann Scherchen had written: "The real artist has to be a slave of his artistic material.... There are not many artists who have been as fascinated by the material of their art as Schönberg." "Der echte Künstler muß Sklave seines Kunstmaterials sein.... Wenig Künstler sind so von der Materie ihrer Kunst besessen gewesen wie Arnold Schönberg" (in *Melos* [1920], p. 9 sq.).

35. Arnold Schönberg: *Theory of Harmony* (see n. 11), p. 19 sq.

36. Arnold Schönberg: *Theory of Harmony* (see n. 11), p. 10 sq.

37. For Schönberg the only one which counts!

38. Arnold Schönberg: *Theory of Harmony* (see n. 11), p. 18.

39. Arnold Schönberg: *Theory of Harmony* (see n. 11), p. 325.

40. Arnold Schönberg: *Theory of Harmony* (see n. 11), p. 414.

41. Arnold Schönberg: *Theory of Harmony* (see n. 11), p. 239.

42. See also Schönberg's statement: "One must reflect that art has set its course not only by the nature of tones but by the nature of man as well..." (A. Schönberg: *Theory of Harmony* [see n. 11], p. 68.

43. Arnold Schönberg: *Theory of Harmony* (see n. 11), p. 238 sq.

44. Theodor W. Adorno: "Reaktion und Fortschritt", in: *Th. W. Adorno und Ernst Krenek: Briefwechsel* (see n. 16), p. 175. ["Das gleiche Obertonverhältnis etwa, das im verminderten Septakkord – oft ist es bemerkt worden – gemessen am Stande des Materials insgesamt zur Zeit Beethovens als stärkstes Spannungsmoment konnte eingesetzt werden, ist in einem späteren Stande des Materials harmlose Konsonanz und bei Reger bereits zum selber unqualifizierten Modulationsmittel entwertet."] In Adorno's *Philosophy of Modern Music* the weighing of the diminished seventh chord correlates to that in "Reaktion und Fortschritt" (see n. 22), 12, p. 40 sq.

45. Cf. Kandinsky: *On the Spiritual in Art*, in Kandinsky: *Complete Writings*, Vol. I (see n. 9), p. 149 sqq. The paragraphs dealing with Cézanne, Matisse and Picasso were the first to be translated into English by Alfred Stieglitz in *Camera Work*, 39 (July 1912), p. 34 (see also G. Levin/M. Lorenz: *Theme & Improvisation. Kandinsky and the American Avant-Garde 1912–1950* [Boston, Toronto, London], 1992, p. 10).

46. See Kandinsky's "Letter from Munich" [V], [May–June 1910], in *Complete Writings*, Vol. I [see n. 9], p. 79 sq. Brisch has emphasized Kandinsky's structural awareness as

witnessed in this letter, stimulating his rating of the historical development in painting (cf. Klaus Brisch: *Wassily Kandinsky* [see note 15], p. 118 sq., 123–135.) As regards the importance of Kandinsky's nineteenth-century forerunners in the emancipation of color and activating "physiological stimuli" see: Peter Anselm Riedl: "Vom Orphismus zur Optical Art", in *Eranos 1972*, 41 (1974), p. 397–427. Gauguin and van Gogh are only two among many who spoke about colors in terms of music; cf. Jean de Rotonchamp: *Paul Gauguin. 1848–1903* (Paris 1906), p. 205; Vincent van Gogh: *Briefe an seinen Bruder* (Berlin 1928), Vol. III, p. 201 (nr. 512), p. 239 (nr. 527), p. 424 (nr. 607). It is of note, too, that in his Bauhaus lecture at Dessau, Kandinsky quotes Cézanne on color "...There is only one way, able to represent all, to translate all, the color" ["....Es gibt nur einen Weg, der alles darstellen, alles übersetzen läßt, die Farbe"]. In his commentary, Zervos writes: "Une telle conception ne pouvait aboutir qu'à la peinture pure." (1925, I. Semster); cf. Getty Center, Resource Collections, Folder 850 910–1.

47. Wassily Kandinsky: *Complete Writings*, Vol. I (see n. 9), p. 154; see also Kandinsky's "On the Question of Form", in *Complete Writings*, Vol. I (see n. 9), p. 237, 239.

48. I want to thank the Schönberg family and the Getty Center, Resource Collections, for permission to publish this and a second letter (see p. 62) which Schönberg wrote on January 15, 1912 to Kandinsky (see p. 64). Joseph Henry Auner who also found these two letters in the Getty Center Archives refers to one of them in his book: *Schönberg's Compositional and Aesthetic Transformations 1910–1913: The Genesis of* Die Glückliche Hand, Ph. Dissertation, Chicago, Illinois, 1991, p. 124, note 79. The first of these two letters however, was written on December 18, not December 28!

49. See p. 63–64.

50. Wassily Kandinsky: *Complete Writings*, Vol. I (see n. 9), p. 157, and passim.

51. Wassily Kandinsky: *Complete Writings*, Vol. I (see n. 9), p. 157, and passim.

52. In *On the Spiritual* Kandinsky stresses the fact that "all these assertions [on colors] are the results of empirical–spiritual experience and are not based upon any positive science" (*Complete Writings*, Vol. I [see n. 9], p. 179).

53. In *On the Spiritual* Kandinsky explicitly mentions literary sources he knew.

54. "Erst will ich verschiedene Farbproben machen: ich will das Dunkle studieren – tief blau, tief violett, tief schmutziggrün usw. Oft sehe ich diese Farben vor mir. Manchmal ahme ich mit Hilfe meiner Lippen tiefe Trompetentöne nach – da sehe ich verschiedene tiefe Mischungen, die das Wort nicht fassen kann und die Palette nur schwach wiedergeben kann." (Johannes Eichner: *Kandinsky und Gabriele Münter. Von Ursprüngen moderner Kunst*, München 1957, p. 127 sq.)

55. Cf. Wassily Kandinsky: *Complete Writings*, Vol. I (see n. 9), p. 156 sqq. One should not forget Kandinsky's knowledge of contemporary literature on this very specific aspect, as indicated by his reference in *On the Spiritual* to Freudenberg and Sabaneev (p. 158, note) as well as to Zakharin-Unkovsky (p. 159, note) and Henri Rovel (p. 196, note).

56. Kandinsky's notions on synesthesia have often been quoted with critical remarks. Admittedly, he is mixing up metaphorical and physiological/psychological aspects of synesthesia. There can be, however, no doubt that Kandinsky's synesthesia was brain-based and not "mindbased". This is emphasized by Richard E. Cytowic's recently published book *Synesthesia. A Union of the Senses*, (New York etc., 1989), p. 270 sq. In *Wassily Kandinsky* (see n. 15, p. 62, note 21) Klaus Brisch quotes Walter Winkler (Psychologie der modernen Kunst, Tübingen, 1949, p. 201–226) for whom "Kandinsky is a synesthete par excellence and in addition he possesses an explicit eidetic gift." ["K. ist ein Synästhetiker par excellence und dazu besitzt er eine ausgesprochene eidetische Begabung."] Frans Evers, dean of the Interfaculty of Image and Sound, Royal Conservatory, The Hague, to whom I wish to extend special thanks for a discussion on this topic, is convinced that Kandinsky was not

a one-hundred-percent synesthete. Usually, Kandinsky's remarks in *Reminiscences*, and his experiences with Rembrandt and Wagner, are quoted; however, in her new book, Jelena Hahl-Koch gives additional interesting information about Kandinsky's synethetic sensibility, *Kandinsky*, (see n. 24), p. 87, 90, 156.

57. Wassily Kandinsky: *Complete Writings*, Vol. I (see note 9), p. 178 sqq. These observations are confirmed by Rudolf Arnheim with special reference to Kandinsky (*Art and Visual Perception. A Psychology of the Creative Eye. The New Version* [Berkeley, Los Angeles, London 1974], p. 369). Arnheim is sceptical, however, insofar as the expressive qualities of colors and forms are concerned: "These characterizations are so heavily overlaid with personal or cultural factors that they cannot claim much general validity" (p. 371). This objection, however, does not automatically exclude the aesthetic and analytical relevance of the qualities of material mentioned by Kandinsky – and other artists. On the contrary, artistic experiences and evocation are much more plausible and convincing as individual and culturally specific traits than in form of common features.

58. The term "structure" was already stressed by Kandinsky in the last (fifth) of his *Letters from Munich* in October/November 1910. Cf. *Complete Writings*, Vol. I (see n. 9), p. 80. See also the analysis by Brisch (*Wassily Kandinsky* [see n. 15], p. 119 sq.).

59. Cf. Wassily Kandinsky: *Complete Writings*, Vol. I (see n. 9), p. 177 sqq.

60. Cf. Wassily Kandinsky: *Complete Writings*, Vol. I (see n. 9), p. 179.

61. Cf. Wassily Kandinsky: *Complete Writings*, Vol. I (see n. 9), p. 163, 165.

62. Cf. Wassily Kandinsky: *Complete Writings*, Vol. I (see n. 9), p. 163.

63. Cf. Wassily Kandinsky: *Complete Writings*, Vol. I (see n. 9), p. 163.

64. Cf. Wassily Kandinsky: *Complete Writings*, Vol. I (see n. 9), p. 167.

65. Cf. Wassily Kandinsky: *Complete Writings*, Vol. I (see n. 9), p. 166 sqq.

66. Kandinsky: *Complete Writings*, Vol. I (see n. 9), p. 178 sqq.; German edition: Kandinsky: *Über das Geistige in der Kunst* (see n. 9), p. 87 sqq. See also: Clark V. Poling: *Kandinsky's Teaching at the Bauhaus. Colour Theory and analytical Drawing* (New York 1986), p. 46.

67. Kandinsky: *Complete Writings*, Vol. I (see n. 9), p. 178 sq.

68. Kandinsky: *Complete Writings*, Vol. I (see n. 9), p. 184.

69. Kandinsky: *Complete Writings*, Vol. I (see n. 9), p. 184.

70. Kandinsky: *Complete Writings*, Vol. I (see n. 9), p. 187 sq.

71. Cf. Heinz Matile: *Die Farbenlehre Philipp Otto Runges. Ein Beitrag zur Geschichte der Künstlerfarbenlehre* (München–Mittenwald 2/1979), 277 sq.; Clark V. Poling: *Kandinsky's Teaching at the Bauhaus* (see n. 66), p. 93.

72. See however the discussion of this point in H. Matile: *Die Farbenlehre Philipp Otto Runges* (see n. 71), p. 369, n. 558a.

73. Kandinsky: *Complete Writings*, Vol. I (see n. 9), p. 163.

74. Kandinsky: *Complete Writings*, Vol. I (see n. 9), p. 201.

75. Kandinsky: *Complete Writings*, Vol. I (see n. 9), p. 193.

76. This aspect of context must not be forgotten. As Pike has written: "Meaning has its locus not in individual bits and pieces of a total structure....None of the bits and pieces has meaning of and by itself. Meaning occurs only as a function of a total behavorial event in a total social matrix." (K. L. Pike: *Language in relation to a Unified Theory of the Structure of Human Behaviour*, prelim. ed., III [Glendale, Calif. 1960], 16, 5.) Cf. also: Reinhold Heller: "Kandinsky and Traditions Apocalyptic", in *Art Journal*, 43/1 [Spring 1983], esp. p. 20 sq. and Yule F. Heibel: "They danced on Volcanoes", in *Art History*, 12/3 [September 1989], p. 342–361. That Kandinsky was deeply affected by political tensions and the threatening war is documented by new material in Jelena Hahl-Koch's book (see Hahl-Koch [n. 24], p. 220 sqq.).

77. "*Kunst* hat 2 Eigenschaften: 1. *abspiegeln* der Gegenwart – also: durch / K[unst]-analyse Gegenwart kennen lernen. / 2. *aufbau* der Zukunft – also: über unsre Zeit /

hinaus erraten des Kommenden. *woher* kommen beide richtlinien?) so kann man / an K[unst] vergang [enheit], aus vergangenheit) Gegenw. [art] u. [nd] Zu-/kunft erkennen." (Cf. Getty Center, Resource Collections, Folder 850 910–2.)

78. "Kunst ist der Notschrei jener, die an sich das Schicksal der Menschheit erleben. Die nicht mit ihm sich abfinden, sondern sich mit ihm auseinandersetzen. Die nicht stumpf den Motor »dunkle Mächte« bedienen, sondern sich ins laufende Rad stürzen, um die Konstruktion zu begreifen. Die nicht die Augen abwenden, um sich vor Emotionen zu behüten, sondern sie aufreißen, um anzugehen, was angegangen werden muß. Die aber oft die Augen schließen, um wahrzunehmen, was die Sinne nicht vermitteln, um innen zu schauen, was nur scheinbar außen vorgeht. Und innen, in ihnen, ist die Bewegung der Welt; nach außen dringt nur der Widerhall: das Kunstwerk." In: A. Schönberg: *Schoepferische Konfessionen* (Zürich 1964), p. 12. The autograph is reproduced in Nuria Nono-Schönberg (ed.): *Arnold Schönberg 1874–1951* (see n. 2), p. 71.

79. Cf. Reinhold Brinkmann: "Schönberg und das expressionistische Ausdrucksprinzip", in *Bericht über den 1. Kongreß der Internationalen Schönberg-Gesellschaft* (Wien 1978), p. 13–19.

80. Cf. Adorno's dictum: "The unresolved antagonisms of reality reappear in art in the guise of immanent problems of artistic form. This, and not the deliberate insertion of objective moments or social content, defines art's relation to society." Adorno: *Aesthetic Theory* [see n. 33], p. 8. ("Die ungelösten Antagonismen der Realität kehren wieder in den Kunstwerken als die immanenten Probleme ihrer Form. Das, nicht der Einschuß gegenständlicher Momente, definiert das Verhältnis der Kunst zur Gesellschaft." German ed. p. 16.)

81. Cf. A. Schönberg: *Theory of Harmony* (see n. 11), p. 127 sqq. and passim. Concerning Schönberg's aspect of compositional "balance" see also Reinhold Brinkmann: *Arnold Schönberg: Drei Klavierstücke op. 11. Studien zur frühen Atonalität bei Schönberg* (Wiesbaden 1969), p. 11 sqq.

82. Cf. "On the Question of Form", in Wassily Kandinsky: *Complete Writings* (see n. 9), p. 237, 239.

83. Cf. A. Schönberg: *Theory of Harmony* (see n. 11), p. 127 sqq.

84. A. Schönberg: *Theory of Harmony* (see n. 11), p. 16.

85. A. Schönberg: *Theory of Harmony* (see n. 11), p. 14. ("... ein gewisses Wertgefühl für Harmoniefolgen" p. 8.)

86. A. Schönberg: *Theory of Harmony* (see n. 11), p. 16. ("... die Gewichtsverhältnisse der Akkorde und Akkordfolgen zu prüfen".)

87. A. Schönberg: *Theory of Harmony* (see n. 11), p. 70.

88. A. Schönberg: *Theory of Harmony* (see n. 11), p. 115 sqq.

89. A. Schönberg: *Theory of Harmony* (see n. 11), p. 127.

90. A. Schönberg: *Theory of Harmony* (see n. 11), p. 203.

91. A. Schönberg: *Theory of Harmony* (see n. 11), p. 150 sqq., 207 sqq.

92. A. Schönberg: *Theory of Harmony* (see n. 11), p. 340 sqq.

93. A. Schönberg: *Theory of Harmony* (see n. 11), p. 370.

94. A. Schönberg: *Theory of Harmony* (see n. 11), p. 384.

95. A. Schönberg: *Theory of Harmony* (see n. 11), p. 420.

96. A. Schönberg: *Theory of Harmony* (see n. 11), p. 421 sq.

97. A. Schönberg: *Theory of Harmony* (see n. 11), p. 238.

98. This aspect has already been mentioned by Werner Hofmann (cf. "Beziehungen zwischen Malerei und Musik", in Catalogue of the exhibition *Schönberg–Webern–Berg* [Wien 1969], p. 109/b).

99. Th. W. Adorno: *Über einige Relationen zwischen Musik und Malerei*, in *Gesammelte Schriften*, 16 (Frankfurt am Main 1978), p. 641. [Daher wird der Konstruktionsbegriff, der die Konvergenz befördert, um so mächtiger, je direkter die Künste dem nackten

Material sich gegenüber befinden, mit dem sie arbeiten, ohne die Zwischenschicht eines Gegenstandes oder eines Idioms....]

100. *Composition II* "during the Winter of 1909–10", *Composition III* September 15th. Hans K. Roethel/Jean K. Benjamin: *Werkverzeichnis der Ölgemälde*, Vol. I, 1900–1915 (München 1982), no. 334, p. 314 and no. 359, p. 336.

101. See for example Roethel/Benjamin: *Werkverzeichnis der Ölgemälde*, Vol. I (see n. 100), no. 359, p. 336; further Klaus Brisch: *Wassily Kandinsky* (see n. 15), p. 238 sq., 281.

102. Cf. Roethel/Benjamin: *Werkverzeichnis der Ölgemälde*, Vol. I (see n. 100), no. 326, p. 305 and plate p. 294. Angelica Zander Rudenstine: *The Guggenheim Museum Collection. Paintings 1880–1945* (New York 1976), no. 82, p. 228–236.

103. Angelica Zander Rudenstine: *The Guggenheim Museum Collection* (see n. 102), p. 228 sq.

104. Wassily Kandinsky: *Reminiscences / Three pictures*, in: Kandinsky: *Complete Writings*, Vol. I (see n. 9), p. 369 sq.

105. Kandinsky's *Impression 3* was accompanied in my lecture by a music example: Schönberg's op. 11, no. 1 (see n. 2).

106. Cf. the analysis of Reinhold Brinkmann: *Arnold Schönberg: Drei Klavierstücke op. 11* (see n. 81), p. 70, 80–96.

107. Cf. especially bars 14–17, 39 sqq.; but also 34 sqq.

108. Clearly this is not only valid for op. 11/1 but, for example for op. 11/3 and the relationship between the three pieces of op. 11 as well. Here, however, within a completely different structural context.

109. Cf. Roethel/Benjamin: *Werkverzeichnis der Ölgemälde*, Vol. I (see n. 100), no. 375, p. 354.

110. Kandinsky: *On the Spiritual*, in *Complete Writings*, Vol. I (see n. 9), p. 218.

111. Cf. J. Hahl-Koch: *Kandinsky* (see n. 24), p. 152 sq.

112. It is important to observe that certain forms, like the large yellow but also the black one, contribute to intersection of diagonals, in that they contain both directions. Concerning the yellow form, it is important to take into account Kandinsky's qualification of "yellow" in *On the Spiritual*, in *Complete Writings*, Vol. I (see n. 9), p. 178 sqq.

113. Kandinsky: *On the Spiritual in Art*, in *Complete Writings* Vol. I (see n. 9), p. 185.

114. "The *second great contrast* is the difference between white and black" (Kandinsky: *On the Spiritual in Art*, in *Complete Writings*, Vol I [see n. 9], p. 189.

115. "Yellow tends toward light (i.e. white)" (Kandinsky: *On the Spiritual in Art*, in *Complete Writings*, Vol. I [see n. 9], p. 179.) See also Jelena Hahl-Koch's annotations concerning Kandinsky's *Impression 3*, in *Arnold Schönberg – Wassily Kandinsky. Briefe, Bilde und Dokumente einer außergewöhnlichen Begegnung*, ed. Jelena Hahl-Koch (Salzburg/Wien 1980), p. 42.

116. Cf. Kandinsky: *On the Spiritual in Art*, in *Complete Writings*, Vol. I [see n. 9], p. 179.

117. Cf. Kandinsky: *On the Spiritual in Art*, in *Complete Writings*, Vol. I [see n. 9], p. 178 sq.

118. This problem is also valid for the Dissertation of Stephen Solom Vise, 'Wassily Kandinsky and Arnold Schoenberg. Parallelisms in Form and Meaning' (Washington University 1969). Vise presents interesting and important insights. His comparisons of musical composition and painting, however, focus too much on specific features of individual works of art. Kandinsky puts a problem which reappears in another, very special form with Mondrian's "affinity to jazz and jazz-dance" which is rooted in the structure of this music as a whole (cf. Karin v. Maur: "Mondrian und die Musik im Stijl", in *Vom Klang der Bilder. Die Musik in der Kunst des 20. Jahrhunderts*, ed. Karin v. Maur [München 1985], p. 404).

119. Wassily Kandinsky: "Cologne lecture". "Kandinsky über seine Entwicklung", in: Kandinsky: *Complete Writings*, Vol. I (see n. 9), p. 400; see also: Johannes Eichner: *Kandinsky und Gabriele Münter. Von Ursprüngen moderner Kunst* (München 1957), p. 108–116, esp. 116.

120. Thomas Zaunschirm: "The painter Arnold Schoenberg", in *Arnold Schoenberg. Paintings and Drawings* (Klagenfurt 1991), p. 77 sqq.
121. Cf. Adorno: "In opposing each other the arts merge into one another." ("In ihrem Gegensatz gehen die Künste ineinander über.") "The arts only converge where each one is genuinely pursuing its immanent principle." ("Die Künste konvergieren nur, wo jede ihr immanentes Prinzip rein verfolgt.") Th. W. Adorno: "Über einige Relationen zwischen Musik und Malerei" (see n. 99), p. 629.)
122. It is noteworthy that the problems of "construction" become especially acute where the relationship of the arts must become very specific, as in both artists' work for the stage around 1910/12; but individual compositions, such as Schönberg's op. 16, no. 3 ("Klänge" – 1909) because of its coincidence of resting time and tone color, and on the other hand a painting like Kandinsky's *Improvisation with horses* (1910), combining terms of painterly structure and musical characters – demonstrating at the same time the painter's cooperation with Th. v. Hartmann – merit special attention. (As for Kandinsky's painting, see his analytical drawing in *Kandinsky. Oeuvres de Vassily Kandinsky (1866–1944)*. Catalogue établi par Christian Derouet et Jessica Boissel, Paris 1984, no. 100, p. 102. The reading of the inscriptions has been rightly corrected by Thürlemann (see note 27, p. 118). Instead of "versch[ieden] f[arbiger] Flecken" one could read perhaps also "verschl(eierte[r]) Flecken".
123. Arnold Schönberg: *Theory of Harmony* (see n. 11), p. 421.
124. Arnold Schönberg: *Fundamentals of Musical Composition*, ed. Gerald Strang and Leonard Stein (London 1967), passim.
125. Apart from his special personal crisis!
126. In 1938 Schönberg declared: "I painted 'Gazes', which I have already painted elsewhere. This is something which *only I* could have done, for it is out of my own nature, and it is completely contrary to the nature of a real painter.... A painter... grasps with one look the whole person – I, only his soul." (Cf. "Painting influences. Los Angeles 11 – II – 1938", in *JASI*, II/2 [1978], p. 237. See also: Klaus Kropfinger: "Schönberg und Kandinsky", in *Arnold Schönberg*, Publikation des Archivs der Akademie der Künste zu Arnold Schönberg-Veranstaltungen innerhalb der Berliner Festwochen (Berlin, 1974), p. 9–14.)
127. See page 18.
128. Wassily Kandinsky: "The Paintings of Schoenberg", in *JASI* (see note 126), p. 182.
129. Schönberg's *Die glückliche Hand* is no confirmation that he was a synesthete. (See also Cytowic: *Synesthesia* [n. 56], p. 271 sq.). For Joseph Henry Auner synesthesia nevertheless is a relevant point (cf. Joseph Henry Auner: *Schoenberg's Compositional and Aesthetic Transformations 1910–1913: The Genesis of* Die Glückliche Hand [see n. 48], p. 122 sqq.) Concerning the interlinking of the different media of expression, see Schönberg's letter to Alma Mahler (October 7, 1910) presented in John Crawford: "*Die Glückliche Hand*: Further Notes", in *JASI* IV/1 (June 1980), p. 73. Furthermore: Harald Krebs: "The 'Color Crescendo' from *Die Glückliche Hand*: A Comparison of Sketch and Final Version, in *JASI* XII/1 (1989), p. 61–67.
130. The question whether Schönberg's conception of the color crescendo was influenced by Kandinsky's *On the Spiritual* has been newly discussed by Joseph Auner (*Schoenberg's Compositional and Aesthetic Transformations 1910–1913: The Genesis of* Die Glückliche Hand [see n. 48], p. 122 sqq.). He convincingly confirms John Crawford's suggestion that Schönberg was influenced by Kandinsky despite the problem of the almost perfect coincidence of time (see note 129). Concerning aspects of "color" in other compositions of Schönberg see Walter Frisch: "Schönberg and the Poetry of Richard Dehmel", *JASI*, IX/2 (November 1986), especially p. 163 sqq.
131. Schönberg didn't use the term "emancipation of the dissonance" earlier than 1925. It is already inherent, however, in his *Theory of Harmony* ("Hence, the distinction between them [consonance and dissonance] is only a matter of degree, not of

kind.... the expressions 'consonance' and 'dissonance', which signify an antithesis, are false." Cf. also Robert Falck: "Emancipation of the Dissonance", in *JASI* VI/1 [1982], p. 106–111).

132. Cf. *Theory of Harmony* (see n. 11), p. 202 sq. where Schönberg emphasizes the "importance of thinking in independent voices" and the "driving power of the motive" as "the only justification, the only *Motor* for the independent movement of voices".

133. Cf. A. Schönberg: *Theory of Harmony* (see n. 11), p. 421 sq.

134. Given the *process* of this emancipation, the relevance of what Brisch called "Flächenkörper" in Kandinsky's early landscapes and other paintings must also be taken in account. "Flächenkörper" is a term taken from Fritz Schmalenbach, which signifies the permeation of colored areas by a structure of differently directed layers (cf. Brisch [see n. 15], p. 99 sqq., especially p. 126 sqq.).

135. Wassily Kandinsky: *Reminiscences / Three pictures*, in *Complete Writings*, Vol. I (see n. 9), p. 391.

136. Wassily Kandinsky: *Reminiscences / Three pictures*, in *Complete Writings*, Vol. I (see n. 9), p. 370.

137. Anton Webern: *Der Weg zur Komposition in zwölf Tönen*, Vorträge 1932, ed. W. Reich (Wien 1960), p. 48.

138. Kandinsky: *On the Spiritutal*, in *Complete Writings*, Vol. I (see n. 9), p. 193.

139. Kandinsky: *On the spiritual*, in *Complete Writings*, Vol. I (see n. 9), p. 207.

140. Even Franz Marc saw Kandinsky's art of "Composition" temporarily in relation to oriental carpets: "It is a pity that one can't hang *Kandinsky's* large composition... beside the Mohammedan carpets in the exposition park.... In Germany we scarcely have a decorative work, let alone a carpet, which we could hang close by. Let's try it with Kandinsky's compositions – they will stand this dangerous test, and not as carpets but as 'pictures'." (Franz Marc: *Schriften*, ed. Klaus Lankheit [Cologne 1978], p. 126 sq.) Very soon, however, Marc changed his view, emphasizing the "purely pictorial" aim with no concern for "decorative effects" (see: David Morgan: "The Idea of Abstraction in German Theories of Ornament from Kant to Kandinsky" [see note 29], p. 241 sq., note 77 with relation to Claus Pese: *Franz Marc. Leben und Werke* [Stuttgart 1989], 30 sq., 117). But Kandinsky himself was taken by surprise when confronted with Eastern, or Persian art (see Kandinsky's "Letter from Munich" in *Complete Writings*, Vol. I [see n. 9], p. 73 sqq.). See also: Kenneth C. Lindsay: "Kandinsky and the Compositional Factor", in *Art Journal* 43/1 [spring 1983], p. 14–18.

141. Kandinsky: *Reminiscences / Three Pictures*, in *Complete Writings*, Vol. I (see n. 9), p. 370.

142. C.f. Kandinsky: *Reminiscences / Three Pictures* in *Complete Writings*, Vol. I (see n. 9), p. 367 and *On the Spiritual*, in *Complete Writings*, Vol. I (see n. 9), p. 162 sqq.

143. "Music, which externally is completely emancipated from nature, does not need to borrow external forms from anywhere in order to create its language" (*On the Spiritual*, in *Complete Writings*, Vol. I [see n. 9], p. 154 sq.).

144. "The direct impression of 'external nature'..." (*On the Spiritual*, in *Complete Writings*, Vol. I [see n. 9], p. 218).

145. "Chiefly unconscious, for the most part suddenly arising expressions of events of an inner character..." (*On the Spiritual*, in *Complete Writings*, Vol. I [see n. 9], p. 218).

146. *On the Spiritual*, in *Complete Writings*, Vol. I [see n. 9], p. 218.

147. Schönberg: *Theory of Harmony* (see n. 11), p. 395. ("Erfinden, nicht aber errechnen! Erdenken darf man, aber man darf es selbst nicht merken, wie man denkt." HL, p. 441) This sentence shows that Schönberg's and Kandinsky's dispute on "construction" was really – as Schönberg put it – above all "a quarrel over words" (*Arnold Schoenberg – Wassily Kandinsky. Letters, Pictures and Documents* [see n. 2], p. 54).

148. Kandinsky: *On the Spiritual*, in *Complete Writings*, Vol. I (see n. 9), p. 215, 218.

149. Represented (partially) by *Impression V Park* (Roethel/Benjamin: *Werkverzeichnis der Ölgemälde*, Vol. I [see n. 100], no. 397, p. 382) and *Improvisation 18 (mit Grabsteinen)* (Roethel/Benjamin: *Werkverzeichnis der Ölgemälde*, Vol. I [see note 100], no. 384, p. 367). The problem of "melodic" and "rhythmic" components in painting, aspects with which Kandinsky dealt more systematically in his Bauhaus-lectures, can be no more than mentioned here.
150. Kandinsky's example for "this complex type of composition" is *Composition II*.
151. See Kandinsky: *On the Spiritual*, in *Complete Writings*, Vol. II (see n. 9), p. 875, note 16.
152. The question of how far the term "composition" may have changed its "inner" meaning, but also its role in the context of Kandinsky's artistic mode needs further investigation; see also Kropfinger: *Romantisches Bewußtsein – Musikalische Modernität – Kandinsky's Große Abstraktion*, in *Zur Aktualität der Romantik*, ed. Brigitte Reuter. Dokumentation. Mit einer Einführung von Ewald Reuter, Tampere 1993, p. 216. Brisch mentions that the first paintings which Kandinsky registered in his handlist were all called "Compositions", "with brief indications of color and object" (see n. 15, p. 165). Roethel/Benjamin more precisely say that the note "C." could be read as "C.[omposition]". For all these cases they have excluded the term "in light of the great importance placed by the artist on his later 'Compositions'" (Roethel/Benjamin: *Werkverzeichnis der Ölgemälde*, Vol. I [see n. 100], no. 181, p. 189). There is, on the other hand, "no evidence that the works belonging to the State Pushkin Museum entitled *Komposition* followed by a Cyrillic letter were assigned their titles by the artist..." (Vivian Endicott Barnett: *Kandinsky, Watercolours*, Catalogue Raisonné Vol. One. 1900–1921 (London 1992), no. 392, p. 350).
153. Vivian Endicott Barnett: *Kandinsky at the Guggenheim* (New York 1983), p. 31.
154. Cf. *Wassily Kandinsky. Sketch for Composition VII. From the Paul Klee Family Collection sold by Alexander Klee*, Sotheby's (London 1992).
155. In *Sketch 2* and *Sketch 3*, as well as in the final version of *Composition VII* the colors are much colder.
156. Cf. *Der Blaue Reiter im Lenbachhaus München*. Herausgegeben und mit einer Einführung von Armin Zweite sowie Bildkommentaren von Annegret Hoberg (München 1991), pl. 46.
157. Cf. Brisch (see n. 15), p. 253.
158. Erika Hanfstaengl: *Wassily Kandinsky: Zeichnungen und Aquarelle*. Katalog der Sammlung in der Städtischen Galerie im Lenbachhaus München (München 1974), no. 249.
159. J. Hahl-Koch: *Kandinsky* (see n. 24), p. 210, no. 255.
160. Erika Hanfstaengl: *Wassily Kandinsky* (see n. 158), no. 248.
161. Kandinsky: *On the Spiritual*, in *Complete Writings*, Vol. I (see n. 9), p. 209. It is clear on the other hand, that "hidden construction" has also a strong spiritual "sound" which, of course, is above all connected with the enhanced expression caused by stringent contrasts and constructive condensation. It is what only instrumental music can afford: to be expressive by means of structurally "logic" development of musical "thoughts" as Friedrich Schlegel put it. Cf. Kropfinger (*Romantisches Bewußtsein...*, [see n. 152], p. 206, 216); cf. also Thürlemann (*Kandinsky über Kandinsky* [see n. 27], p. 86 sq.). Interestingly, "latent construction" did not lose its value for Kandinsky when the constructive elements in his paintings had come to the fore. In a letter to J. B. Neumann of October 21, 1935 he writes: "I know and love it: balancing, however in a way, which makes the thing externally appear as to be unbalanced." ["Es sind 'dramatische' und sehr 'lyrische' Blätter dabei, heisse und kühle und sehr kalte, schwere und haarleichte, aber fast durchwegs mit dem mir geeigneten 'Gleichgewicht', das, wie Zervos sagt, immer rätselhaft bleibt. Ich weiss und liebe es: ausbalancieren, aber so, dass das Ding äusserlich unbalanciert erscheint."] (Getty Center, Resource Collections, folder 850 910–69.)

162. Erika Hanfstaengl: *Wassily Kandinsky* (see n. 158), no. 252. It may be one of the earliest – if not the first – sketch, according to the general note on the upper right border: "Erst schematisch fest !!/aufstellen. Dann Verbindungen / + Unterbrechungen/Grenzen positive (?) / u[nd] negative (?)."

163. Erika Hanfstaengl: *Wassily Kandinsky* (see n. 158), no. 251.

164. There are of course also watercolor studies for *Composition VII* (see Vivian Endicott Barnett: *Kandinsky, Watercolours* [see note 152], fig. 358 sqq.). Especially interesting in this case are figs. 359 and 360, which are clearly connected with *Sketch I*.

165. Concerning his analysis of *Painting with White Border* (cf. *Reminiscences / Three Pictures*, in *Complete Writings*, Vol. I [see n. 9], p. 390, 391. One is reminded of what Kandinsky says in his "Cologne lecture" of 1914 about the enormous immediate and contextual qualities of the color white, "turning the whole of painting upside-down" (in *Complete Writings*, Vol. I [see n. 9], p. 397 sq.).

166. Kandinsky: *Reminiscences / Three Pictures*, in *Complete Writings*, Vol. I [see n. 9], p. 385.

167. Hanfstaengl: *Wassily Kandinsky* (see n. 158), no. 250. See also Thürlemann: *Kandinsky über Kandinsky* (see n. 27), p. 197, who is certainly right in referring Kandinsky's words "Analysis of the last sketch" to *Sketch 3*.

168. Cf. J. Hahl-Koch: *Kandinsky* (see n. 24), p. 212 sq. On the photographs, when compared with reproductions of the final version, strangely enough a small strip of the upper border of the painting is missing.

169. The annotation "Abgrund" in the lower *right* corner is an argument against Thürlemann's identification of Hanfstaengl no. 273 as a further preparatory study for *Composition VII* because of the same note in its lower *left* corner (cf. Thürlemann: *Kandinsky über Kandinsky* [see n. 27], p. 140).

170. The relation of the diagonals in Sketch 1–3 and final version is: 1 : 1.06 : 1.06 : 1.11.

171. W. Kandinsky: "Letters from Munich", in *Complete Writings*, Vol. I (see n. 9), p. 80.

172. A. Schönberg: *Theory of Harmony* (see n. 11), p. 70.

173. Especially in Schönberg's *Gedanke* – manuscript (cf. Alexander Goehr: Schönberg's *Gedanke* Manuscript, in *JASI* II/1 (1977), p. 4–25.

174. See among others: Carl Dahlhaus: "Ausdrucksprinzip und Orchesterpolyphonie in Schönberg *Erwartung*", in *Bericht über den 1. Kongreß der Internationalen Schönberg-Gesellschaft* (Wien 1978), p. 34–38.

175. These are, of course, not the only shaping elements and features; cf. John Crawford: "*Die Glückliche Hand*: Schoenberg's *Gesamtkunstwerk*", in *Musical Quarterly* LX/4 (1974); Karl Wörner: *Die glückliche Hand* (Bonn 1970) and more recently: Joseph Henry Auner: *Schoenberg's Compositional and Aesthetic Transformations 1910–1913: The Genesis of* Die Glückliche Hand (see n. 48), passim.

176. Cf. Reinhold Brinkmann: "Schönberg und George. Interpretation eines Liedes", in *Archiv für Musikwissenschaft* 26/1 (1969), p. 1–28.

177. Cf. Brinkmann: "Schönberg und George" (see n. 176), p. 16.

178. This letter is published here for the first time (see notes 1 and 48 and p. 62+64).

179. *Arnold Schönberg: Style and Idea*, ed. Leonard Stein, (Berkeley / Los Angeles, 1984), p. 144.

180. Cf. Rudolf Stephan: "Über Schönbergs Arbeitsweise", in *Arnold Schönberg Gedenkausstellung 1974*, ed. Ernst Hilmar (Wien 1974), p. 119 sqq.; R. Stephan: "Über die Klangvorstellungen Arnold Schönbergs", in *Klang und Komponist. Ein Symposium der Wiener Philharmoniker*, ed. O. Biba u. W. Schuster (Tutzing 1992), p. 191–199.

181. Arnold Schönberg. *Self-Portrait. A Collection of Articles, Program Notes and Letters by the Composer about his Work*, ed. Nuria Schönberg-Nono (Belmont Publishers, Pacific Palisades 1988), p. 54.

182. Arnold Schönberg. *Self-Portrait* (see n. 181), p. 55.

183. Arnold Schönberg: "The Relationship to the Text", in *A. Schoenberg: Style and Idea*, ed. Leonard Stein, (Berkeley / Los Angeles 1984), p. 144 sq.

184. It is clear that this may differ from artist to artist.
185. Arnold Schönberg. *Self-Portrait* (see n. 181), p. 55.
186. This can be taken for granted when we compare Kandinsky's descriptions in *Reminiscences / Three Pictures* (in *Complete Writings*, Vol. I [see n. 9], p. 371) and Haber's criteria for eidetic images as referred to by Cytowic in *Synesthesia* (see n. 56, p. 100).
187. Kandinsky: *Reminiscences / Three Pictures*, in *Complete Writings*, Vol. I (see n. 9), p. 371.
188. Cf. Ernst Gombrich: *Art and Illusion*, Reprint (London 1993), p. 155.
189. See Gombrich: *Art and Illusion* (see n. 188), p. 155 sqq.
190. Comparable artistic efforts like those of Hölzel, Delaunay, Klee, Mondrian and others cannot be taken into account here.
191. This is a position held by Johann Friedrich Herbart und Robert Zimmermann, based on Kant and Moritz; cf. Morgan (see n. 29, p. 232 sq.). With these and other comparisons with puzzling aspects from the history of ornament, no catalogue of influences is intended!
192. A position which, to a certain degree, recalls that of Vischer and Fechner; cf. Morgan (see n. 29, p. 233).
193. Cf. Klaus Kropfinger: "The Shape of Line", in *Art Nouveau and Jugendstil and the Music of the Early 20th Century* (Adelaide 1984) (=Miscellanea Musicologica. Adelaide Studies in Musicology, Vol. 13), p. 136 sqq.; ibid.: "Wagner – van de Velde – Kandinsky", in K. Kropfinger: Über Musik im Bilde [see note 31], p. 434 sqq.
194. Cf. Morgan (see n. 29), p. 236 sq.
195. An approach which reflects Roessler's position (cf. Morgan [see n. 29], p. 238) and that of van de Velde (cf. Kropfinger: "The Shape of Line" [see n. 193], p. 136 sq.) as well. On the importance of Hoelzel cf. Peg Weiss: *Kandinsky in Munich. The Formative Jugendstil Years* (Princeton 1979), p. 43 sqq.
196. Cf. Morgan (see n. 29), p. 234. That does not mean, however, that Kandinsky was (directly) influenced by van de Velde, Endell, Roessler and/or Lipps.
197. Cf. Rose-Carol Washton Long (*Kandinsky* [see n. 29], passim), but also Langner's ("Gegensätze und Widersprüche – das ist unsere Harmonie" [see also n. 1]), Zweite's ("Kandinsky zwischen Tradition und Innovation" [see n. 29]) and Peg Weiss's studies (cf. Edward J. Kimball and Peg Weiss: "A Pictorial Analysis of 'In the Black Square'", in *Art Forum*, 43/1 [1983], p. 36–40).
198. Rudenstine rightly states that: "Kandinsky's works of 1913 were, until the early 1950s, traditionally regarded as totally abstract." (Rudenstine: *The Guggenheim Museum Collection* [see n. 102], 173.)
199. Kandinsky: "On the Question of Form", in *Complete Writings*, Vol. I (see n. 9), p. 243 sq.
200. In both versions: "...einmalige Erscheinung einer Ferne, so nah sie sein mag." "Walter Benjamin: Das Kunstwerk im Zeitalter seiner technischen Reproduzierbarkeit", in *Gesammelte Schriften*, Vol. 1(2), ed. Rolf Tiedemann / Hermann Schweppenhäuser (Frankfurt am Main, 3/1990), p. 440, 479. "Auratic Iconography" matches what Kandinsky calls the "particular spiritual sound" that objects do indeed have, which he could not immediately get rid of because he was "not yet sufficiently mature to experience purely abstract form without bridging the gap by means of objects." (Kandinsky: "Cologne lecture", in *Complete Writings*, Vol. I [see n. 9], p. 396.) In my view, the aspect of "auratic iconography" does not match Steiner's idea of "aura" (cf. Sixten Ringbom: *The Sounding Cosmos* [see n. 29], p. 63, 81 sqq., 96 sqq.). For another interpretation of "aura" in Kandinsky's paintings of this time see Yule F. Heibel: "'They danced on Volcanoes': Kandinsky's Breakthrough to Abstraction, the German Avant-Garde and the Eve of the First World War", in *Art History*, 12/3 (September 1989), esp. p. 354 sq.

201. This could have been the reason why Kandinsky in 1936/37 insisted that a painting like *Composition VII* should be called "non-objective" in spite of the figurative relics still visible (cf. Rudenstine (see n. 102), p. 273 sqq.).
202. Cf. Ernst Gombrich: *Art and Illusion* (see n. 188), p. 314.
203. This sentence of Schönberg's is related to his First String Quartet, op. 7 (cf. *Schoenberg – Berg – Webern. The String Quartets. A Documentary Study*, ed. Ursula v. Rauchhaupt (Hamburg 1971), p. 36.
204. Cf. Kropfinger: "The Shape of Line" (see n. 193), passim.
205. Cf. *Reallexikon zur deutschen Kunstgeschichte*, Vol. V, ed. L. H. Heydenreich und K.-A. Wirth (Stuttgart 1967), cols. 88 sqq.
206. No less significant is the analytical sketch of *Composition II* (cf. Rudenstine [see n. 102], p. 233).
207. Heller lays stress on the fact that "Apocalyptic thought patterns appear with increasing vehemence in Kandinsky's imagery – both verbal and pictorial – during 1910–13. Prior to 1910, neither his writings nor his paintings reveal such tendencies." ("Kandinsky and Traditions Apocalyptic", in *Art Journal* [see n. 76], p. 20.)
208. Cf. Peg Weiss: "Editor's Statement: Are we ready to memorialize Kandinsky?", in *Art Journal*, 43/1 [Spring 1983], p. 11.
209. Sixten Ringbom is surely exaggerating the importance of anthroposophy and theosophy for Kandinsky's spiritual art (cf. *The Sounding Cosmos* [see n. 29], passim). This aspect is also valid in Ringbom's text "Überwindung des Sichtbaren. Die Generation der abstrakten Pioniere", in *Das Geistige in der Kunst. Abstrakte Malerei 1890–1985* (ed. Maurice Tuchman and Judi Freeman, Stuttgart 1988, p. 131–154), where he even credits Theosophy with Kandinsky's wish to become [!] a synesthete. There is no doubting Kandinsky's interest. But Kandinsky certainly did not need to be inspired by Besant's and Leadbeater's Thought- and Colour-Forms or Dr. Freudenberg's occult descriptions. This is a methodologically, and because of the artist's biography and self-observations, not justified exaggeration of "influence".
210. Cf. J. Hahl-Koch: *Kandinsky* (see n. 24), p. 178.
211. Ringbom: *The Sounding Cosmos* (see n. 29), p. 172 sqq.; Majorie Reeves / Beatrice Hirsch-Reich: *The Figurae of Joachim of Fiore* (Oxford 1972), 314 sqq.
212. Wassily Kandinsky: "Cologne lecture", in *Complete Writings*, Vol. I (see n. 9), p. 400.
213. Cf. the typescript of a Bauhaus lecture (13/IV/32) with the concluding remark, following a discussion of the "unthinkable distances", where he writes: "... despite this 'the cosmos holds together', it doesn't fall apart, therefore: endless telekinesis" (Getty Center, Resource Collections, folder 850 910–5) (... trotz dem 'hält der Kosmos zusammen', zerfällt nicht, also: unendliche Fernwirkung."). There is also a reading list among Kandinsky's papers (not in his own handwriting) that includes Johannes Kepler's *Harmonices Mundi* and his *Prodromus dissertationum cosmographicarum continens Mysterium cosmographicum* (Getty Center, Resource Collections, folder 850 910–42).
214. Kandinsky: *Reminiscences / Three Paintings*, in *Complete Writings*, Vol. I (see n. 9), p. 377 sq.
215. Cf. Erwin Panofsky: *Idea* (Berlin 1960), p. 44 sq.
216. Kandinsky: *Reminiscences / Three Paintings*, in *Complete Writings*, Vol. I (see n. 9), p. 373.

Lieber Herr Kandinsky,

   ich kann leider (das ist sehr schade für mich) nicht an Ihrer Ausstellung teilnehmen, denn ich habe ja zu dieser Budapester Ausstellung zugesagt und die wird am 2. Januar eröffnet. Deshalb muß ich Sie bitten alle meine Bilder mit Ausnahme jenes Porträts, das Sie ''Dame in Rosa'' nennen [sic!], durch einen Spediteur und unter Nachnahme der Spesen *sofort nach Erhalt dieser Karte* (bitte vielmals) nach Budapest an folgende Adresse zu senden:

Müvesz – haz, Budapest IV. Kristóf-ter 2

Die ''Dame in Rosa'' dagegen an mich, auch gegen Nachnahme. Nicht wahr bitte, Sie sind so freundlich, das sofort zu tun. Schade, daß ich nicht bei Ihrer Ausstellung dabei sein kann, aber ich habe dort schon zugesagt und es ist das auch günstiger für mich, weil ich dort einen eigenen Raum bekomme (23 Bilder) wo ich nicht von den starken Farben der andern Maler erschlagen werde.

Ihr Buch habe ich jetzt schon ganz gelesen und werde es ein zweites Mal lesen. Es gefällt mir außerordentlich, denn wir stimmen in fast allen Hauptsachen, wie Sie ja auch aus meinem Buch entnehmen werden überein. Ich bin übrigens sehr neugierig, was Sie zu meinem Buch sagen werden. Ich schreibe Ihnen demnächst ausführlicher.

Ich weiß nicht, ob ich Ihnen schon gesagt habe, daß ich für den ''blauen Reiter'' doch etwas ''Musik'' (ein Lied) hergeben kann.

Für heute Schluß. Herzliche Grüße auch an Ihre Frau Ihr Arnold Schönberg.

18/12.1911

[darunter mit dickem Schreibzeug, offenbar von Kandinskys Hand]:
''bestellt 20I XII''
ARNOLD SCHÖNBERG, BERLIN-ZEHLENDORF-WANNSEEBAHN
MACHNOWER CHAUSSEE, VILLA LEPCKE

ARNOLD SCHÖNBERG, BERLIN-ZEHLENDORF-WANNSEEBAHN
MACHNOWER CHAUSSEE, VILLA LEPCKE

15/1.1912

Lieber Herr Kandinsky,

in größter Eile, denn ich muß mich auf meinen heutigen Vortrag vorbereiten. I. Sie erhalten aus Wien von Herrn Ullmann einen Aufsatz von mir für den "Blauen Reiter" über "Das Verhältnis zum Text ['']! Den hatte ich einem wohltätigen Zweck eines akademischen Vereins zugesagt. Doch ziehen die, da es sich um eine Karnevals – Angelegenheit handelt, lieber etwas lustiges vor. Ich sandte ihnen bescheidneren. – Wollen Sie mir nun gleich mitteilen, ob Sie diesen Aufsatz im "Blauen Reiter" bringen möchten. II. Die Noten kann ich Ihnen erst in ein paar Tagen schicken. III. Mit meinen Bildern das ist ein kolossales Mißverständnis. Ich bat Sie *alle* meine Bilder, mit Ausnahme jenes Portraits nach Budapest zu senden. Bitte lesen Sie meinen Brief noch einmal. Das ist mir höchst unangenehm. Denn die in Budapest warten wohl noch immer auf die Bilder. Wenn Sie das noch ändern können, so bitte ich Sie dringend es zu tun und alles, auch die "Landschaft" (die ich übrigens "Nachtstück" nenne) nach Budapest zu schicken. Nur die Dame in Rosa nicht. Aber die könnten Sie mir zuschicken! Darf ich Sie darum bitten? IV. Preise habe ich nicht genannt, weil ich glaubte es habe wegen der paar Tage keinen Zweck. War denn eine Verkaufsmöglichkeit? Auch weiß ich nicht genau genug welche Bilder Sie ausstellten. Haben Sie Fotografien von den Bildern gemacht? Ich meine für den "Bl. [auen] R. [eiter]" – Wann soll der denn erscheinen? Daß Sie mir vorwerfen, ich hätte Ihren Brief nicht beatnwortet ist ungerecht. Aber ich gebe zu: nicht ganz. Aber jetzt schreibe ich doch öfter, als Sie!!!! – Es ist schade, daß Sie nicht nach Berlin kommen. Ich hatte mich sehr darauf gefreut! Könnten Sie in Rußland nicht etwas für meine Musik anfangen? Ich meine: Daß man mich einladet, meine Werke zu dirigiren? Viele herzl. Grüße Ihnen und Ihrer Frau Ihr Arnold Schönberg. Auch von meiner Frau!

Dear Mr. Kandinsky,[1]

I am regrettably unable to participate in your exhibition – a very great pity for me – due to the fact that I have just agreed to an exhibition in Budapest,[2] which opens on 2 January. Thus, I must ask you to send all of my pictures – save for the one you call "Lady in Pink"[3] – to the following address in Budapest by forwarding agent, C.O.D., *immediately upon receipt of this postcard* (and with many thanks):

Müvesz – haz, Budapest IV. Kristóf-ter 2[4]

The "Lady in Pink," on the other hand, to my address, also C.O.D. It is so very kind of you to do this. Regrets that I cannot be present for your exhibition, but alas I had already accepted the other, which is indeed more favorable for me, as I will have a room of my own (23 paintings) where I will not be overshadowed by the strong colors of the other painters.

I have just read your book from cover to cover,[5] and I will read it once more. I find it extraordinarily pleasing that we agree on nearly all of the

---

[1] This and the following letter are located in the Getty Center, Research Collections (Folder 850 910–70) (see also notes 1 and 48 of my text).

[2] Schönberg had been invited by Paris von Gütersloh to participate in an exhibition in Budapest with "15–20" of his paintings (cf. Nuria Nono-Schönberg, ed., *Arnold Schönberg 1874–1951. Lebensgeschichte in Beschreibungen*, Klagenfurt, 1992, p. 90). Von Gütersloh also writes that Schönberg would have a whole room at his disposal. Schönberg mentions the invitation first in his letter to Kandinsky of 14 December 1911, where he speaks of 24 pictures to be exhibited (cf. *Arnold Schoenberg–Wassily Kandinsky. Letters, Pictures and Documents*, ed. Jelena Hahl-Koch, trans. John Crawford, London and Boston, 1984, p. 39). Included in the same exhibition were pictures by Schiele, Kolig, and Faistauer (cf. *Schoenberg–Kandinsky. Letters, Pictures and Documents*, p. 190, n. 20). Von Gütersloh wrote an essay entitled "Schönberg der Maler" for the *Festschrift Arnold Schönberg*, Munich, 1912, p. 65–74, with contributions by Alban Berg and others.

[3] The identification of the painting in question is still unclear, though it may have been the portrait of Klara von Zemlinsky, if one can make such a judgment from the reproduction (cf. *Arnold Schoenberg. Paintings and Drawings*, ed. Thomas Zaunschirm, Klagenfurt, 1991, Fig. 98, p. 241, and p. 372). Kandinsky tried to get a photo of the "Lady in Pink" for the "Blue Rider" (letter of February 6, 1912; cf. *Schoenberg–Kandinsky. Letters, Pictures and Documents* [see n. 1, p. 46]). But neither this plan nor Kandinsky's intent to present the painting in an exhibition of *Der Sturm* (letter of March 4 1912; ibid. p. 47) was successful. Marc may have seen the portrait in Schoenberg's dining room, when he visited the composer in Berlin, January 28, 1912. According to Kandinsky, Marc was "always talking about it with great enthusiasm" (ibid.).

[4] This is the address that von Gütersloh mentions in his letter to Schönberg (see n. 1).

[5] This is a reference to Kandinsky's book *On the Spiritual in Art*, which the artist had sent to Schönberg with his photograph and dedication on 4 April 1911.

main issues, as you too will gather from reading my book.[6] I am, incidentally, extremely curious to know what you will have to say about my book. I shall write to you in more detail soon. I am not sure whether or not I have already told you that I will, after all, compose some music (a song) for the *Blue Rider*.

For now, that sums it up. My kindest regards to your wife, Yours, Arnold Schoenberg.

18 December 1911

[below, in bold script, apparently in Kandinsky's own hand]:
"ordered 2̶0̶1 XII"
ARNOLD SCHÖNBERG, BERLIN-ZEHLENDORF-WANNSEEBAHN
MACHNOWER CHAUSSEE, VILLA LEPCKE

ARNOLD SCHÖNBERG, BERLIN-ZEHLENDORF-WANNSEEBAHN
MACHNOWER CHAUSSEE, VILLA LEPCKE

15 January 1912

Dear Mr. Kandinsky,
   In great hurry, as I must prepare my lecture for today.
I. You [will] receive from Mr. Ullmann in Vienna[7] an essay of mine for the *Blue Rider* dealing with "The Relationship to the text!" – Something I agreed to do for an academic association. However, as it should have concerned Carnival, they preferred something amusing. I've sent them a more modest piece. Would you let me know right away whether or not you would like to include this article in the *Blue Rider*?

---

[6] Schönberg's *Theory of Harmony*, which he had sent to Kandinsky with his picture and a dedication, dated 12 December 1911, in which he quotes from the last movement of his Second String Quartet.

[7] Here Schönberg surely does not speak of *Viktor* Ullmann, who would later be his pupil, but who at this time was just 13 years old; rather he means *Ludwig* Ullmann, who belonged to the editorial staff of the *Akademischer Verband für Literatur und Musik*. It is therefore also clear that Schönberg had originally intended the text for publication by the *Verband*. The more "modest" text Schönberg speaks of consisted of his "Aphorisms," which appeared in the *Karnevalsnummer 1912* of *Der Ruf*, the journal of the *Verband* (cf. *Arnold Schönberg. Gedenkausstellung 1974*, ed. Ernst Hilmar, Vienna, 1974, nos. 235 and 236, p. 245. See also Schönberg's Berlin Diary of February 14, 1912; cf. "Attempt at a Diary", in *JASI* IX/1 [June 1986], p. 28]).

II. The music I will send to you in a couple of days' time.[8]

III. As for my paintings, this is a colossal misunderstanding. I asked you to send *all* of my pictures, with the exception of this single portrait, to Budapest. Please, read my letter once more. It is of the greatest embarrassment to me. For in Budapest, they surely will still be waiting for the pictures. If you are yet able to correct this, I urgently ask you to do it, and to send all, including the "Landscape" (which, by the way, I call "Night [Nocturnal?] Piece"[9]) to Budapest. The only exception is the "Lady in Pink." As for her, however, could you send her to me! May I please ask you this?

IV. I gave no prices, because I believed that for a couple of days there would be little chance. Was there indeed the possibility of a sale? Neither do I know exactly which pictures you exhibited. Did you take photographs of the pictures? I mean for the "Bl. R." [*Blue Rider*] – When is it expected to appear? That you blame me for not having answered your letter is unjust. But I grant you: not entirely. But now I write more often than you!!! – It's a pity that you aren't coming to Berlin. I had very much looked forward to it! Couldn't you initiate something in Russia for my music?[10] I mean: Arrange for someone to invite me to conduct my works? Many cordial regards to you and to your wife, Yours, Arnold Schoenberg. Also from my wife!

---

[8] Not earlier than February 6, 1912 could Kandinsky thank for Schönberg's music ("Herzgewächse") for which Gabriele Münter had once more urgently asked on January 27, 1912.

[9] Apparently the signed and dated picture of 1910 which in the catalogue of the recent comprehensive Schönberg exhibition has been listed as "Night landscape" (*Arnold Schoenberg. Paintings and Drawings*, p. 301, 380, no. 194.)

[10] Kandinsky's letters of January 16, 1912 (cf. *Schoenberg–Kandinsky. Letters, Pictures and Documents*, p. 43), March 28 (ibid., p. 50 sq.) and October 23 (ibid., p. 58) show that he was seriously concerned to obey Schönberg's demand.

Kandinsky, Schönberg and their Parallel Experiments

JELENA HAHL-KOCH

We are currently celebrating the 82nd anniversary of Schönberg's concert of early January 1911 in Munich. Kandinsky attended this concert, and few days later he painted his famous *Impression III (Concert)* (fig. 1) and wrote his first letter to the composer. Fortunately these two geniuses became friends and left us an extraordinary correspondence on a whole range of subjects that intrigued them, at that crucial period between 1911 and 1914 when Kandinsky founded abstract art and Schönberg atonal music.

The subjects dealt with in their letters were Kandinsky's and Schönberg's *paintings*, their *stage* plays and their *theories* (which they were working on at the same time, but independently). Also their search for a *common denominator* of art and music with the final aim being the SYNTHESIS OF THE ARTS, then the creative act itself and the question whether *intuition* or construction, the more intellectual approach, should take the lead.

Figure 1 Kandinsky, *Impression III (Concert)*, 1911, oil on canvas., Städt. Galerie im Lenbachhaus, Munich © W. Kandinsky c/o Beeldrecht Amsterdam

In this colloquium report, you might expect to hear a general outline of all the interesting themes between these two innovators. But, don't worry, I won't repeat what I wrote in the edition of their correspondence, because I prefer to concentrate on those subjects where there is new material or where new research has been done.

One small piece of new information. It was Kandinsky's companion, the artist Gabriele Münter, who had found Schönberg's address, so Kandinsky could write to him. She mentioned this at a later occasion, when she was observing the contact between Kandinsky and 'Volker' (Erich Gutkind, a German-Jewish philosopher) who tried – together with Kandinsky and a few others – to found a peace initiative in 1914 shortly before the outbreak of World War I. Münter, who intended to establish a contact between Gutkind and Schönberg, wrote to the latter on August 20, 1912: "I think such people should get to know each other, just as I had found your address"[1]. Certainly Kandinsky himself had wished to meet Schönberg, but also his companion, who knew him well since they lived and travelled together from 1904 on, had occasionally taken the initiative and made the first practical steps. As for comparable contacts there was, except for the two just mentioned, only one more in these years: to the Russian artist, musicologist, physician and organizer of the younger Cubofuturist artists, Nikolai Kulbin. In general, however, Kandinsky was rather shy and reserved. So we can conclude that he took such initiatives only when it seemed really important for him to meet someone. He wrote to Kulbin because he had heard that his new art association in St. Petersburg, the Triangle, was as progressive and daring as his own *New Artists Asociation* in Munich. The later contact with Gutkind had already been established, since Gutkind had sent his book *Siderial Birth* to the *Blue Rider* group in 1912.

So we can see that: in Schönberg's case, Kandinsky (and with him Münter) made a major effort to meet an individual person. Why? Was it just the progressiveness of Schönberg's music that fascinated Kandinsky to such an extent? Or did he understand enough about music to be able to judge (and better than most other contemporaries of Schönberg) the high quality of that music? Or was it, because he was eager to find another fellow fighter for new ideas in art – art in its largest definition? All this was certainly the case, but it only answers the question partially. Another reason was Kandinsky's tremendous interest in music, which surpassed by far his theoretical knowledge (he played both the piano and the violoncello, but considered himself rightly as a dilettante). His preoccupation with music had already become evident in his friendship with the Russian composer Thomas von Hartmann, with whom he had worked on his experimental 'stage compositions' since 1909.

But before we investigate Kandinsky's and Schönberg's "dilettante" innovations, i.e. those beyond their professional activities, let us start with the first subject matter of their letters: Should intuition or construction take the lead in the creative process? Listen to how Schönberg in 1911 still pleaded for the intuitive solution: "But art belongs to the *unconscious*! One must express *oneself*! Express oneself *directly*! Not one's taste, or one's upbringing, or one's intelligence, knowledge or skill. Not all these *acquired* characteristics, but that which is *inborn, instinctive*"[2].

Schönberg – as we have always known – had worked with tremendous difficulty on the musical score of his opera *Die glückliche Hand* (The Lucky Hand) and did not finish it until fully 3 years after writing the text, in November, 1913. In between he had composed *Pierrot Lunaire*. A very thorough investigation into all obstacles for Schönberg's delay was published recently in the *Schoenberg Journal* by Joseph Auner. The reason he gives is intriguing: "The breakdown of Schönberg's intuitive aesthetics and the emergence of a new approach to composition...This is reflected by the strikingly large number of sketches (while otherwise he had little to none) and by the fact that Schönberg had substantially modified his earlier views"[3]. In 25 pages Auner proves the enormous difference from the spontaneous, genial achievement of *Erwartung*, Schönberg's previous monodrama that he composed within an astonishingly short time period (17 days) with hardly any sketches or corrections. But now the path seemed obstructed and obscured, the intuitive solution was no longer in reach. Was it only because of the personal crisis (his wife's love affair in 1908)? Auner says the change was much more fundamental; I agree. While on the whole I maintain my opinion that there was no influence between Kandinsky and Schönberg, now I am proposing an hypothesis, which when I edited the correspondence, I did not yet dare to make, because there were not enough facts then known. My hypothesis is: Schönberg could after all have thought about, why Kandinsky continued to insist on the necessity of construction in the creative process and contradicted him a few times: "Fundamentally, I agree with you. That is, when one is actually at work, then there should be no thought, but the 'inner voice' alone should speak and control. But up to now the painter has thought too little in general...But the painter (and precisely so that he will be able to express *himself*) should learn his whole material so well and develop his sensitivity to the point where he recognizes and vibrates spiritually..."[4]. Actually this was the only point of disagreement. And especially since they otherwise showed remarkable parallels in their ideas and creative acts, and because Schönberg thought highly of the nine year older artist, he could at least have been somewhat disturbed by Kandinsky's words, with the result that his new aesthetic concept in 1913 included a lot more preparatory work and construction. So in his *Lucky Hand*, whose theme is precisely the opposition between effortless, genial creation and the more superficial, laborious and less inspired handicraft, the author had lost to some extent his own 'lucky hand'.

Now let us shift to the subject of *synesthesia*. Once, in an unpublished letter of 1903 to Gabriele Münter, Kandinsky described the city of Venice thus: "...this twilight, where blue, purple, gold, orange, copper develop the most pensive symphony!"[5] One is reminded of similar comparisons between color impressions and a Symphony, the fortissimo of an orchestra and so forth, in his *Reminiscences*. Such comparisons are neither arbitrary nor deliberately poetic: Kandinsky's whole correspondence, his theoretical writings and also the titles of his paintings (Impression, Improvisation, Composition, Pastorale, Fugue and so on) attest to the continuous presence of music.

The first drafts for *On the Spiritual in Art* are dated 1904 (they have never been published); they deal with the effects of color on the human mind (also in relation to sounds in general and music in particular). In his letters to Münter of the same year, he stresses that he needs inner peace and tranquillity to concentrate on and perceive such subtle vibrations, before writing down his observations – just the same as for creating a work of art.

Among Kandinsky's yet unpublished and undated manuscripts in his Munich estate is a strange double-sheet (figs. 2–4) with 3 notes, 2 corresponding figures and 4 explanatory texts. On the first page Kandinsky states that the depicted note "means a complaint, a desire, a non-satisfaction, [a little] pain, a little suffering". The second page with the straight figure at the bottom reads: "Solemnity of a supernatural character with coldness and indifference towards men. Its symbol is nature as a whole. This sound is like an answer to the question (see above), which however remains incomprehensible and unsatisfactory.
Graphically = [line, dash, arrow]."
On the third page with the figure in motion Kandinsky explains: "Enthusiasm, passion, joy. It is like a joyous apprehension of a voice from above, but which does not come from a familiar and definable source. Graphically [a spiral moving upward]."
The fourth and final page consists only of text: "The soul poses a question and looks for an answer in the surrounding sensual nature. The answer is given, but does not satisfy. Suddenly the supernatural answer comes that calls into higher realms. *Accord* D major is peacefulness, satisfaction after having received the answer"[6].

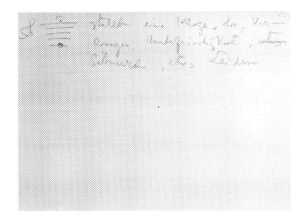

Figures 2–4 Undated manuscripts by Kandinsky. (Gabriele Münter- and Johannes Eichner-Foundation, Munich.) © W. Kandinsky c/o Beeldrecht Amsterdam

Here we have in a 'shorthand' formula Kandinsky's whole conception of art, namely that the material aspect of our world is not sufficient: the essential answer lies in transcendance (which artistically, of course is closer to abstraction than to the depiction of the material world). But one is puzzled by the musical notes; what does the painter mean by associating three single notes to emotions or states of mind? If one might still follow and guess his feelings about the Accord D major, one wonders how an isolated sound can mean anything. [I would very much like to hear more about it from musicologists: is Kandinsky experimenting in a totally naive and absurd manner? Or is there something to it?]

In any case, all this is symptomatic of Kandinsky's fascination with music and shows the leading role it played in his thoughts and sensitivity. In a letter to Schönberg in 1911 he gives the reason for this leading role that music had for him: "How fortunate musicians are with their well advanced art. Real ART, long fortunate in having foregone purely practical means. How long will painting have to wait for this? Though it is entitled (obliged) to it as well: colors and lines for and by themselves – such limitless beauty and power"[7].

Kandinsky ranks music as the leading art form, because it is the most abstract and does not imitate the outer world (... for instance a rooster's crow is not necessary to suggest a morning mood). The Russian Symbolist poet Andrei Bely had stated already in 1902: "Beginning with the lowest forms of art and ending with music, we witness a slow but sure weakening of the image or reality. In architecture, sculpture and in painting these images play an important role. In music they are absent. In approaching music, a work of art becomes deeper, broader"[8]. It is likely that Kandinsky knew Bely to some extent, since many publications of the Russian symbolists are still in Kandinsky's library.

Music can teach painting the principle of using colors, lines, and shapes in and for themselves. This was precisely what he longed to do even before he made the final step toward abstract painting. And this is why he sought out progressive composers like Thomas von Hartmann and mainly Schönberg. He was so enthusiastic about the first atonal compositions, which revealed to him the affinities between their respective aspirations, that he saw the need to get to know more about this composer who was causing scandals, just as he himself was with his exhibitions.

That very year, when he established the contact, in 1911, Kandinsky states in *The Spiritual in Art*: "Schönberg's music takes us to a realm where musical experience is not acoustic but purely spiritual." And he translated parts of Schönberg's *Theory of Harmony* into Russian for the catalog of Vladimir Izdebsky's second *International Salon* 1911 in Odessa and added an important observation: "...how keenly this revolutionary composer feels the inviolable, *organic* link, the inevitable natural development of the new music out of the old...There is a limit, however, to the attainments of every age, every chord, every progression is permissible, 'but – Schönberg says – I feel even today that there are certain limits which determine my use of this or that dissonance.' Schönberg combines in his thinking the greatest freedom with the greatest belief in the ordered development of the spirit"[9]. Here Kandinsky naturally speaks for himself as well.

Let us go back to 1907, to more unpublished documents. He spent that year with Gabriele Münter in Paris, where he came to realize that the Fauves were far ahead of him. His relationship with Gabriele had also reached a dead end. After their return to Germany, Kandinsky had to recover from this emotional crisis alone in a resort: "I would like to be able to feel again, to cry again before nature, to kneel down, to give thanks...I cannot live like a blind and deaf person, after having had eyes and ears...I have become insensitive. And only music can save me...I have to have good music (we know for instance that he was very fond of Beethoven's 3rd symphony). It stimulates me so"[10].

Kandinsky also inquired into the recently founded Munich sanatorium's use of color therapy, which applied music as well: "At times the patient was given single sounds or particular chords in rhythmic repetition during the treatment" – reports Alexander Strakosch, Rudolf Steiner's secretary and husband of Kandinsky's former student Maria Giesler[11]. We know now that Kandinsky owed to Maria his acquaintance not only with Rudolf Steiner, the founder of anthroposophy, but also with the Russian musicologist and theosophist Alexandra Zacharina-Unkovskaya. In 1910 Maria gave a color scale with which Unkovskaya used to demonstrate the vibration of sounds in accord with the vibration of colors (this scale is preserved in Kandinsky's Munich estate). Kandinsky mentions in a letter of October 1910 from Moscow to the previously mentioned Petersburg physician, painter, musicologist and organiser of the young Futurists, Nikolai Kulbin: "I may go to Kaluga to speak with Alexandra Vasilievna Unkovskaya (that is, to meet her)"[12]. – and to Münter he wrote that Unkovskaya was eager to show him her system, her investigations into the numerical, mainly the no. 7, and he reported that his woodcuts seem to her "purest painterly music"[13].

In the *Spiritual in Art* Kandinsky describes the work of Unkovskaya: "to impress a tune upon unmusical children with the help of colors...She has constructed a special, precise method of 'translating the colors of nature into music, of painting the sounds of nature, of seeing sounds in color and hearing colors musically". This method has been recognized as useful by the Petersburg Conservatory – On the other hand, Scriabin has constructed empirically a parallel table of equivalent tones in color and music, which very closely resembles the more physical table of Mrs. Unkovskaya. Scriabin has made convincing use of his method in his *Prometheus*." More critical is a private letter to Münter: "Recently I heard Scriabin's music. Interesting but – in my eyes – too beautiful. He too, thinks a lot about correspondences between the musical and the color tones, but, as I understand, not profoundly enough"[14].

In a phase of slow progress with abstraction – when he was tormented by self doubts and uncomprehending critics – Kandinsky turned increasingly to music, as his first musician friend Thomas von Hartmann reports:" This period (before 1910) was marked by his ideas of a certain relationship between the doctrine of painting and musical theory, and by his constant dissatisfaction with the contemporary theatre (particularly opera)"[15]. From 1909 on, Kandinsky collaborated with Hartmann on his stage compositions, with the idea of creating a work of art in which sound/music, color/painting, movement/dance and lighting were at times used together or against each other, in all variations. This synthesis aimed at achieving more than the sum of the parts, not just an addition or subordination of one part to another – as was, according to Kandinsky, still the case with Wagner and Scriabin. The best known of these stage compositions was *The Yellow Sound*, which Kandinsky took out of the close context with two other stage plays and developed it further, until he finally published it in 1912 in the *Blue Rider* Almanac.

At the same time, between 1909 and 1913, Schönberg who went through a crisis before reaching his 'free atonality', turned increasingly to painting and also worked on small operas with the aim of a *Gesamtkunstwerk*. In 1909 it was the short monodrama *Erwartung*, then he began the work on *Die glückliche Hand* (The Lucky Hand), interrupted by *Pierrot Lunaire*. It is especially the 3rd scene of *Die glückliche Hand* which reveals Schönberg's pursuit of the *Gesamtkunstwerk* and which at the same time is most comparable with several scenes of Kandinsky's *Der gelbe Klang*. It is the combined crescendo of the orchestra with lights of changing colors, which, however, according to Schönberg's words, seems to be brought about by the Man's (the main character's) changing emotions, and thus to that extent still shows, by means of psychology, a last link with reality. This is no longer the case in Kandinsky's play. We should also remember that at the same time, Kandinsky stated that in his opinion Wagner (who of course was of great importance for both Kandinsky and Schönberg) showed only the first steps towards a real synthesis of the arts, because he did not use the media completely independently, but in an additive manner, with music always having the leading role.

When Schönberg compares Kandinsky's *The Yellow Sound* with his own *Lucky Hand*, he calls its renunciation of a realistic plot a "great advantage" and affirms that he had *fundamentally wanted the same thing*. This is certainly credible, since he gave for instance the following direction: "The entire effect should not imitate nature, but rather be a free combination of colors and forms" (exactly as Kandinsky), but then – what a contradiction – Schönberg describes a detailed realistic stage-setting[16]. Such crass collisions between purely symbolic actions and frankly naturalistic passages are astonishing and, one must admit, weak points of the work. So it is good to learn from Schönberg's letters to Kandinsky that basically he intended to be more abstract as well as coming closer to a real 'Gesamtkunstwerk'. This was to a greater extent achieved by Kandinsky's stage compositions: it was already a random play of independent color, movement and noise/or music. It must have fascinated him to add to the elements of color and form, which were familiar to him from painting, the temporal elements of music as well as movement and lighting, both of which could modify form and color and make them come alive. His results, and to some extent also those of Schönberg, went beyond everything that had been achieved so far in the field of the synthesis of the arts (a field of interest since the Romantic and mainly the Symbolist period).

For sure Kandinsky and Schönberg – together with Oskar Kokoschka, the sculptor Ernst Barlach and some others – must be included in that series of 'dilettantes' who gave to the German Expressionist theatre its most significant impetus and opened new creative possibilities to the professional theatre. Sometimes the most daring innovations are made as it were on a side track, by dilettantes which both Kandinsky and Schönberg were in the field of the theatre, because in a neighboring art they can experiment more playfully and without the need and stress of being successful.

Kandinsky, in order to investigate the internal relationship between the different realms and to examine the 'translatablity' of one art into the other, experimented with Hartmann and Alexander Sakharov, a young Russian dancer. Sakharov, later a famous 'modern dancer', modified his role in Kandinsky's very first stage play, *Daphnis and Chloe* for his first recital in Munich in 1911 (Kandinsky had given up this project, after Diaghilev and Fokin had started their version, which in Kandinsky's eyes was already outdated). While they of course used ballet, Sakharov, as a kindred spirit of Kandinsky's, eliminated every decorative and secondary detail and tried to crystallize the essence and (religious) origin of dancing.

Kandinsky described his experiments with Sakharov and Hartmann: "The musician chose among my pictures the one that seemed to him the most musically eloquent and clear. He interpreted it without the dancer. Then the dancer returned, listened to the music and translated it into dance, whereupon he was asked to guess which watercolor he had danced"[17].

Not by chance, Kandinsky's first and most intensive involvement with these questions falls in the critical transitional phase between representational and abstract painting. From his autobiographical writings we know that these were anarchical, agonizing years of searching, doubting and sometimes of despair and great loneliness. But Kandinsky did not publish the quoted account until about 10 years later in Russia, when he attempted to finally give a scientific basis to his still active preoccupation with the synthesis of the arts. He quoted the composer Alexander Shenshin as an exponent of a true scientific relationship between music and the plastic arts, one who had found mathematical correlations between a Michelangelo sculpture and a Liszt composition on the same theme. Kandinsky continued to experiment in the INKHUK: "Musicians chose 3 basic chords, painters were invited to depict them first in pencil, then...each chord in color." We are reminded of his early experiments (Fig. 2–4).

Back to the Munich period, when such experiments led to an innovative use of music and noises in his stage compositions. As early as 1909, in *Green Sound*, we find the following: "a terrifying noise behind the stage, as if the sky were falling down." And in *Black and White* also from 1909: a short and strange horn sound, while figures, clad in black, execute rhythmic mouvements. Then a high guttural voice utters inarticulate sounds. A later version of *Yellow Sound* of 1912 uses the guttural tenor of 1909 in two tension-filled moments: shrill and high, it shouts absolutely incomprehensible words, containing a multitude of a-vowels (Kandinsky gives only as a suggestion "Kalasimunafakola")[18].

In October/November 1910 Kandinsky was in Moscow and continued to work with Hartmann on those stage compositions. At the Conservatory they were given a demonstration of the difference between a harmonium with tempered tones and one with natural tones (an invention of a Mr Smirnov). Kandinsky found that what today is considered utterly dissonant and impossible, sounds very fine and even harmonious on the natural keys (for instance si-do-re). He concludes: "From this can result a basic upheaval of the theory of harmony and counterpoint"[19]. From Moscow he also reports that Hartman had played the *Giants* (i.e. the first draft of *Yellow Sound*) to the composer Boleslav Yavorsky, who was full of praise: "stage it immediately, he said." It turned out that Yavorsky had similar plans, in fact the prelude of the *Giants* was almost identical with his, and Kandinsky considered letting him write the music to the prelude and Hartmann for the *Giants*, the postlude and *Black and White*. They applied at Stanislavsky's 'Artists Theater', but were refused. Kandinsky called that theatre too realist, and the recent staging of his much admired Belgian poet Maurice Maeterlinck's *Blue Bird* was disappointing: "a children's fairy tale plus philosophical-occult patchwork". Kandinsky calls Yavorsky the best pupil of Taneyev: "He is quite somebody. He revolutionized the whole musical theory and has inaugurated new principles (by drawing upon the oldest ones)." [Remember what Kandinsky said about Schönberg's awareness of the old principles in spite of his innovations!] "[Yavorsky's] theory is a sister of my painterly theory: the direct application of the physical-psychological effect."[20] Kandinsky's interest in such matters goes back as far as 1897, when the perception-theorist Theodor Lipps was teaching at the Munich university. Lipps spoke about immediate psychic experience, stressing the role of empathy as against intellectual perception.

Remember, too, Kandinsky's remarks in his *Spiritual*, which echo Maeterlinck – about the pure sound of a word, for example, when a word is repeated often enough, its meaning becomes secondary and ceases to intrude on its acoustic aspect. Only then does one perceive the inner sound, the word's perhaps mystical meaning.

The Kandinsky-literature since Sixten Ringbom's book *The Sounding Cosmos* (Abo 1970) stresses more and more the theosophical and anthroposophical connections and some art historians pay more attention to supposed 'thought forms' and auras than to the paintings themselves. [Some of you may remember the large exhibition which borrowed the title of Kandinsky's main theoretical work *On the Spiritual in Art* a few years ago here in Den Haag, coming from the County museum in Los Angeles: a Dutch theosophical journal at that time as it were took over Kandinsky, treating him as if he were the purest theosophist and their intimate fellow. No, there is evidence that Kandinsky never joined the Theosophical or Anthroposophical Society and his interest in it soon faded after a short fascination. In fact the artist never joined *any* non-artistic association. But there is another spiritual connection, one that has not yet been investigated. His encounter with the composer Hartmann in 1908 or earlier led to a *life-long, very close friendship*. Hartmann and his wife Olga, a singer, were close to the Sufi movement even before joining

Gudjieff's esoteric group in 1917. Sufism was still a secret teaching at this time. Members were not permitted to reveal much to the uninitiated to avoid misuse. But such a stable personality as Kandinsky (who was Hartmann's senior by 17 years) could certainly be trusted. Also it was clear to any initiate that Kandinsky was 'extra lucid', as Steiner is supposed to have observed. So it is quite likely that the Hartmanns alluded to the important role the so-called Wazifas played in their life. A Wazifa (or Latifa) is a sound which carries an age-old significance, naming one or another of God's aspects, which man partakes of to some extent. It acts upon the different chakras or energy-zones of the body: for instance those including the i-sound stimulate the third eye, the seat of affective perception. The a-sound (as Kandinsky emphasized in the incomprehensible words of his stage plays), opens the heart chakra in loving affection to the world. At the initiation the master often attributes one or several such sounds to the pupil as a daily exercise, according to what the student must strengthen or still discover within himself. Now why should Hartmann have kept such matters secret from his friend, who since 1904 had been studying similar phenomena and their relation to colors, and who used them in his stage compositions? In fact Hartmann's wife Olga firmly stated that the movement of the last *giant* in Kandinsky's *Yellow Sound* (when he raises both arms slowly till his figure reaches the form of a cross) was inspired by a Sufi spiritual exercise. This seemed to me rather to have a Christian root, and I remember fighting over this question with Olga, when I stayed with her to study Hartmann's contribution to the common stage plays. Still I must do justice to Olga's memory and judgement, and as surprising as I found her statement, it has historical value. There is no sure way anymore to reconstruct the truth.

Aside from light, sound (music) is for the Sufi the most important manifestation of the spirit that can be perceived by our senses and is used for prayer, healing etc. In the Sufi tradition, just as in the Tibetan etc., exercises in overtones are very important, they are considered to be the finest, most spiritual manifestation of sound (I am so curious to know what the professional musicologists attending this colloquium will say about the reasons...is it because overtones are extremely subtle or because they are *indirect* and supplementary tones to the one created main tone/sound...?). It is not proven but it is likely that Kandinsky had heard about that from his friends – and that was prior to his acquaintance with Schönberg.

The subtlety of effect can be compared with microtonal compositions. They supposedly influence the psyche in barely perceptible ways without detouring through the brain. This is precisely how Kandinsky wanted to reach people through his art. In June, 1910, he wrote his first letter to Nikolai Kulbin, believing – as he did with Schönberg – that they had common goals. Perhaps Kandinsky was already familiar with Kulbin's publication *Studio impressionistov* (*Studio of the Impressionists*), with its passages on hearing colors and coordinating spectral colors with the music scale. Kulbin sent Kandinsky his brochure *Free Music. Application of the New Art and Music*. Kandinsky promptly translated parts of it for the *Blue Rider* almanac. In essence, these say that, like the 'music of nature', free music uses *all* tones, quarter, eighth, even thirteenth tones. The microtonal composer's ability to act on the mind is enriched in particular by 'small intervals' which are not perceived by the brain. Such ideas were 'in the air' at that time, but Kulbin was probably one of the first to have noted them and experimented with them. I wonder to what degree this can be compared with Schönberg's invention of the 'Sprechstimme', the 'speaking' voice that he used more and more in his works.

The sensitivity for microtonal effects might have been particularly strong in Russia, perhaps because every Russian was subjected to them in church from childhood on. Not through the choir, but through the priest's finely elaborated way of chanting (an ear for music is an absolute requirement for priesthood in the Orthodox church). The priest's voice rises in pitch imperceptibly at particularly dramatic or solemn moments, not through steps or half steps but through something close to 'microtonal glissandi' (for non-musicologists like myself this can be explained oversimply as the violin technique of gypsy music). Russian Poets create a similar effect with their rhapsodical howling way of declamation. Nowadays it has become more rare, but I remember hearing Yosip Brodsky a few years ago recite in exactly this tradition, and it sent strange shivers up and down my spine.

Kandinsky's first contact with microtonal effects goes back to 1900 – but in painting. There is new evidence concerning Paul Signac's famous treatise *From Delacroix to Neo-Impressionism*, published in 1899, which Kandinsky quotes often, starting from *On the Spiritual* right up to 1928. His early close friend Benja Bogaevskaya translated the book into Russian probably on his instigation (her manuscript was found in Kandinsky's estate with several early pencil sketches of his). Signac emphatically demonstrates that 'petits intervalles' are found in Delacroix's work, where they help to create hitherto unknown effects and remarkably pure shades of color: i.e. intervals between a) light/dark, tone in tone, b) close shades, like warmer/colder.

When Kandinsky in 1914 expanded his stage compositions to what was to become *Violett*, his composer friend Hartmann was not in Munich.

Kandinsky endeavored to deal with the music himself, giving only global indications about instruments (like: a violin plays a scale) and concentrating on noises and voices. Example: "A child's voice, very high and somewhat in the manner of a church song". Before the next act there are voices and noises in full darkness which announce the changing of the scene: nails being pounded in, an artisan whistling, commands like: "Bring the wall, the domes – careful! Lower the sun (something rolls around with a muted noise)."[21] These are 'alienating effects' similar to those produced much later in Bertolt Brecht's theatre. The darkness on the stage and in the theatre increases the perception of the sounds. Kandinsky specifies the human voices with precision: a breathless child's voice; a warm alto; whispers. The modulations of an old beggar's voice go from "nasal, almost howling" to "hacked, dragging" and "cello-like glissando". A shawm imitates a human voice, then the same theme is quietly played on a trumpet.

There is a large wooden cow on stage which first moos either sadly or stolidly and later in a very high range, "complaining pathetically as if she had lost her calf", first alternating with the choir, later on together. The action of *Violett*, if "action" is the right term, could be termed "pre-dadaist". There is an attempt at producing surprise, and shock too, by baffling the audience, confronting it with the unfamiliar and a deliberate lack of coherence between different elements. When one is not distracted by meanings or plot, one is more open to the direct effect of the art form, the media itself, Kandinsky believed, particularly if it contains new and unusual elements.

Not having Hartmann to work with, Kandinsky composed a little music for the first and only time in his life. So take it more as a curiosity, when you now witness as a one minute pause in my report the few notes which Kandinsky wrote as a recitativo for one voice.

For Schönberg painting was a marginal, but from 1907 till 1912, very important activity. When Kandinsky contacted the composer, he was not aware that he painted too. And surprise! Schönberg painted not only realistic pictures, mainly portraits and self-portraits, but also some abstract ones (figs. 5, 7, 9, 10, 12). The critics judged: "Schönberg's music and Schönberg's pictures – then one must lose both one's hearing and sight at the same time." But Kandinsky was one of the first people who recognized the value of these highly expressive and genuine paintings, and he dared to show three of them in his first *Blue Rider* exhibition and almanac next to professional works. But he prefered the realistic ones!

Peter Gorsen's opinion: "Standing in the way of an art-historical understanding of Schönberg's visionary painting is... the fact that it reveals

Figure 5 Schönberg: *Vision*
© A. Schönberg
c/o Beeldrecht Amsterdam

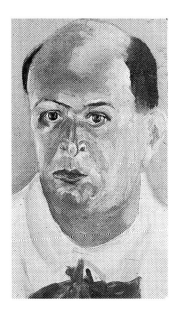

Figure 6 Schönberg: *Self-portrait*
© A. Schönberg c/o Beeldrecht Amsterdam

Figure 7   Schönberg: *Red Gaze* © A. Schönberg c/o Beeldrecht Amsterdam

Figure 8   Schönberg: *Self-portrait* © A. Schönberg c/o Beeldrecht Amsterdam

Figure 9 Schönberg: *Thinking* © A. Schönberg c/o Beeldrecht Amsterdam

Figure 10 Schönberg: *Die glückliche Hand* © A. Schönberg c/o Beeldrecht Amsterdam

Figure 11 Schönberg: *Mahler's Funeral* © A. Schönberg c/o Beeldrecht Amsterdam

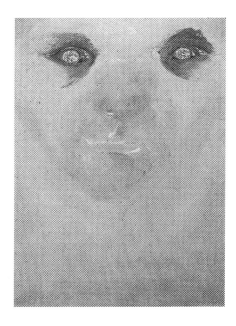

Figure 12 Schönberg: *Vision (Gaze)* © A. Schönberg c/o Beeldrecht Amsterdam

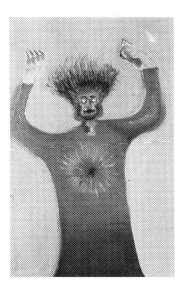

Figure 13   Schönberg: *Hatred* © A. Schönberg c/o Beeldrecht Amsterdam

itself in its introversive pictorial language as decisively unhistorical and regressive, but at the same time as the creative self-healing attempt of a depressive individual, who finds his actual artistic justification only in his musical work, in which the painter's psychogrammes are integrated and dissolved."[22] "The comparison of his visionary pictorial poems with self-portraits of the depressed may reveal that we have primarily a phenomenon of therapeutic painting and not that of artistic volition here." And why is this the case only within a certain time period? And why is his painting a self-healing process, but not his music? Isn't *every* artistic exercise in some way a self-healing process (a process which concerns no one but the author himself and can be totally disregarded, if the result is art)?

In contrast to this and to many other opinions, the contemporary Austrian artist Oswald Oberhuber stated in 1984 that Schönberg was the most important painter of his time[23]. He sympathizes with Schönberg's tendency to *withdraw*, and whose share in the history of art in turn was witheld. Let us reflect upon the idea of withdrawing – literally we might think of Schönberg's withdrawal when Kandinsky wanted to continue exhibiting his paintings, for instance in Berlin after 1912. The composer said he does not feel right to be among professional artists. But also: to withdraw indirectly, to draw and paint more awkwardly and naively than to his ability. But why is there such a difference in quality (a purely art-historical point of view of course)? Does it mean that Schönberg sometimes withdrew more, sometimes less?

Last year, finally a huge catalogue was published, showing most of Schönberg's artistic production. And when one sees it all, one wonders even more about the contrast between absolute masterpieces and so many weak works. The editor, Thomas Zaunschirn, mainly discusses the difficulty of distinguishing the composer from the painter. To protect the painter from the composer, it seems important to inquire about the belief in the homogeneity of the person. What is the actual meaning of the statement: "There was only one Schoenberg whichever he did: compose, teach, write or paint (Sorell, 1958). But the totality of the person does not necessarily constitute the homogeneity of the individual facets. A religious genius does not have to be an outstanding artist, and a person's ability to cook does not become more impressive by peak performances in sports." A very good and witty question. But still it is a fact that talents are usually *not* equally distributed: one person is a good cook, another a great musician. Unfairly, it is true that a genius is also quite often talented in many other fields than his own, as Schönberg's and Kandinsky's examples show! Also let us ask the naive but logical question: why is it necessary to separate Schönberg the musician from Schönberg the painter? He was a great composer, that is a fact; does he therefore have no right to be a good painter? Or at times a weaker painter? Why cut a person to pieces artificially?

For control let us come back to Schönberg's own words. When in 1907 he announced he wanted to paint portraits and even earn money with his new profession, he later admitted: "It was a way of expressing myself, of presenting emotions, ideas. As a painter I was absolutely an amateur. And I had no theoretical training and only a little aesthetic training, this only from general education...This is the difference between my painting and music"[24]. To Stokowsky he concedes in 1949 that his painting "deviates considerably" from other styles. He considered his own style as "making music with colors and forms." As opposed to his own frequent repeated suppositions, the peculiar position of his painting lies in the lack of a style. The various ways of painting a self-portrait deserve the same attention as the art- historical failure in the search for models, Zaunschirn claims. Was it Ensor, Jawlensy, Kubin? Kokoschka started much too late, and Schönberg got to know Kandinsky, when the main part of his painting was accomplished. From Richard Gerstl he might have learned a little technique. No, Schönberg had practically no models, and that might be the main reason why, as a painter he has been spared appropriation. He probably would have liked that: how resistant he still is to all strategies of reception and classification. "He shows an awkward originality, in light of which it is not permitted to differentiate between the successful *Red Gaze* and unsuccessful portraits, between quality and things it would have been better not to show"[25]. In my opinion not only the few paintings of *highest* quality may be shown, but also the truly dilettante pictures. The fact is that even minor and marginal activities of geniuses have an interest, especially if they are innovative.

NOTES

1 Letter from G. Münter to Schönberg, Aug. 20, 1912, in: Arnold Schoenberg/Wassily Kandinsky, *Letters, Pictures and Documents*. Ed. J. Hahl-Koch, London/Boston 1984, p. 55f.
2 Letter to Kandinsky, ibid. p. 23.
3 J. Auner: "Schoenberg's Aesthetic Transformations and the Evolution of Form in *Die glückliche Hand*", in: *Journal of the Arnold Schoenberg Institute*, Vol. XII, No. 2, Nov. 1989, p. 2.
4 Letter to Schönberg, in: Schoenberg/Kandinsky, *Letters*...p. 25.
5 Letter to Münter, September 3, 1903, pp. 103 ff. (Gabriele Münter- and Johannes Eichner-Foundation, Munich.)
6 (Gabriele Münter- and Johannes Eichner-Foundation, Munich).
7 Letter to Schönberg, April 9, 1911. in: Schoenberg/Kandinsky, *Letters,*...p. 27 f.
8 A. Bely, "Formy iskusstva", in: *Mir iskusstva*, St. Petersburg No. 8, 1902.
9 "Paralleli v oktavakh i kvintakh", in: *Salon 2*, Ed. Vladimir Izdebsky, Odessa 1910/1911, p. 16.
10 Letter to Münter, July 7, 1907 (Gabriele Münter- and Johannes Eichner-Foundation, Munich).
11 A. Strakosch, *Lebenswege mit Rudolf Steiner*. Strassburg/Zuerich 1947, pp. 16 f.
12 Letter to Nikolai Kulbin, October 18, 1910 (Russian Museum, St. Petersburg).
13 Letter to Münter, October 23, 1910 (Gabriele Münter- and Johannes Eichner-Foundation, Munich).
14 Letter to Münter from Moscow, October 10, 1910 (Gabriele Münter- and Johannes Eichner-Foundation, Munich).
15 Thomas von Hartmann, "Der unentzifferbare Kandinsky" (The undecipherable Kandinsky), 1913, manuscript (Gabriele Münter- and Johannes Eichner-Foundation, Munich).
16 Letter of Aug. 19, 1912, in: Schoenberg/Kandinsky, *Letters,*...p. 54.
17 Report in: Vestnik rabotnikov iskusstv, No. 4–5, Moscow 1921, p. 74f.
18 Manuscript, Centre Georges Pompidou, Paris.
19 Letters to Münter, October 3 and November 17, 1910 (Gabriele Münter- and Johannes Eichner-Foundation, Munich).
20 ibid.
21 Manuscripts of "Violett", Centre Georges Pompidou in Paris.
22 Quoted from: *Arnold Schoenberg, Paintings and Drawings*, Ed. Th. Zaunschirn, Klagenfurt 1992, p. 43.
23 ibid.
24 Th. Zaunschirn, "The Painter Schoenberg", in: *Arnold Schoenberg, Paintings and Drawings*, Ed. Th. Zaunschirn, Klagenfurt 1992, p. 53.
25 Ibid.

Kandinsky and Schönberg: The Problem of Internal Counterpoint

BULAT M. GALEYEV

Most people connect the name and theoretical works of Kandinsky with the problem of synesthesia. Moreover he is often called an artist-synesthesist. And indeed he constantly referred to the analogies between music and painting, compared concrete musical timbres with certain colors all the time. Further, it appears that he made special research of the synesthesia problem in the "laboratory of monumental art" (INHUK), founded by him after the Revolution, and then in the Bauhaus. These facts are known to many researchers, but, unfortunately, they disregard the main deductions of Kandinsky which are connected with his brilliant idea of "internal counterpoint". The idea appeared to be very fruitful and I have proved that Kandinsky had discovered the fundamental esthetic law, which is very important for modern artistic practice, for all arts, including the new ones too.

Thus, let us first recollect what synesthesia is. As a psychological phenomenon and as a product of culture synesthesia is intermodal, intersensory (specifically–audio-visual) associations most actively formed and cultivated in human intercourse (language, and especially in art). I have already said at the symposium during the "Impakt-91" festival, that among audio-visual synesthesias it is possible to select the following most common for all people appropriate associations:

dynamics of sound, changing of music loudness	– dynamics of "gesture" (this is both its movement in depth and the changing of brightness);
melodical development	– dynamics of plastics, of picture;
music tempo	– speed of motion and of transformation of visual images;
timbre development	– colour development of plastics;
changing of tonality	– development of colouring of the whole picture or of colour planes (during polytonality);

| shear on registers | – changing of size and lightness of the drawing; |
| changing of modes (major, minor) | – changing of lightness of the whole picture. |

Many artists and theoreticians of art consider, that in the new arts based on the audio-visual synthesis it is quite sufficiant to follow the "prompts" of synesthesia and to continually realize, model on the screen or on the stage these accordances, mentioned above, in order to obtain a highly artistic result. These tendencies are especially evident in cinema without a plot, abstract cinema, in animation (specifically in computer animation of recent years), where there is even a special term for it here in the Netherlands – "synesthetical film". In those films there is constant synchronism in the motions of music and complicated visual images, which is considered not only as a merit, but occasionally turns into an end in itself.

Yes, these films are attractive as a kind of "visual portrait" of well-known musical works (let's recall certain fascinating films of O. Fischinger, N. McLaren, the Whitney brothers). But the experience of other audio-visual arts prompts the notion that possibilities of the audio-visual synthesis are not exhausted by audio-visual synchronism (or, so to say, by an audio-visual "unison").

Stanislavsky in theatre, Fokine in dance, Eisenstein in cinema, Scriabin in light-music have all shown what great possibilities are hidden in the methods of audio-visual polyphony when, side by side with moments of audio visual "unison" (i.e. of synchronism of "audio" and "vision" by some mutual signs), the moments of premeditated, conscious digression from the "unison" are used too. I mean the moments of "audio-visual counterpoint", when "audio" and "vision" come into conscious (thought out) conflict. This conflict can manifest itself (be put into effect) in either "horizontal plane" (unsuperpositions in time structure) or in "vertical plane" (unsuperpositions in emotional and sensible influence). In other words, synthesis in these moments is put into effect purposefully against "prompts" from synesthesia, achieving by this the necessary feeling of contrast, conflict, distress, etc., finally forming thus a complicated dramaturgy of synthetical work (composition). But these propositions can also be considered as universally recognized by the theory and they will, I hope, introduced into practice of all the new audio-visual arts step by step.

The genius of Kandinsky is based on the fact that he went further, opened deeper regulations of the synthesis by turning his attention to phenomena of so-called "internal counterpoint", on the basis of which I have developed his ideas, having continued with research into the principles of the so-called "internal polyphony" (for all temporary arts, including audio-visual).

In connection with this I would like to highlight that, side by side with the usual known to all *inter*modal synesthesias, there are also less evident, less appreciated, but equally important *intra*modal synesthesias. What I would like to touch upon are the psychological associations between the separate components inside *one* sensory material! Thus, for example, V. Kandinsky noted that the active yellow color is close by its emotional effect to an active sharp figure of a triangle, the calm dark blue color is close to a calm circle, and a monolithic square is close by its effect to the red color, etc. By analogy one can see the presence of "internal" synesthesia for hearing too: the timbre of trumpet is similar to an active melodical drawing, to the major tonality, and the timbre of cello is similar to a slow tempo, to an elegiac melody, etc.

If we follow the prompts of the "internal" synesthesia we shall reach a constant strengthening, duplicating of the effect (e.g. if we make a triangular figure yellow, a circle dark blue, etc.). This method can be called an "internal unison". But we have hardly considered the effect of constant strengthening a worthy artistic task. Because the drama, the final aim, the content of the art work may demand other methods too, where an artist consciously avoids "internal unison".

Leaning upon his experience as a painter, Kandinsky explained this term: "internal counterpoint", invented by himself, in the following way. He imagined the painting "Sudden grief", in which there is a woman, who has recieved a letter, informing her that she has suddenly become a widow. Kandinsky considers it would be banal to depict the "feeling of grief" with the "grief" plot itself and with the "grief" composition and with the "grief" drawing and with the "grief" colouring. He thinks that a much more powerful effect could be reached if against the theme of grief the widow's dress would suddenly become bright red, it would stress the suddenness of grief and the drama of the moment. If one looks attentively on Kandinsky's abstract pictures one would note that Kandinsky widely used the whole range of contrasts – from zero during internal unison (red square, blue circle) to the sharpest contrasts (yellow circle, green square), etc. All this lets us perceive his abstract pictures as a real symphony, "music for the eye".

I have supposed that a similar situation is common for all arts, where, probably, it is also possible to discover the moments of purposeful, premediated "internal counterpoint" of various degrees of complexity in different periods of the development of these arts.

The most evident **architecture** examples: the outward appearance of Egyptian pyramids does not conflict with our habitual feeling of the ponderability, the solidity of the material used: namely stone (we are dealing here with "internal unison"). And on the contrary, in the structures of "flaming Gothic" and in whimsical, flowing windings of baroque, the visual image is synesthetically antagonistic to the material used ("internal counterpoint"), something that defines the aesthetic peculiarity of these styles.

In **poetry**, when unintentionally highlighting ("marking out") the phonic qualities of words in verses (onomatopoeia and alliteration), it is possible to make these qualities of sound continuously fall in "unison" with the meaning – as was sometimes done by the Russian Symbolist poets at the end of the 19th century. But it is also possible to interwine these two "voices" (sounding and meaning) in other, more complicated and different relations, dictated not only by a formal task, but by an internal artistic necessity. Brilliant examples of harmony of sound and meaning were given by the great Russian poet Alexander Pushkin. And it was our contemporary poet Boris Pasternak, who filled the notion of "music of verse" with a polyphonic, but not a trivial flat content. He wrote: this "phenomenon is not acoustic at all and it consists not in euphony of vowels and consonants, taken separately, but in the correlation of the meaning of speech and its sounding". I should like to note, that the creative work of Pasternak himself proves that the character of these correlations in his work is not limited by a despondent "internal unison".

In another temporal art – in **theatre**, similar arguments were used by Stanislavsky, who violently opposed the method of "merry meriment", which is frequently used in actor's recitation, when "merry semantics" regardless of the authors intentions – whether it is necessary or not – is presented phonically in a "merry" sounding.

And, finally, **music**, where it appears, even one-voice melody can be split into, so to say, "internal voices", if mental plots are made of the charges in every component (melodical development, loudness, tempo etc.). They can be parallel (i.e. follow the "prompts" of intramodal synesthesia – e.g., supposed to sound-pitch activity by loud sounding, quick tempo, buoyant timbre and mode) or remain in an antiphase (quick tempo in pianissimo, lyrical melody in nasal timbre and so on). The Russian composer Rimsky-Korsakov in his works on orchestration has made profound research into this problem. He dwelled on the necessity to apply both methods (according to our terminology the method of "internal unison" and "internal counterpoint" which, taken together, permit us to say, concerning the temporal art of music, about the existence of "internal polyphony" in music). By the way, according to my comparing analysis of music of different epochs, it is possible to note the following fact: a step by step change from the primary usage of the "internal unison" methods to wider turning to "internal counterpoint" methods is observed in music evolution (compare for example the music of Bach, Beethoven, Scriabin). To my mind in a most evident form it has become apparent in the "Klangfarbenmelodie" of Schönberg, where such a characteristic as timbre has also got an opportunity for independent development (although it was done within a purely formal method).

Probably similar evolution is common in the development of every art. Nevertheless we finally see that even the experience of non-synthetic art proves the possibility and necessity of deepest penetration of counterpointical, polyphonical thinking in the structure of audio-visual, synthetic arts. These arts can now use, alongside the evident merits of audio-visual polyphony, the merits of "internal polyphony" of every art participating in the synthesis. This will let us reach the closest polyphonical unity of "external" and "internal" voices for the realisation of the most complex artistic ideas.

Such are the conclusions resulting from my reflections upon a subtle and profound observation made by Kandinsky on the problem of "internal counterpoint".

Bibliography

1. *V. Kandinsky*. Concerning the Spiritual in Art (Painting). – In: Petrograd All-Russian artists congress proceedings (December 1911–January 1912), 2 volumes, Petrograd, 1914.
2. *V. Kandinsky*. Stages: Artist's Text. – Moscow, 1918
3. *V. Kandinsky*. On Stage Composition. – Figurative art (*Izobrazitelnoe iskusstvo*), 1919, 1.
4. *V. Kandinsky*. Concerning the Spiritual in Art. – New York, 1967
5. *S.D. Khan-Magomedov*. Kandinsky on Perception and Effects of Means of Artistic Expression – In: VNIITE proceedings, Technical aesthetics issue No. 17, Moscow, pp. 77–96
6. *V. Kandinsky*. Exhibition Catalogue. – Leningrad, Avrora, 1989. From the contents:
   Letters of V.V. Kandinsky to D.N. Kordovsky
   D.V. Sarabjanov. About V.V. Kandinsky
   S.D. Khan-Magomedov. V.V. Kandinsky in the section of monumental art at INHUK (1920)
   T.M. Pertseva. V.V. Kandinsky and GAHN
   L.P. Monakhova. V.V. Kandinsky in the Bauhaus (1922–1933)
   M.P. Vikturina. About the question of V.V. Kandinsky's painting technique
7. *V. Kandinsky*. Concerning the Spiritual in Art. – Leningrad, 1990

Where does "The Blue Rider" Gallop? Schönberg, Kandinsky and Scriabin on the Synthesis of Art

IRINA L. VANECHKINA

1992 is notable for the fact that it was the anniversary for the almanac "The Blue Rider" (Der Blaue Reiter) – the first and last issue of which was published in 1912 in Munich, edited by V. Kandinsky and F. Marc. This collection of articles of known artists and musicians greatly influenced the theory and practice of 20th century art, which explains constant attention to it up to the present times. There exists prominent research about "The Blue Rider" and its authors (e.g. see [1]). Our interest in it is stimulated by the fact that on the pages of this collection met the three great artists of the 20th century, who tried, each of them in his own way, to embody in their creations the idea of synthesis of arts (meaning the painter Kandinsky, and composers Schönberg and Scriabin). Kandinsky is represented by two articles – "To the Question of Form" ("Über die Formfrage") and "About Stage Composition" ("Über Bühnenkomposition")[2] and also by the practical work – the scenario of his composition"Yellow Sound" ("Der gelbe Klang")[3]. Schönberg had published here the article "Correlation with Text" ("Das Verhältnis zum Text"). Ideas of A. Scriabin are introduced by his friend and biographer L. Sabaneyev in the article "Prometheus by A. Scriabin" ("Prometheus von Skrjabin")[4].

The aim of our report is to bring to light the similarities and, at the same time, reveal the differences in their understanding of aims and ways of synthesis, to compare the results of their practical experiments, evaluating both from the positions of modern synthesis theory[5]. In short, we have to ascertain where "The Blue Rider" started its run from and where it is really galloping now, regarding the title of the collection itself as a symbol of modern ideas of arts synthesis.

First of all the similarity lies in the fact that they themselves were creators of the Leonardo type – variously endowed men. Thus the painter Kandinsky wrote verses and scenarios, and was a musically educated man. Musician Schönberg took painting seriously, and wrote verses and librettos for his stage works. Musician Scriabin also wrote poetry and philosophical programmes for his writings. It is also remarkable that all of them paid attention on making analogies between the hearing and seeing (Kandinsky and Schönberg compared musical timbres and colors; it is known an original system of parallels between colors and tonalities had been born in Scriabin). In a certain measure their mutual passion for theosophical studies influenced all this. Nevertheless we can only establish that, side by side with the fact that every one of them was a pioneer in his main sphere of activity (Kandinsky – abstract painting, Scriabin – new modes, Schönberg – dodecaphony), all of them, each in his own way, be it in painting or music, inevitably and naturally came to the synthesis of arts.

Thus, let's begin with the theoretical standpoint of Kandinsky. Discussing the essence of synthetic art (for some reason he used another unusual term – "monumental art") he imagined the real embodiment of the synthesis as some kind of "stage composition". As we can see, Kandinsky uses just these words and it is the summing up, on the stage only, of the following three abstract elements:

"1.   Musical tone and its movement.
 2.   Corporal-spiritual sounding and its movement, expressed by means of a human body or object.
 3.   Color tone and its movement, which obtain independent significance and are used as a means processing equal rights."

Thus, his stage "composition" differs from the usual theatre performances just because all the synthesized elements are "abstract". "Abstract" soundings of music and "abstract" movements of human body were used in the traditional theatre too, but the new component of synthesis here is the "color", coming from "abstract" painting and which has to get the movement, lacking in the painting itself. Explaining the principles of the interaction of these three "abstract" elements, Kandinsky warns, that in spite of their independence they must not repeat each other, being at the same time subordinated to the one "internal aim". Kandinsky wrote, that, for example, "music can be completely subdued or moved to the background, if action, e.g. movement, is expressive enough and its effect is only weakened by an active presence of music. Decreasing the motion in a dance may lead to the growth of motion in music". In these conceptions Kandinsky demonstrates one of the most important and deepest ideas of his theory – the idea of counterpoint in different arts. He points out, that the unusual force of influence of synthetic art lies just between "consonance" and "anti-consonance", i.e. between unison and counterpoint of means used.

For all that, Kandinsky as a painter thought that only the light is that main means, through which it is possible to influence the human spirit. "Color as a key, eye is a little hummer, spirit is a multistrung piano". This phrase was written by V. Kandinsky in his work "Concerning the Spiritual in Art", which preceded "The Blue Rider". Being based on the idea, that the spirit is the whole and that sight is connected with all other senses, Kandinsky suggested detailed comparisons not only between colors and feelings, colors and symbols, colors and timbres, but also between colors and temperature qualities, colors and different kinds of motion. These synesthetical notions of his form are the content of a special chapter "Language of Colors" in the above mentioned work "Concerning the Spiritual in Art"[6].

Exactly the principles of two program works by Kandinsky – "About Stage Composition" and "Concerning the Spiritual in Art" lay at the base of the creation of the scenario for his composition "Yellow Sound". Though the composition has its plot it is quite abstract. Live actors participate in it, but they are only character-symbols. The use of colors in the dresses of the personages is symbolical too. So a child in white and a man in black symbolize Life and Death. Groups of people in red and blue symbolize the earthly and spiritual and giants in yellow – the instant and base. Light must be present in Kandinsky's work too, but it is just the beams, lighting the characters and helping to connect stage action with music by their dynamics. (As for the significant reasonings of Kandinsky about "moving abstract painting", it appears, he meant first of all appreciation of abstract dance in color costumes.) They are also examples of counterpoint of means which are contained there. So in the third picture the musical diminuendo corresponds to the light crescendo, while bright and variable light is contrasted with the low whisper of the giants. In the fifth picture, Kandinsky advises to use the method of conscious divergence in the tempo of music and dance etc.

Kandinsky himself had no time to see the realization of his "Yellow Sound"[7]. Foreseeing the difficulties of possible embodiment of the abstract stage composition according to his verbal (by means of words only) description, Kandinsky thought, that the main thing in the scenario published by him are the proposed principles. As one could foresee, all the attempts to perform the "Yellow Sound" in different countries in further years were very different one from another. And this is not surprising if we keep in mind that different musical bases were used there (in the USA – T. Khartman, in France – A. Webern, in the USSR – A. Schnittke). But it is important for us to note the following: in all of them the use of light was accomplished according to the theatre canons, and the thesis about moving abstract painting (I would like to stress it) was reduced to the appreciation of a dance in colored dresses. This primacy of material color and material plastics was preserved in the performance of Kandinsky's composition, staged by him to the music by Mussorgsky "Pictures from an Exhibition" in Dessau in 1928[8]. Scenography here became more complicated – not only did the actors move on the stage but also color decoration elements, lamps, were moved by the actors to music. Thus, in such an unusual way Kandinsky tried to achieve the animation of the abstract painting. In this he was close to experiments of O. Schlemmer with abstract ballet. It is surprising that Kandinsky did not use the experience of his other colleagues in the Bauhaus – L. Khirsh-veld-Mak, I. Khartvig, who had already achieved some real animation of the most complex figures of abstract painting by the use of nonmaterial light projection.

Now let us address ourselves to Schönberg. His article in "The Blue Rider" is devoted to the interrelations of music and word, where he stands for the use of different most complex forms of their union. Also in those years, as it is known, he worked on the synthetic monodrama "The Lucky Hand" ("Die glückliche Hand"), where to music and word he added mimicry, picturesque decorations and peculiar scenography, subordinated to music. A. Schönberg is astonishingly close to V. Kandinsky in the symbolic character of the plot. But his idea is more developed and complete. Leit-motives, leit-timbres, leit-colors are conformed to all personages. The timbre of the cello always corresponds to the Man; violins, flutes, harps – to the Woman. In the dynamics of the stage-light the composer used the following color-timbre parallels: yellow – trumpet, blue – English horn, violet – clarinet, bassoon and so on. Schönberg refers to purely light-music methods at the culminating moment of the drama, when tension of the action and expressionist music reach such a limit that the sounds appear to "go out of themselves" into the sphere of different feeling, into the sphere of light. It takes place in the scene of the storm. The logics of correlation between color, timbres and emotions incarnated in this light-musical episode is consonant with Kandinsky's system of color-timbre synesthesias. (It is clear – they were friends and spiritually close.) The storm in nature, tension of human emotions are accompanied by the sound and light crescendo. In timbres the movement goes from violins and oboes through clarinet, bassoon, tambourine, harp to the triumph of trombones and trumpets. The episode is brought to a finish by a pacifying English horn. Accordingly this is mirrored in color, which goes from black and brown through dull green, violet and red to orange and yellow. The light crescendo is closed by a soft blue color. As we see,

Schönberg like Kandinsky remained close to the usual theatre traditions, although as a musician having worked for a long time for the stage, he was more detailed in the study of light-musical (music-kinetic) synthesis methods.

But it was Scriabin who completely reduced the whole visual component to the light. In the above mentioned article about the "Prometheus" by Sabaneyev there is some information about the line of "Luce" (light), according to which all the space had to be changed into colors parallel and synchronously with the changing of chords and tonalities in music. It is known besides that just after the "Prometheus", Scriabin already spoke about the necessity to introduce into the part of light some complex light forms, light plastics and, what is vital, he rebukes the initial idea of audio-visual counterpoint methods in the future synthetic works.

Scriabin had no time to put his principles into practice, the same as he had not realized his idea of "Mystery". This great synthetic performance had to be presented in some temple, built of ephemeral, unsubstantial material. By the way, Kandinsky also dreamt about some fantastic temple where there would be presented and united all the arts. It was remarkable what name Kandinsky had given to this temple – "The Great Utopia"[9]. The last synthetic idea of Schönberg's was "Accompanying Music to a Cinema Scene" ("Begleitmusik zu einer Lichtspielszene") which was also left unrealized. Without a doubt, the successors will turn to these projects again and again – out of respect for the pioneers of audio-visual synthesis.

If we evaluate the positions of our three "riders" on a global scale, and if we speak about synthesis of arts on the music base, then it was best discovered by Scriabin. Only by turning to ephemeral material – i.e. the light, can one achieve that pliability and freedom in the management of visual material, which has already been achieved in respect to the sound. Only in this case the synthesis of "audio" and "visual" will have equal rights both in articulating and artistic possibilities. Only by the use of light one can get a moving abstract painting with the most complex dynamics of the most complex figures, which are no longer subordinate to the forces of gravity. (This is the difference between "screen" and "stage", where the action of the gravity forces is preserved for both the usual and abstract ballet.)

I should like to highlight of the inferences of modern scientists about the light-music genesis. It is certain today that men have already had for a long time an opportunity to perceive music through eyes – in dance[10]. And light-music is a further, instrumental development of a musical gesture. Today, having received such material as controlled light one can turn to "instrumental light choreography", to the dance of abstract light images, as it is possible to characterize briefly the essence of the new art – light-music. Art works of A. Laszlo, O. Fischinger, T. Wilfred, the best abstract computer films convince us of that only on the screen, just by the use of light, it became possible to obtain a harmonious and complete unity of "music for ear" and "music for eye", having made a decisive step towards the reaching of a qualitatively new level of synthesis. "The Blue Rider" had come to its end and passed on the baton to the other riders – to the riders of the computer era.

REFERENCES

1. *E. Roters*: Wassily Kandinsky und die Gestalt des Blauen Reiters. – Jahrbuch der Berliner Museen, vol. 5, 1963, No. 2.
2. This text was published in Russian later with abridgments:
   В. Кандинский. О сценической композиции. – Изобразительное искусство, 1919, N. 1.
3. This was not published in Russian. Only in collected works of S. Eisenstein (1964–1971) there were wide extracts from it (vol. 2, p. 2213–215).
4. This article was earlier published in Russian:
   Л. Сабанеев. "Прометей" Скрябина. – Музыка, 1919, N. 13.
5. In some measure it has been done already in confronting analyses of their creative works: *H.H. Stuckenschmidt*. Kandinsky und Schönberg. – Melos, vol. 31, 1964, Nos. 7–8; *H. H. Stuckenschmidt*. W. Kandinsky und A. Schönberg. – Universitas, vol. 32, 1977, No. 3; *F. Weiland*. Der gelbe Klang. – Interface, vol. 3, 1981, No. 1; *D. Pecaud*. Le temps d'un espace: Scriabin, Kandinsky. – Schweizerische Musikzeitung, vol. 117, 1977, No. 3; *J. C. Crawford*. Die Glückliche Hand: Schönberg's Gesamtkunstwerk. – The Musical Quarterly, vol. 60, 1974, No. 4; *K. H. Wörner*. Arnold Schönberg and the theatre. – The Musical Quarterly, vol. 48, 1962, No. 4; И. Л. Ванечкина. В. М. Галеев. Позма огня (о концепции светомузыкалвного синтеза А. Н. Скрябина). – Казань. Изд-вб КГУ, 1981.
6. This classic work of Kandinsky was published for the first time in Germany in 1912 in German, but firstly it was proclaimed in Russian (see *Trudui Vserossiiskogo sezda khudozhnikov* in January 1911–Dec. 1912. – St. Petersburg, 1914). In the USSR it was published in the *Tvorchestvo* (Creative work) magazine (1988, No. 8–10 and 1989, No. 1) and as a separate book it was printed in Leningrad in 1990.
7. About attempts to perform the "Yellow Sound" see in article: И. Л. Ванечкина: Судьба ценической композиции В. Кандинского "Желтый звук". – In the book: Светомузыка в театре и на зстраде (тезисные доклады). – Казань, КАИ, 1992.
8. See about this in the article: Hartman – Mussorgsky – Kandinsky – Ravel. – Neue Zeitschrift für Musik, 1963, No. 10.
9. В. Кандинский. О великой утопии. – Художественная жизнь, 1920, N. 3.
10. В. Галеев. Светомузыка: становление и сущность ноього искусства. – Казань, Таткнигоиздат, 1976.

Public Loneliness: Atonality and the Crisis of Subjectivity in Schönberg's Opus 15

ALBRECHT DÜMLING

The Relationship to the Text

As a key-work of contemporary music Schönberg's *"Fünfzehn Gedichte aus 'Das Buch der hängenden Gärten' von Stefan George"* op. 15 documents not only a turning point in music history, but also in the development of the modern artist. The esoteric poems by Stefan George and the dissonant musical aphorisms by Arnold Schönberg at first look seem to be out of this world, far away from the European reality. But it is just this isolation, this strangeness, which reflects the personal situation of both artists and which in fact was the basis of their inspiration. This, together with the more and more chromatic development of the musical material following Wagner, gives an explanation for the necessity and authenticity of this first atonal composition. Rather than repeat the different chromatic stages between tonality and atonality, I will in the following focus on the more neglected aspect, how the connection to specific poetry helped Schönberg to redefine his role as an artist. This new role consequently authorized him to give his musical language such a considerable change.

In Schönberg's oeuvre text-related compositions clearly dominate. Out of the fifty works that carry an opus number twenty-eight are based on texts, on poems, novels or dramas, not to mention unnumbered works such as the *"Gurrelieder"*, the oratorio *"Jakobsleiter"* and the opera *"Moses und Aron"*. In the composers' early period the dominance of vocal works is even more striking. From opus 1 to opus 22 only five compositions are not related to texts.[1] The majority of the early works are songs, *Lieder* and *Gesänge*. Nevertheless some musicologists try to see Schönberg primarily as a composer of 'absolute music' in the tradition of Brahms, who then in turn is also regarded as an autonomous composer. For these historians the string quartet and not the song represents the center of his evolution, and they are happy to quote from the composer's essay "The Relationship to the Text" (1912)[2] in order to show that poetry had no influence on his artistic development. But does Schönberg's aesthetic theory really correspond to his works, does his essay appropriately describe the creation of

his George Songs op. 15? Was the poetry that he selected only of secondary importance for him?

In his early years Schönberg had set a great variety of poems, by
romantic and realistic poets which are forgotten now and whose influence
on him was less important. In 1897 however he turned to an author who
even today is known as one of the heads of German Modernism ("*Die
Moderne*"): Richard Dehmel (1863–1920). In December 1899 he finished a
string sextet entitled "*Verklärte Nacht. Gedicht von Richard Dehmel / für sechs
Streichinstrumente*" (Transfigured Night. Poem by Richard Dehmel, for six
string instruments). In the first performances this relationship to the text
was always prominently mentioned (Figures 1–2).

In a letter to Dehmel, dated December 13, 1912, Schönberg wrote:
"Your poems have had a decisive influence on my musical development.
They forced me for the first time in my life, to search for a new sound in
lyric music. That is to say, I found it spontaneously by reflecting musically what your verses stirred and agitated in me. People who know my
music will confirm that my first experimental settings of your *Lieder*
contained more hints at my future development than many of my much
later compositions."[3] The composer confessed, that the experience of the
new texts had inspired a new musical language. Schönberg in those years
almost exclusively composed using texts of this poet, acquiring at the
same time greater sensibility for instrumental colors and for impressionistic harmony.

The second great step forward in his development as a composer of
Lieder occurred in 1908 and was connected with a poet, who figures as a
counterpart to Richard Dehmel, namely Stefan George (1868–1933).
Although Schönberg later tried to dispute this influence, there is some
evidence that the decisive step to atonality was closely connected with his
choice of George's poetry. One may suggest that his influence was even
greater than that of Dehmel.

The background of George's poetry

There is no bigger contrast conceivable than between the straightforward
and even adventurous nature of Dehmel on one side, and the esoteric
distance and self-stylization of George on the other. Dehmel disliked the
godlike attitude of his colleague. In 1895 he wrote in a letter: "George
claims to have reserved the one way to real art for himself. We object to
that since we believe that there are many dwellings in the house of our
father Apollo. George wants art for art's sake whereas we search for a
connection between art and life. Life doesn't consist only of exclusive

Concert-Bureau Alexander Rosé

I. Kärntnerring 11.

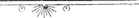

Kleiner Musikvereins-Saal.

Dienstag den 18. März 1902

abends halb 8 Uhr

VI. (letzter) Kammermusik-Abend

Quartett Rosé

Arnold Rosé	**Anton Ruzitska**
(1. Violine)	(Viola)
Albert Bachrich	**Friedrich Buxbaum**
(2. Violine)	(Violoncell)

Programm:

1. HERMANN GRÄDENER Quartett D-moll, op 33.

   Allegro con brio.
   Adagio (im Balladenton).
   Scherzo.
   Rondo. Finale (Allegro moderato).

2. ARNOLD SCHÖNBERG Sextett nach **Richard Dehmels** Gedicht
   ›Die verklärte Nacht‹.
   (Manuscript, erste Aufführung.)

   2. Viola: Herr **Franz Jelinek** ⎰ Mitglieder des k. k. Hof-
   2. Cello: Herr **Franz Schmidt** ⎱   Opernorchesters.

3. JOHANNES BRAHMS . Quintett F-dur, op. 88.

   Allegro non troppo ma con brio.
   Grave ed appassionato.
   Allegretto vivace.
   Allegro energico.
         2. Viola: Herr Franz Jelinek.

Während der Vorträge bleiben die Saalthüren geschlossen.

Figure 1 Program of the first performance of Schönberg's op. 4. Vienna, March 18, 1902. (Arnold Schönberg Institute Los Angeles)

Kammermusik-Verein in Prag.
XXVIII. Jahrgang.

Zweites Konzert

Montag den 21. März 1904 um 7 Uhr abend

im Konzertsaale des Rudolfinums,

unter gefälliger Mitwirkung des Quartetts der Herren:

Konzertmeister **Arnold Rosé** (1. Violine), **Albert Bachrich** (2. Violine), **Anton Ruzitska** (Viola) u. **Friedr. Buxbaum** (Violoncell)

und der Herren:

Franz Jelinek (2. Viola) u. **Franz Schmidt** (2. Violoncell) aus Wien.

PROGRAMM.

1. „**Verklärte Nacht,**" nach dem gleich-
   namigen Gedichte DEHMELS in dessen
   ·WEIB UND WELT· für sechs Streichinstrumente . . . . **Arnold Schönberg.**

2. **Italienische Serenade G-dur** (Streich-
   quartett) . . . . **Hugo Wolf.**

3. **Zweites Streichsextett G-dur, op.
   36** (1866) . . . . **Johannes Brahms.**
   a) Allegro non troppo.
   b) Scherzo. Allegro non troppo.
   c) Poco Adagio.
   d) Poco Allegro.

Drittes Konzert am **12. April** unter Mitwirkung des **Henri Marteau-Streichquartetts** aus Paris.

Figure 2   Program of a performance of op. 4 in Prague in 1904. Here even the source of the poem, the volume "Weib und Welt", is mentioned. (Arnold Schönberg Institute Los Angeles)

temples...''[4] Despite these objections he did not hesitate to list George along with Hofmannsthal, Mombert, Dauthendey, Arno Holz, Scheerbart, Detlev von Liliencron and Przybyszewski as one of the important poets of the turn of the century.[5] George never showed that same tolerance.[6]

To understand this attitude we must look at the biographical background to his poetry. In 1892, after the completion of his book "*Algabal*", he suffered a profound crisis in Vienna, when the young Hugo von Hofmannsthal rejected his offer of friendship. Just in that moment of isolation, he heard there lived in his hometown Bingen on the river Rhine a person who knew and liked his poems. This person was Ida Coblenz, the extravagant daughter of a rich Jew, who resided in a palatial home just opposite the Georges.[7] In an unpublished novel titled "*Daija*" she has portrayed the young Stefan George who from 1892 visited her several times and left on her a strange, cold impression. Nevertheless she could not deny her admiration for the formal mastery and musicality of his poems.[8] George for his part was highly impressed by the young woman who not least by the oriental style of her dressing, differed significantly from the other inhabitants of this provincial town.

In the summer of 1894 he presented her with fifteen poems which later became the center of the "*Buch der hängenden Gärten*". She found herself portrayed in the dominating Semiramis figure, and the Hanging gardens seemed to be a poetic version of the elegant surroundings of her father's home. A broad iron gate, ornated with a coat of arms and two stone vases in antique style, gave the entrance its grand feudal character.[9] In his Semiramis songs George mentioned this gate as the "*beblümte Tor wo wir nur das eigene Hauchen spürten*". The young poet stayed here whenever he could. For him this garden was the only possible place of happiness. Among the many George photographs there are only two that portray him not as a serious priest or prophet, but as a human being that could even smile. These unusual portraits (Figure 3) were taken by Ida Coblenz in her parents' garden in the summer of 1896.

There is no single picture that shows George smiling again. Rather typical is the facial expression shown in Figure 4.

In my book on Schönberg and George I have investigated and characterized the relation between the poet's life and his poetry in greater detail, and explored the strange irony that subsequently led Ida Coblenz to marry Richard Dehmel. The same woman that had inspired George's "*Buch der hängenden Gärten*" later provoked Dehmel's famous volume "*Weib und Welt*", which included "*Verklärte Nacht*". Had George's highly

Figure 3 Stefan George in Ida Coblenz's garden, summer 1896. (Photos: Ida Coblenz) From: Robert Boehringer, Mein Bild von Stefan George. Düsseldorf und München, 2nd ed. 1968, plate 43

Figure 4 Photograph of Stefan George. (Photo: Sabine Lepsius) From: Boehringer, plate 57

artificial verses been the product of an unreal dream, Dehmel's poetry could more easily be identified with his real life. In November 1896 the last letters where exchanged between Ida Coblenz-Auerbach and Stefan George. He asked her to return the volume *"Das Jahr der Seele"* that he had dedicated to her. After that he did not address love poems to any other woman. Instead he built up a circle of disciples from which women were excluded. So was music.

The early *"Blätter für die Kunst"*, the esoteric journal of the circle, had started in a Wagnerian atmosphere[10] and had contained some musical settings of George poems like this composition by Karl Hallwachs.

Figure 5   From "Lieder im geschmack eines fahrenden spielmanns von Stefan George / in Musik gesetzt von Karl Hallwachs". Reprinted in "Blätter für die Kunst" 1894, II 2.

Like Zelter in his equally simple and homophonic Goethe settings, Hallwachs also preserved in his composition the rhythm of the poem and of course maintained its verse structure.[11] He must also have planned to compose some poems from the "Book of the Hanging Gardens". In December 1894 Ida Coblenz asked George, if Hallwachs had already finished the *Semiramis-Lieder*. If they were composed at all they were never published. After Ida Coblenz had made her decision for his rival, George developed a concept of poetry as a cultural form totally in contrast, in direct opposition to music. He never again asked composers to set his verses nor did he ever want to have the name of Ida Coblenz mentioned.[12] Only after George's death did she dare to recollect her early encounters.[13] And their correspondence was first published in 1983.

Schönberg's transition from Dehmel to George

Although Schönberg certainly was unaware of these hidden connections between *"Verklärte Nacht"* by Richard Dehmel and the *"Buch der hängenden Gärten"* by Stefan George, he nevertheless must have felt the contrast in style and attitude. This contrast was also reflected in the different audiences of both poets. At the turn of the century Dehmel's poetry, which abandoned the strict moral laws of the middle-class, was popular among progressive intellectuals and workers alike. In contrast George's encoded, snobistic poetry appealed to a minority, to an elite of connoisseurs, some of whom – like Hugo von Hofmannsthal and Clemens von Frankenstein – actually came from the nobility. George viewed the public success of his rival with despair and contempt. The greater Dehmel's popularity, the sharper would he insist on exclusivity and not allow any newspaper to reprint his poems. Instead he invented special letter-types for his verses and a unique form of reciting which was limited to a few selected houses.[14]

Although in the George circle one was not even allowed to mention the name of Dehmel, there existed one man who managed to maintain good relations with both poets. The pianist and composer Conrad Ansorge (1862–1930), a pupil of Liszt, had set poems both by Dehmel and George and was acknowledged for his understanding, not only of music but also of the other arts. To promote this connection between modern music and modern poetry the *Ansorge-Verein* of Vienna was established, supported by poets and composers alike, by literay critics and music historians, among them Peter Altenberg, Detlev v. Liliencron, Karl Wolfskehl, Wilhelm Kienzl and Max Graf. They all aimed at equal rights for poetry and music. In December 1904 the *Verein* organized a Stefan George-program, including Ansorge's settings of the cycle *"Waller im Schnee"* (Pilgrims in the Snow). The success however was limited. For the musically interested listeners the songs were too simple, whereas the literary element in the audience had difficulties with George's esoteric style.

Arnold Schönberg and his friend Alexander von Zemlinsky were connected to the *Verein* from the outset. One of his earliest programs, dated February 11, 1904, had included a selection of Schönberg songs (from op. 2 and op. 3), mostly based on Dehmel, together with excerpts of Ansorge's George cycle *"Waller im Schnee"*. Schönberg in contrast to his friend Zemlinsky appreciated that composition.[15] Whether or not he appreciated George's poetry, too, is unknown. But when, a few months later, in July 1904, the 600th anniversary of Petrarca was celebrated, he decided to set a translation of Petrarca's *"Nie ward ich, Herrin, müd"*, which he included in his op. 8. The aristocratic style of this poem marks a first step towards the similarily stylized poetry of George.[16] It took however more than three years till on December 17, 1907, Schönberg really set a George poem. It was his op. 14 Nr. 1 *"Ich darf nicht dankend an dir niedersinken"*.

The poem belongs to George's cycle *"Waller im Schnee"*. Since Schönberg had kept the concert program from February 1904,[17] he must also have known the program notes which explained *"Waller im Schnee"* as the lament of a lonely artist who is going to lose his friend. This was just his own situation that December in 1907 when Gustav Mahler, his most influential supporter, left the Austrian capital. The decision to compose a George poem a few days after this sad event is not only justified by the common subject of lament and loneliness; it also signified the decision to redefine his identity as an artist.

Years of Crisis

In a slow and very difficult process Schönberg had to accept his lone-liness. The scandal that followed the first performance of his Chamber symphony op. 9 in February 1907 had deeply hurt him. One critic had characterized this composition as "wild noises of democrats that no human being with any self-respect would ever mistake for music".[18] But not only in concert-life did he feel more and more rejected; the same was true in his private life, the summer of 1907 being a turning point. The Schönbergs spent that summer together with the Zemlinskys and the painter Richard Gerstl near Gmunden at Lake Traun. Influenced in his ideas by Otto Weininger and Sigmund Freud, in his paintings by Zuloaga and van Gogh, Gerstl was radically opposed to all academism.[19] His interest in music was such, that once even the position of a music critic was offered to him.[20] Over that summer he gave lessons in painting to Arnold Schönberg and his wife Mathilde. When, a few months later, Gerstl lost his studio, he found a new one in Liechtensteinstraße, in the same house according to Wellesz, where his friends the Zemlinskys and the Schönbergs lived.[21] A closer relationship to Mathilde must have developed.

Even in the early days of his marriage, Schönberg had found it difficult to integrate his wife in to the circle of his friends. Now this wedlock must have come to a crucial point. There is some evidence that he had this in mind when, in the autumn of 1907, he wrote down for the first time the quotation from the popular song *"O du lieber Augustin, alles ist hin"* (Everything is lost). As we know, this quotation belongs to his second String Quartet which – ironically – he dedicated to his wife. His sad or even bitter feelings were intensified when shortly later, on the 9th of December, Gustav Mahler left Vienna. As a consequence the *"Vereinigung schaffender Tonkünstler"* was disbanded.[22] Mahler, the honorary president of that organization, had promoted performances of the compositions of his younger colleague. Without him there was only a single Schönberg concert in Vienna that next year. In December 1907 Schönberg recognized

sharply his deep isolation which left no more room for Dehmel's opti-
mism, for his feeling of liberty and freedom. He no longer felt free but
was looking for new authorities. In his early years Schönberg had not
been a very religious man. Human love represented for him a far greater
value. Yet in 1907 and 1908, his years of crisis, he began to change this
orientation. Instrumental in the transition was George's poetry. While
Dehmel since 1897 had represented for him the model of the modern
artist, who with his free and optimistic spirit reaches mankind, he now
turned to George as the model of the isolated artist creating the future
and no longer caring for a contemporary audience.

The difficult path to a new musical language

To understand the inner logic of this process, it seems necessary to take a
look at the chronological order of his compositions between 1907 and
1909. His third sketch-book, covering just that critical period, may serve
as a source. As already Reinhold Brinkmann has pointed out,[23] Schönberg
was occupied with several compositions at the same time. In this process
instrumental works were pushed away more and more by vocal projects.
Again the texts brought up new ideas which then changed the musical
language.[24]

The Second String Quartet must have been planned originally as a
purely instrumental composition. Schönberg started to compose the first
movement on the same day in which he completed his Conrad Ferdinand
Meyer chorus *"Friede auf Erden"* (Peace on Earth) op. 13: on March 9, 1907.
This work was several times interrupted by *Lieder* which seem to have
influenced the concept of the String quartet. It lost in this process it's
abstract, formal character and became semantic.

The first interruption had already taken place in March and April 1907,
when Schönberg composed his two ballads op. 12 in order to participate
at a ballad contest organized by the popular Berlin journal *"Die Woche"*. It
indicates that, at that time, he was still longing for success and appreciation. In July 1907, when he spent his holidays with his family, with the
Zemlinskys and Gerstl at Traun Lake, he interrupted the string quartet to
start another instrumental composition, his Second Chamber Symphony.
He finished neither the string quartet nor the chamber symphony.

In the autumn of that same year, he noted on page 98 of his sketch-book
a Goethe setting *"Kennst Du das Land, wo die Zitronen blühen"*, Mignon's
yearning for the land of dreams. Just two pages later we find the quotation of the popular song *"O du lieber Augustin, alles ist hin"*, mentioned
above, which was to be the first semantic element in his Second String

Quartet. It could easily do without words since everyone in Vienna would automatically associate them with the melody. There is an inner connection between those two sketches, which also explains the growing portion of vocal music and of dissonances at the same time. The dreamland of the Goethe text seems to represent the ideal world of art, whereas the popular song hints at the despairing banality of everyday life. Since Schönberg did not feel at home in his own surroundings any more he looked for a new orientation. In this situation George's poetry offered him a new system of values that was far removed from banality. Schönberg himself confirmed this in his essay "How one becomes lonely": "I had started to compose a second chamber symphony. But after I had nearly finished two movements, about half of the whole work, poems by Stefan George, the German poet, inspired me to set a few of them, and surprisingly, without any expectations of that kind, those *Lieder* revealed a style that was totally different from everything I had written before. This was the first step on a new, but very difficult path."[25]

The first George song that he composed, *"Ich darf nicht dankend an dir niedersinken"* as his op. 14, 1, enters new fields of harmony, but does not yet, however, represent his definite arrival at the poet's world. In the beginning of the next year (February 1908) he created the song *"In diesen Wintertagen"* which expressed new hope. The style of this poem by Karl Henckell (which was also set by Richard Strauss) reminds one of the poetry of Dehmel. As the poem ends with the idea of love, the composer in his setting gave this word *"Liebe"* the most prominent position. The composition ends in a pure C-major-consonance, symbolizing the desired harmony (Figure 6).

Already in March 1908 Schönberg turned again to George. He then composed *"Da meine lippen reglos sind und brennen"*, as the first song of his "Book of the Hanging Gardens". It no longer ends with a consonance, but rather with a musical question-mark, with a harmony that is as mysterious as the signal mentioned in the last line of the poem (Figure 7).

Figure 6 Schönberg, op. 14, Nr. 2, last bars. (© Universal Edition, Wien)

Figure 7   Op. 15, 4, bars 23–26. (© Universal Edition, Wien)

The Choice of the Text

Schönberg's selection of a poem from George's *"Waller im Schnee"* could be explained since the composer knew this cycle from Ansorge's composition. How he met with the poet's *"Buch der hängenden Gärten"* can only be a matter of speculation. Neither Zemlinsky nor Gerstl would have recommended this book to him since both disliked George's poetry. Schönberg himself may have discovered the poetical image of the garden as a parallel to the dreamland from Goethe's Mignon song or Henkell's island of love. But the "Book of the Hanging Gardens" not only consists of the central fifteen Semiramis poems; it is surrounded by descriptions of the hero's fight as a crusader against his enemies. In these poems (which he did not set) Schönberg could find a symbolic version of his conflict with the conservative musical world of Vienna. This assumption is being underlined by the fact that there exists an undated sketch of a song *"Friedensabend"*, depicting the Hanging Gardens as the peaceful contrast to the battlenoise from below.

The opposition of garden and city around 1900 was a central concern in the arts. Many architects of the time made a strict division between living and working quarters. For *Jugendstil* artists like Olbrich, Muthesius and Schultze-Naumburg the suburban villa represented the ideal form of living. Schönberg who in his early years always lived in the city center, changed this habit after the crisis of 1908. Neither in Vienna nor in Berlin or Los Angeles did he prefer to dwell in downtown areas. Instead he chose residential districts like Zehlendorf, Mödling and Brentwood. The short period of a more urban life in Berlin was an exception to this rule.

Another form of isolation was characteristic for the original Hanging gardens at Babylon, once one of the Seven Wonders of the World. The sensation seems to have been derived primarily from the high position over the ground, which demanded technical solutions for the watering of

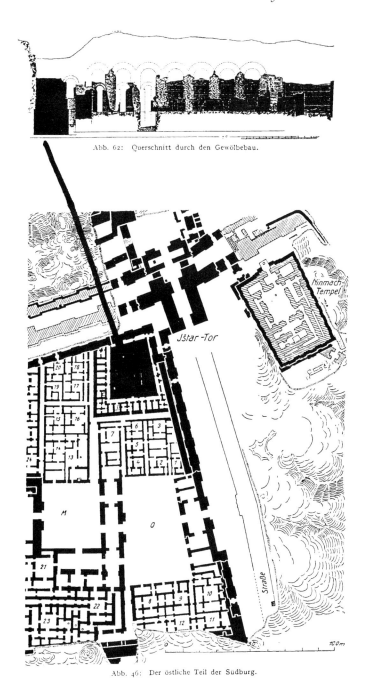

Abb. 62: Querschnitt durch den Gewölbebau.

Abb. 46: Der östliche Teil der Südburg.

Figure 8 Map of Babylon, from: Robert Koldewey, Das wieder erstehende Babylon, Leipzig 1913

flowers and the isolation of cellars below against encroaching waters. The Babylonians managed this by combining several layers of reed, asphalt, bricks and even lead. Only five years before Schönberg started his composition the vaults which carried the Hanging Gardens were excavated by the German archeologist Robert Koldewey.

Although the discovery and reconstruction of old Babylon was the greatest project of German archeology after 1899, there is no indication that Schönberg had any information about it. For him the Hanging Gardens were not an historic place but the symbol of a protected sphere that contrasted with the aggressive banality of everyday life. The garden also represented the contrast between necessity and refinement. Another motif that may have influenced his choice of text was the motif of noble exclusivity, which corresponded to his development from a democrat to a monarchist.[26] Most important however was the motif of love which George represented totally differently than Dehmel in his poetry. Instead of partners with equal rights, we find the young man as an inexperienced slave who adores a mighty queen.

> *Tell me on what path today*
> *She will come and wanders by . . .*

the poor man utters and then submissively continues:

> *That I lean my cheek to lie*
> *Underfoot for her repose.*

While Stefan George approached Ida Coblenz in a subservient tone, Richard Dehmel, later her husband, addressed her in a more spontaneous way. Also he idealized love, but to glorify rather than to disguise reality. Both poets had spoken to the same woman in two very different ways. Schönberg took over their attitudes in two contrasting situations but also in context of one woman: Mathilde. In the early years of his marriage he could identify his love with Dehmel's enthusiastic tone. In 1908 he found the pessimistic and submissive attitude of George more appropriate. In one of his aphorisms, published one year later, he explained: "When oriental people want to honor a friend, they use as extreme and powerful means the method of self-humiliation. 'Your slave, your servant; I am not worthy, to loosen your shoe-string.' – if a servant says this to a prince, it is not especially flattering, because it is true. But if a prince says it to a prince, it means: 'You know, who I am and how I am admired. Look, I place you even higher than myself. I step down to let you be seen better.

From this you may recognize, how much I like you.' "[27] Schönberg concluded: "Only the superior who is sure to loose nothing can praise in such an unrestricted way." Since he now regarded himself as the superior, the method of self-humiliation could be used by himself.

Start with an open end: op. 15, No. 4

Like the poet also, Schönberg first did not mean to create a whole cycle of songs. So instead of No. 1 he started with No. 4 of the Semiramis songs. This is the poem:

> *Da meine lippen reglos sind und brennen*
> *Beacht ich erst wohin mein fuss geriet:*
> *In andrer herren prächtiges gebiet.*
> *Noch war vielleicht mir möglich mich zu trennen,*
> *Da schien es, dass durch hohe gitterstäbe*
> *Der blick, vor dem ich ohne lass gekniet,*
> *Mich fragend suchte oder zeichen gäbe.*

This is a rough verbal translation:

> *Since my lips now are motionless and burning,*
> *I only now take notice of where my feet have brought me:*
> *To other master's splendid realms.*
> *It was perhaps still possible to turn back.*
> *Then it seemed, that between the high fence palings*
> *The glance, before which I knelt all the time,*
> *Would search for me and give signs.*

The seven lines seem to contain two complete phrases. Closer investigation shows however that the first line of the second phrase "*Noch war vielleicht mir möglich mich zu trennen*" is a complete phrase, too. In its reflective character it contrasts to the rest. The syntactic as well as semantic structure of the poem can therefore be described as a symmetrical three-part form ABA.

Contents/syntax: $3 + 1 + 3$ Lines
    A   1 *Da meine lippen reglos sind und brennen*
        2 *Beacht ich erst wohin mein fuss geriet:*
        3 *In andrer herren prächtiges gebiet.*

    B   4 *Noch war vielleicht mir möglich mich zu trennen,*

A   5 *Da schien es, dass durch hohe gitterstäbe*
    6 *Der blick, vor dem ich ohne lass gekniet,*
    7 *Mich fragend suchte oder zeichen gäbe.*

The slightly different rhyme structure, as shown in the following example, consists of two parts, which are interconnected by a rhyme-element b:

Rhyme: 4 + 3 Lines
    1 Da meine lippen reglos sind und   *brennen*   a
    2 Beacht ich erst wohin mein fuss *geriet:*   b
    3 In andrer herren prächtiges   *gebiet.*   b
    4 Noch war vielleicht mir möglich mich zu   *trennen,*   a

    5 Da schien es, dass durch hohe gitter – stäbe   c
    6 Der blick, vor dem ich ohne lass *gekniet,*   b
    7 Mich fragend suchte oder zeichen gäbe.   c

This unusual structure already shows influences of oriental poetry. But the musical quality of the poem is not limited to rhythm and rhyme. Under the influence of Mallarmé and Verlaine George controlled the vowel structure also within the lines:

Rhymes supported by vowels and consonant endings
    a   s - i-nd   u-nd b-rennen
    a   m-i-ch z-u   t-rennen

    b   fuss ge – r   iet
    b   . . . s ge – b   iet.
    b   . . ss ge – kn iet.

    c   d u r ch   hoh e gitter – st äbe
    c   s u   ch te od er zeichen g äbe

Rhyme "a" includes the vowels "i" and "u":
    sind und brennen – mich zu trennen
Rhyme "b" includes the final consonant "s":
    fuss geriet – ges gebiet – lass gekniet
Rhyme "c" has the most relations: "u", "ch", "o", "e" and "äbe":
    Durch hohe gitterstäbe, suchte oder zeichen gäbe.

One can even analyze the whole poem as a sequence of vowels, as demonstrated in Figure 9, 4.

1 contents/syntax: 3 + 1 + 3

A 1 Da meine lippen reglos sind und brennen
   2 Beacht ich erst wohin mein fuss geriet:
   3 In andrer herren prächtiges gebiet.

B 4 Noch war vielleicht mir möglich mich zu trennen,

A′ 5 Da schien es, dass durch hohe gitterstäbe
    6 Der blick, vor dem ich ohne lass gekniet,
    7 Mich fragend suchte oder zeichen gäbe.

2 rhyme: 4 + 3

  1 Da meine lippen reglos sind und   brennen   a
  2 Beacht ich erst wohin mein fuss   geriet: b
  3 In andrer herren prächtiges   gebiet.   b
  4 Noch war vielleicht mir möglich mich zu trennen,   a
  5 Da schien es, dass durch hohe gitter – stäbe   c
  6 Der blick, vor dem ich ohne lass gekniet,   b
  7 Mich fragen suchte oder zeichen gäbe.   c

3 rhymes supported by vowels and consonant endings

```
a  –X – X – X – X–          s – i – nd       u – nd   b – rennen
a                           m – i – ch  z – u        t – rennen,
b                                    fuss  ge – r   iet
b                                    ···s  ge – b   iet
b                                    ···ss ge – kn  iet
c                    d u r ch     hoh e     gitter –  st äbe
(Mi) ch   ······     s u  ch te    od er    zeichen g  äbe
```

4 Vowels

	A	I	E	O	I	U	E
1	DA(meine)	lIppen	rEg –	1Os	sInd	Und	brEnnEn
2	Be–						
	Acht	Ich	Erst	wO–	hIn(mein)	fUss	gE–
		rIet:					
3		In					
	Andrer						
			hErrEn (pr		chtI…ge…s)		gE–
		bIet.					

4   NOch
        wAr   vIel(leicht)   mIr
                                              mOeglIch
                                                 mIch   zU   trEnnEn,
        DA   schIen   Es,
        dAss   dUrch
                                     hOhe
                                         gItter . . . . . .   (stäbE)
                         dEr
6   blIck,   vOr   dEm
                                            Ich
                                   Oh   − nE
        lAss ge− knIet,
7   MIch
        frAgend   sUch −   tE
                              Oder
              (zeichen)   (g)äbe
i=lippen − sind − ich − wohin − gitter − blick − mich

Figure 9   Book of the Hanging Gardens: Analysis of poem No. 4.

The model may be found in the first line:
Da meine lippen reglos sind und brennen
The sequence of the German vowels a-i-e-o-i-u-e is comparable to a
melodic theme, that is being varied in the following lines. The second
line resembles closely the original theme whereas in the following lines
the order of vowels changes more and more.

In the beginning of his musical composition (Figure 10) Schönberg
preserves the structure of the poem, by setting it line by line. Already in
the second line his manuscript contains a significant mistake. Instead of
"*beacht ich* erst, *wohin mein fuss geriet*" he wrote down "*beacht ich* nicht
wohin mein fuss geriet". He thus underlined the blindness of the lyrical
Ego, staggering into unknown territory. This corresponds to the lack of
any clear meter at the beginning of the composition. Only after three bars
can a regular rhythm and a regular bar system be recognized.

In no other song from his op. 15 did the composer use the tempo mark
"*gehend*" (in walking speed). He hereby seemed to state that the rhythms
symbolize the walking of our hero. His movement starts irregularily and
syncopated, but then becomes a regular two–four–time. Already from bar
12 this regular pulse dissolves into five–eight–time. At the reprise in bar
18 begins the last section, based on a four–four–time, an expanded

version of the beginning. So already the changing times show the three-part-structure A B A.

The three sections are characterized by different movements which represent different emotional situations. Whereas the first part shows the man walking into unknown territory, in the second part his regular movement comes to a standstill. The five–eight–time evokes, instead of walking, a more reflective mood. The voice here changes from singing to a kind of nervous whispering, which now definitely changes the verse structure into prose. This marks the turning point: the hero asks himself if he had not better return (*Noch war vielleicht mir möglich...*). Yet the third part brings the decision to stay in these strange surroundings. Someone is

Arnold Schönberg, op. 15, nr. 4

Figure 10   Schönberg, op. 15, No. 4 (© Universal Edition, Wien)

looking, giving mysterious signals (marked in Figure 10). As in a dream
the hero neither knows who is looking at him nor what the signals mean.
But he wishes to discover the answers.

This staggering movement towards an unknown destination corresponds to the lack of any tonal orientation. On March 18, 1908 Schönberg renounced for the first time a distinct tonality. Although in this song melodic as well as harmonic elements are based on the interval of the third, they are no longer connected to a basic tonality. The end offers no tonal solution. Like the poet, the composer too, makes no effort to solve the riddles. It is up to the listener to add a consonant chord, an ending in G-major or F-sharp-major, in his imagination, or to accept the unresolved dissonance. The end is left open.

The Ascent from the Sensuous to the Spiritual

Five days after this song No. 4 (*"Da meine Lippen..."*) Schönberg had completed No. 5, by the end of the month No. 3. On 13th of April he finished No. 8, based on a highly emotional poem:

> *Wenn ich heut nicht deinen leib berühre*
> *Wird der faden meiner seele reissen...*

Those four songs he wrote down on a double-sheet under the heading *"Vier Lieder"*.[28] All four poems express a burning longing for a mysterious woman that does not say a single word. They express expectation, *Erwartung*.

The two vocal movements from the string quartet op. 10, *"Litanei"* and *"Entrückung"*, which were created in the early summer of 1908, represent a totally different attitude. Schönberg selected these two poems from the books *"Maximin"* and *"Traumdunkel"* which belong to George's volume *"Der siebente Ring"*, written years after the poet's last contact with Ida Coblenz. *"Litanei"* no longer addresses a human being but a god. The central line of that poem reads: *"Töte das sehnen, schließe die wunde! nimm mir die liebe, gib mir dein glück!"* Or in the translation by Ernst Morwitz:

> *Whole be the wounded, yearning shall perish!*
> *Ease me of passion, give me your joy!*

Yearning shall perish...This movement marks the departure from the idea of love towards religion. Even more open and clear this is expressed in the last movement *"Entrückung"*:

> *I only am a spark of holy fire,*
> *A thunder only of the holy tongue!*

The last line recalls Schönberg's confession: "Art is the outcry of those, who in their fate experience the fate of mankind... In their inside is the movement of the world; to the outside comes only the reflection: the work of art."[29] Impotence in real life changed into phantasies of omnipotence. Art replaced love and religion. The most private was transformed into the universal.

Schönberg himself has characterized this process, which can be found in his Second String Quartet and his "Book of the Hanging Gardens" alike, as the "ascent of the sensuous into the spiritual".[30] To understand his atonal compositions and the writings of that period, it is of great importance to know their chronological place in this transitional process from the sensuous to the spiritual, a process that Schönberg also mentioned in his dedication of the "*Harmonielehre*" to Kandinsky[31] or in his famous letter to Dehmel, where he looked back to his development from materialism through anarchism to spiritualism.[32] Whereas the "Book of the Hanging Gardens" marks an early point in this development, his correspondence with Kandinsky[33] and his essay "The Relationship to the Text" are already on a higher level of abstraction. Before correlating this essay and his op. 15 it is therefore necessary to take into account the degree of self-stylization that we find in this later period.

Creation of a new Ego

The year 1908 was certainly the darkest in Schönberg's life.[34] His wife left him for Gerstl, and only when she was appealed to as the mother of his two children did she finally return. Schönberg drafted several last wills that show how near he was then to suicide. To prevent this he made up a new definition of himself. Separating body and soul, private person and the artist, he created a new Ego. The real Schönberg, he declared in this document, is the artist and not the private person. The artist, by his solution, had never been betrayed by his wife; he did not even know her. "So this event has not happened to me, but to some ridiculous creation from the imagination of a woman. My wife has betrayed the man, she wanted to see in me. But I was far away. She has never seen me, nor have I ever seen her. We have never met."[35]

In an act of violence Schönberg constructed a new artificial world from which banality, as he put it, was excluded. It was also an act of purification and self-protection that made him express the following in his last will: "He who sticks to facts will not get beyond them, to the heart of things. I deny facts. All, without exception. For me they have no value; for I elude them before they can draw me down to them."[36] In the crisis of subjectivity Schönberg created a new Ego, that no longer cared for the outside world.

In an aphorism, published in 1909, he wrote: "A human being is what he experiences; an artist experiences only what he is."[37] This self-definition prevented him accepting his bad experiences as part of reality. Since they nevertheless were present in his mind and his work, Schönberg now emphasized the unconscious elements in the process of artistic creation. He proclaimed that the unconscious dominated the conscious, which meant the collapse of the principle of subjectivity, of autonomy and self-control that he up to that moment had claimed for himself. But only by denying control of his unconscious could he in his critical period keep control over himself.

After the completion of my Schönberg–George study, Otto Breicha[38], Jane Kallir and Patrick Werkner have published books on Richard Gerstl, that give more complete information about that autumn of 1908. But also the compositions and paintings, that were produced that September in Schönberg's flat and in Gerstl's studio, apparently both in Liechtensteinstraße 68–70, give an impression of the uneasy atmosphere. Here (Figure 11) is a deliberately provoking self-portrait of Gerstl, dated September 12, 1908.[39]

After finishing the Four George Songs, consisting of Numbers 4, 5, 3 and 8, in the spring of 1908 and after also completing the *"Litanei"* in the summer, Schönberg in that September continued his composition of the "Book of the Hanging Gardens". He started with No. 13, a number he had always connected with bad luck. In this poem all hope of opening the heart of the mighty Semiramis has disappeared.

> *No. 13*
> *Du lehnest wider eine silberweide*
> *Am ufer, mit des fächers starren spitzen*
> *Umschirmest du das haupt dir wie mit blitzen*
> *Und rollst als ob du spieltest dein geschmeide.*
> *Ich bin im boot das laubgewölbe wahren*
> *In das ich dich vergeblich lud zu steigen..*
> *Die weiden seh ich die sich tiefer neigen*
> *Und blumen die verstreut im wasser fahren.*

George carefully tried to avoid repetitions of words within a poem, and even within the cycle. It is especially surprising therefore, that the word *"Weiden"* (Willows) appears twice. Willows hanging into the water are in German called *"Trauerweiden"* (willows of sorrow). By this repetition the poet seemed to point at them as symbols of sorrow and grief. Schönberg

Figure 11   Richard Gerstl, *Self-portrait in full size*, 1908, oil (Private Collection)

finished his No. 13 on the 27th of September. The same day a letter had arrived from Richard Strauss, saying that he could not accept the Chamber symphony op. 9 for his concerts in Berlin.[40] Two days later Gerstl made two desperate self-portraits, both dated September 29. They differ only in the expression of the eyes.

Figure 12 Richard Gerstl, *Self-portrait*, 29 September 1908, pen, pencil, ink (Graphische Sammlung Albertina, Vienna)

Schönberg in his self-portraits also concentrated on the expression of the eyes, as for example in Figure 14.

It seems that Schönberg only now decided to set all fifteen of the poems. In direct connection with No. 13 he sketched No. 14 and No. 15. On the 11th of October he interrupted his work and began first drafts to his drama with music *"Die glückliche Hand"*. Here in his own words he portrayed the artist as the supernatural being, that no longer needs

Figure 13 Richard Gerstl, *Self-portrait*, 29 September 1908, shifted ink and carbon (New York, Galerie St. Etienne, Nachlaß Kallir)

Figure 14 Schönberg, *Self-portrait*, pastel on paper (Schönberg Family) (© A Schönberg, c/o Beeldrecht Amsterdam)

earthly happiness. Now that he had found his new Ego he did not really need George any more, but could write his own text instead. He could now also renounce the tonal associations which still had been implicit in his earlier George settings. Tonality, which for the majority of european listeners represented the basis of all music, was for him only a *"Mittel der Darstellung"*, a medium of representation. Since it no longer corresponded to his *"Ausdruckswillen"*, his expressive volition, he no longer used it.

Schönberg definitely abandoned tonality in his George Songs No. 11 to 15, which also in the poetic cycle represent the turn from summer to autumn, from fulfillment to departure. Parallel to the decay of love in the songs, parallel to the approach of autumn in art and reality, the emancipation of dissonance took place. However the more Schönberg advanced from sensualism to spiritualism, the more he believed in his new artificial priest-like Ego, the more he denied any reflection of reality in his work.

When on November 4, 1908, there was a concert of Schönberg's pupils the critics again reacted very hostilely. On the night after that concert Gerstl committed suicide in his studio in Liechtensteinstraße.[41]

A few weeks later, on the 21th of December, the year's only Viennese Schönberg concert took place, containing the first performance of the Second string quartet, which the composer had finally finished and dedicated to his wife.[42] This work reflected the terrible private crisis but also a new vision of himself as an artist. Despite an incredible scandal the composer tried to be calm. In a letter to Arnold Rosé, the primarius of the ensemble, he wrote: "The unshakable courage of a moral being is deaf to the licentiousness of a bestial pack."[43] In himself and in his pupils Schönberg now developed a faith that could no longer be questioned by anything.

The experiences of that year completely changed his relation to reality – and to himself. From that moment on he felt he was fighting almost alone against a world of enemies. As he confessed in a letter to Karl Kraus, his attitude to the public was ambivalent. On one hand he regarded it a tall order to write for an audience, on the other hand he envied other artists their positive reviews. He did not want to consider the listeners, who he believed were mostly incompetent, and yet he needed their response. He explained away his lack of success in concert life and the accompaning scandals as confirmation of his lonely way.

In the program notes for the first performance of his fifteen Songs from the "Book of the Hanging Gardens", the composer wrote: "I suspect, that even those, who have trusted me so far, will not understand the necessity of this development." One of those friends, who no longer followed him on his way to a new musical language, was Alexander von Zemlinsky, his brother-in-law and once his teacher.[44] Since Zemlinsky could no longer help him, Schönberg looked for other ways to develop a strong belief in himself. He found examples of lonely brilliance in Gustav Mahler, Otto Weininger[45], Karl Kraus[46], Stefan George, Parzival and even Jesus Christ.[47]

The inner logic of expression

Schönberg's George reception was essentially based on the subjects of his poetry, on his poetic images, on his personality, his definition of the artist and his *"Weltanschauung"*. Yet the aesthetic views of both were very different. When they created their respective "Book of the Hanging Gardens" both had to control a critical personal situation. The different ways they treated it in their art works, can be explained by their divergent personalities, but also by their different artistic media. Since music in the creational process seems to be more open to subconscious elements than literature, George turned away from this "dionysic" art.[48] Artistic form for him meant either strict self-control or repression of the instinctive.

On the other hand Schönberg in his atonal period, understood music as a record of dreams that didn't need an interpretation. "On its highest level art deals exclusively with the reproduction of the inner nature."[49] Another quote from the *"Harmonielehre"* underlines this attitude: "The creation of the artist is instinctive. Consciousness has little influence on it. He gets the impression, that everything what he does is dictated to him. As if he was following the will of some inner power, whose laws he does not know. He is only the executor of a will that he does not understand, of the instinct inside himself."[50]

Here, as in his testament, Schönberg renounced any responsibility for his instinct. But he certified that the resulting work of art was necessary; it represented a form of catharsis essential for his existence. His compositions preserve a truth that the composer himself did not want to take for granted. What characterizes most of his works in this period, is that they are very private and at the same time highly stylized, tremendously open and also hiding secrets. Whereas the unity of both sides creates the spontaneous intensity of these works, Schönberg himself tried to overlook the biographical aspects. This strange simultaneousness of openness and strict reserve can also be found in his paintings and in later works. In October of 1910 in a letter to Alma Mahler, he confessed, apparently reflecting *"Die glückliche Hand"*: "Colors, noises, lights, sound, movements, gazes, gestures – in short, those things which compromise the material of the stage – are to be lined up in a colorful way. Nothing else. In my feeling it had a meaning to me when I wrote it down. If the components result in a similar picture when they are put together, that's alright with me. If not, this is even better. For I do not want to be understood. I want to express myself but I hope I will be misunderstood. It would be dreadful to me if I could be seen through. That is why with my things I prefer talking about technical matters..."[51]

While George allowed his personal feelings to enter his art only in a highly controlled way, Schönberg burst open the stylized form of that poetry and thus, through his music restored to the poems the spontaneity which they had lost in the artistic process. Against the aesthetics of the beautiful and of the ornament, which were represented by George, he developed the aesthetics of truth. In his essay *"Probleme des Kunstunter-richts"* he mentioned truthfulness as the highest criterion of art, a principle that was personified in his drama *"Die glückliche Hand"*. The beautiful woman there cannot have the least understanding for the lonely man, the truthful artist. Strangely enough Schönberg related truthfulness no longer to artistic subjectivity but to the subconscious. Explaining that he was determined by his inner nature, he said farewell to the responsibility of the subject.[52]

He deprived George's poems of the beauty of their strictly controlled form and identified the true essence of the plot. In his musical settings these documents of poetic symbolism became expressionistic texts. Softened feelings of noble melancholy were transformed into terrible outcries, as in the *fortissimo* beats of the last piano epilogue. Since Schönberg – or rather: the expressive forces in himself – aimed only at the truth, i.e. the essence of his psychic processes, he dissolved the rhythmic discipline of George's verse in prose and recited this prose in a way that could best express his inner perplexity.

Tonality and anarchism

In contrast to George, Schönberg revolted around 1908 against clearcut forms without trying to establish a new form. He did not want to establish a new style either. Corresponding to the domination of the subconscious there was a strong anarchic element in his aesthetics. His father was already an anarchistic idealist. His own collaboration with Ernst von Wolzogen and his setting of a poem by John Henry Mackay, author of a biography of Max Stirner, are hints at his ongoing interest in anarchistic ideas.[53] In 1912 in a letter to Dehmel he had confessed, that behind him was a period of anarchism. This background is revealed also in his attitude towards tonality, which Schönberg not only understood as a symbol of harmony, but also of rule and dominion. He interpreted tonality as a portrait of the conflicts of society. So his description of modulation in his *"Harmonielehre"* strikingly resembles an analysis of the struggles between the different nationalities in the Austro-Hungarian monarchy. Mentioned are the borders, "where the powers of the governors diminish and the right of self-determination of the subordinates can under some circumstances call forth revolutions, changements in the constitution of the whole structure."[54] It is quite revealing to find already in the *"Harmonielehre"* the composer's conflict between anarchism and monarchism. While at one point he explains the dissolution of tonality as the emancipation of the subordinates, he subsequently describes it as a reform that is owed to a liberal sovereign. It is this relationship between anarchism and atonality, which was stressed by Ernst Bloch in his *"Geist der Utopie"* and later by Heinz-Klaus Metzger, who saw atonality as the preview of a political revolution still to come.[55]

George had demanded strict discipline in the arts. Schönberg, in contrast, did not want to be limited by any borderline. Since he compared infinity to eternity, he also needed in his music elements of infinity. Already in the last movement of his Second String Quartet, titled *"Entrückung"* (transport), he came near to the idea of an infinite musical space, where tonal centers as well as centers of rhythmic gravity had to be regarded as outdated limitations.

New Music expresses the New Man

Schönberg's departure from lyrical modernism – as represented by Dehmel – and his passing over to modern lyrics – as represented by George – marked the beginning of New Music in its emphatic sense.[56] It is characteristic for the key-works of New Music that they emerged from extreme isolation and loneliness, a situation, which questioned not only the identity of the artist, but also his language and his possibilities to communicate. As in Hofmannsthal's "Chandos"-letter[57] or in the quoted draft of Schönberg's last will, the artist met this crisis by creating a new Ego. He became a new being with a new artistic language – he became a modern artist. Schönberg's George Songs are fundamentally different from those by Franz Schreker, Egon Wellesz, Karl Hallwachs, Armin Knab or Conrad Ansorge, since they reflect an existential perplexity. Since Schönberg and George had to cope with real communications problems, they developed their very own artistic languages that differed from the generally used code. In his *"Harmonielehre"*, which is also a prime source for his aesthetic views, Schönberg wrote: "To the new and unusual of a new chord the real 'Tondichter' is driven only by the following reasons: he must express the new, unheard of, that is moving him. What for coming generations is only a new sound, a technical element, represents far more: it is the unvoluntarily found symbol, that announces the new man, who is expressing himself."[58] In a strange combination of anarchism and theosophy Schönberg proclaimed that the laws created by the genius should be the laws of future mankind.[59] His creations then were a kind of prophecy, Schönberg himself being the prophet, in both an artistic and religious sense. "We are to remain blind", he explained in his speech on Gustav Mahler, "until we have acquired eyes, eyes that see the future."[60]

Since the 'new man' had to be an alternative to the former existence of George and Schönberg, he was characterized by elements of nobility and even holiness. The very high self-regard of the modern artist stands in strange contrast to his proclaimed renounciation on any public effect. Since this artist did no longer try to communicate, this activity was now passed over to the listener or the reader. It was their duty to recognize the artist's code and to try to understand what he had wanted to express.

Unlike other composers of *Lieder*, Schönberg in his George Songs, did not want to create musical settings that were stylistically equivalent to the poetry. By reading the poems he was actually reading himself, or rather: his self. His songs were very private, even intimate creations. This intimacy comes in conflict with the enhancement and the climax of the mediums of expression. The balance of lyric expressions and lyrical technical means which was characteristic for the romantic *Lied*, no longer exists here.

What makes it so difficult to perform the songs, are not only their dissonant harmonies which are no longer related to a clearly recognizable tonal center. It is also the contrast between lyric intimacy – like in the fourteenth song – and great dramatic expression – like Numbers 7 and 8. The wide range of ambitus and dynamics transcends by far that of a 'normal' *Lieder*-recital.[61] The conflict between distance and nearness, which led to those different concepts of interpretation, is inherent in the juxtaposition of the artistic concepts of George and Schönberg. The composer was even uncertain for some time if he should publish his new composition at all. When finally he decided to have his Opus 15 performed in public[62], he added a preface that underlined the central position of these songs for his artistic development:

> "With the George Songs I have succeeded for the first time, to approach an ideal of expression and form, that I have already had in mind for years. Until now I had not enough energy and assurance to realize it. But since I have finally entered this path, I am aware that I have crossed all borders of the old aesthetics; although I am going towards an destination that to me seems clear, I already feel the opposition that I have to encounter; I feel the heat of rebellion, which even moderate temperaments will produce, and I anticipate, that even those, who have so far believed in me, will not understand the necessity of this development."

EHRBAR-SAAL, 1910, 14. Jänner, ½8 Uhr abends

VEREIN FUER KUNST UND KULTUR

NEUE KOMPOSITIONEN VON ARNOLD SCHOENBERG

DIE SOPRANSTIMMEN SINGT FRAU MARTHA WINTERNITZ-
DORDA

DIE TENORSTIMMEN HERR HANS NACHOD

FRAU ETTA WERNDORF SPIELT DREI KLAVIERSTUECKE
UND BEGLEITET DIE LIEDER NACH GEORGE

HERR KAPELLMEISTER ARNOLD WINTERNITZ BEGLEITET
DIE GURRE-LIEDER UND DIE FUENF EINZELNEN GESAENGE

HERR DR. ANTON VON WEBERN UND HERR DR. RUDOLF
WEIRICH VEREINIGEN SICH MIT DEN BEIDEN LETZTGENANN-
TEN ZUR AUSFUEHRUNG DER FUER ZWEI KLAVIERE ACHT-
HAENDIG GESETZTEN VOR- UND ZWISCHENSPIELE IN DEN
GURRE-LIEDERN

VORWORT

Die Gurre-Lieder habe ich anfangs 1900 komponiert, die Lieder nach George und die Klavierstücke 1908. Der Zeitraum, der dazwischen liegt, rechtfertigt vielleicht die große stilistische Verschiedenheit. Die Vereinigung solch heterogener Werke im Aufführungsrahmen eines Abends bedarf, da sie in auffälliger Weise einen bestimmten Willen ausdrückt, vielleicht ebenfalls einer Rechtfertigung.

Mit den Liedern nach George ist es mir zum erstenmal gelungen, einem Ausdrucks- und Form-Ideal nahe-zukommen, das mir seit Jahren vorschwebt. Es zu verwirklichen, gebrach es mir bis dahin an Kraft und Sicherheit. Nun ich aber diese Bahn endgiltig betreten habe, bin ich mir bewußt, alle Schranken einer vergangenen Ästhetik durchbrochen zu haben; und wenn ich auch einem mir als sicher erscheinenden Ziele zustrebe, so fühle ich dennoch schon jetzt den Widerstand, den ich zu überwinden haben werde; fühle den Hitzegrad der Auflehnung, den selbst die geringsten Temperamente aufbringen werden, und ahne, daß selbst solche, die mir bisher geglaubt haben, die Notwendigkeit dieser Entwicklung nicht werden einsehen wollen.

Deshalb schien es mir angebracht, durch die Aufführung der Gurre-Lieder, die vor acht Jahren keine Freunde fanden, heute aber deren viele besitzen, darauf hinzuweisen, daß nicht Mangel an Erfindung oder an technischem Können, oder an Wissen um die anderen Forderungen jener landläufigen Ästhetik mich in diese Richtung drängen, sondern, daß ich einem innern Zwange folge, der starker ist, als Erziehung; daß ich jener Bildung gehorche, die als meine natürliche mächtiger ist, als meine künstlerische Vorbildung.

Arnold Schönberg.

Figure 15 Program of the first performance of Schönberg's "Fünfzehn Gedichte aus 'Das Buch der Hängenden Gärten' von Stefan George" op. 15 on January 14, 1910, in Vienna (Arnold Schönberg Institute Los Angeles)

The expression of extreme loneliness, which was raised from the lyric intimacy to great dramatic dimensions, became a public art form after January 1910. This public loneliness stemmed from the contradiction between the powerlessness of the artists as men and the overestimation of their power as artists: from the contradiction between isolated single elements and beings on one side and the tendency towards infinity at the other. The modern artist transgressed by far his personal limits, those of his art and the limits of his audience, which changed from a community to a lonely crowd. He proclaimed that public and loneliness were a unity.

NOTES.

1. Opera 7, 9, 11, 16 and 19.
2. A. Schönberg, Das Verhältnis zum Text. In: Der Blaue Reiter. Ed. by W. Kandinsky and F. Marc. New edition by Klaus Lankheit. München 1965, p. 60–75.
3. Schönberg, Ausgewählte Briefe. Mainz 1958, p. 30. Cf. Joachim Birke, Richard Dehmel und Arnold Schönberg. Ein Briefwechsel. In: Die Musikforschung 1958, pp. 279 ff.
4. R. Dehmel, Ausgewählte Briefe 1883–1902. Berlin 1923, p. 207.
5. Dehmel, Briefe. pp. 365 f.
6. Cf. A. Dümling, Die fremden Klänge der hängenden Gärten. Die öffentliche Einsamkeit der Neuen Musik am Beispiel von Arnold Schönberg und Stefan George. München 1981. p. 284, note 560.
7. Julius Bab, Richard Dehmel. Berlin 1926, p. 126.
8. Ida Dehmel, Über Richard Dehmel und seine Zeitgenossen. Reprinted in: Richard Dehmel, Dichtungen, Briefe, Dokumente. Hamburg 1963, p. 264.
9. Ida Coblenz-Dehmel, Daija. Unpublished novel at the Dehmel Archiv of the Staatsbibliothek Hamburg. p. 19.
10. At least one member of the George circle, Karl Wolfskehl, the friend of Kandinsky, remained a Wagnerian throughout his life. A strong Wagnerian was also George's early friend Georg Fuchs, who later founded the Münchner Künstler-Theatre. Cf. Peg Weiss, Kandinsky in Munich. The Formative Jugendstil Years. Princeton 1979, pp. 93 f.
11. Cf. A. Dümling, Umwertung der Werte. Das Verhältnis Stefan Georges zur Musik. In: Jahrbuch des Staatl. Instituts für Musikforschung Preußischer Kulturbesitz 1981/82. pp. 29–32.
12. Only in recent years has the strong impact of Ida Coblenz on George been studied in more detail. Cf. Friedrich Thiel, Vier sonntägliche Straßen. A study of the Ida Coblenz problem in the Works of Stefan George. Utah Studies in Literature and Linguistics, vol. 19. New York 1988.
13. Ida Dehmel, Über Richard Dehmel und seine Zeitgenossen. In: Richard Dehmel, Dichtungen, Briefe, Dokumente. Hamburg 1963.
14. Cf. Dümling, Die fremden Klänge der hängenden Gärten. pp. 233 ff.
15. Paul Stefan, Das Grab in Wien. Eine Chronik 1903–1911. Berlin 1913, p. 24.
16. Cf. Peter Horst Neumann, Arnold Schönberg, Stefan George, Petrarca. Zu des Komponisten Textwahlen zwischen 1904 und 1924. In: Neue Züricher Zeitung, Sept. 15, 1974, p. 50.
17. Program in Schönberg Collection, Library of Congress, Washington D.C.
18. Illustriertes Wiener Extrablatt, February 9, 1907.

19. Patrick Werkner, Physis und Psyche. Der Österreichische Frühexpressionismus. Wien/München 1986, pp. 51 f., 57.
20. Gerstl was also a friend of Conrad Ansorge. Cf. Werkner p. 53.
21. Cf. Dümling, Die fremden Klänge, p. 161. See also Jane Kallir, Arnold Schöenberg's Vienna. New York 1984, p. 24.
22. Walter Pass, Schönberg und die "Vereinigung schaffender Tonkünstler in Wien". In: Österreichische Musikzeitschrift, June 1974.
23. R. Brinkmann, Arnold Schönberg: Drei Klavierstücke op. 11. Studien zur frühen Atonalität bei Schönberg. Wiesbaden 1969, p. 16.
24. As Elmar Budde has demonstrated, this priority of vocal music also exists in Webern's oeuvre. Cf. Budde, Anton Weberns Lieder op. 3. Wiesbaden 1971.
25. Schönberg, Wie man einsam wird. In: Vojtech (ed.), Arnold Schönberg. Stil und Gedanke. Aufsätze zur Musik. Frankfurt/M. 1976, p. 354.
26. Already in his essay "Probleme des Kunstunterrichts" he contrasted nobility and "plebeians". Cf. Vojtech, p. 166.
27. Schönberg, Aphorismen. In: Die Musik IX, 21 (1909/10), p. 162.
28. Original manuscript at the Pierpont Morgan Library New York. Cf. Dümling, Die fremden Klänge..., p. 289.
29. Schönberg, Schöpferische Konfessionen. Ed. Willi Reich. Zürich 1964, p. 12.
30. Cf. Hubert Stuppner, Schönberg, oder: Der Aufstieg des Sinnlichen ins Geistige. In: Musik-Konzepte Sonderband Arnold Schönberg. München 1980, p. 100–116.
31. cf. Hartmut Zelinsky, Der "Weg" der "Blauen Reiter". Zu Schönbergs Widmung an Kandinsky in die "Harmonielehre". In: Jelena Hahl-Koch, Arnold Schönberg – Wassily Kandinsky, Briefe, Bilder und Dokumente einer außergewöhnlichen Begegnung. Salzburg 1980.
32. Schönberg, Briefe. p. 31.
33. Cf. Hahl-Koch.
34. According to Jelena Hahl-Koch, Kandinsky had similar experiences in 1907.
35. Testamentsentwurf. Excerpts quoted in Kallir p. 28, and Thomas Zaunschirm (ed.), Arnold Schönberg. Paintings and Drawings. Klagenfurt 1991, p. 47f.
36. Cf. Thomas Zaunschirm, Arnold Schönberg the Painter. In: Zaunschirm, p. 47.
37. Schönberg, Aphorismen. In: Die Musik IX, 21 (1909/10), p. 162.
38. Otto Breicha, Gerstl – Kursorisches zum "Fall". In: Richard Gerstl (1883–1908). 85. Sonderausstellung des Historischen Museums der Stadt Wien. Eigenverlag der Museen der Stadt Wien 1983.
39. Werkner p. 63f.
40. H.H. Stuckenschmidt, Schönberg. Leben, Umwelt, Werk. Zürich/Freiburg 1974, p. 64.
41. Jane Kallir p. 28.
42. This dedication is as strange as his painted portraits of Mathilde. John Russell discovered in them "an asymetrical, off-center quality that may seem to us to portend the breakdown of the marriage and its eventual tragic end." Zaunschirm p. 125.
43. Pierpont Morgan Library New York.
44. In 1909 Zemlinsky, who up to this year had been Schönberg's neighbor in Liechtensteinstraße 68, left this apartment.
45. Cf. Jaques Le Rider, Der Fall Otto Weininger. Wurzeln des Antifeminismus und Antisemitismus. Wien 1985.
46. Like Kraus, Schönberg also now regarded the spiritual as a male quality, the sensuous on the other side as primarily female. Cf. Nike Wagner, Geist und Geschlecht. Karl Kraus und die Erotik der Wiener Moderne. Frankfurt/Main 1982.
47. "In 'Pierrot lunaire'...Schönberg established the identification of the artist and Christ by a related religious symbolism: that of the Mass." Carl Schorske, Die Explosion im Garten: Kokoschka und Schönberg. In: Wien – Geist und Gesellschaft im Fin de Siècle, Frankfurt/M. 1982, p. 355.

48. Cf. Dümling, Umwertung der Werte (cf. Note 11).
49. Schönberg, Harmonielehre, 7th ed. Wien 1966, p. 13.
50. Ib. p. 497.
51. Zaunschirm p. 437.
52. Cf. Norbert Nagler, Restauration und Fortschritt. Schönbergs monarchistische Demo-kratisierung der Musik. In: Musik-Konzepte Sonderband Arnold Schönberg. München 1980, p. 166.
53. Besides Wolzogen Hans von Bülow, Richard Strauss and Rudolf Steiner also propagated the ideas of Stirner. Cf. Hartmut Zelinsky, p. 232f.
54. Schönberg, Harmonielehre. p. 176.
55. Heinz-Klaus Metzger, Arnold Schönberg von hinten. In: Musik-Konzepte Sonderband Arnold Schönberg, p. 33.
56. Cf. C. Dahlhaus, Musikalische Moderne und Neue Musik. In: Melos/NZ 1976, p. 90.
57. Dümling, Die fremden Klänge..., pp. 35f.
58. Schönberg, Harmonielehre. p. 478.
59. Zelinsky, p. 228.
60. Schönberg, Mahler. In: Vojtech, p. 24.
61. Carla Henius, "...und alles Vornehmen unter dem Himmel hat seine Stunde." Erfahrungen mit Schönbergs "fünfzehn gedichten aus dem buch der hängenden gärten" von Stefan George. In: Musik-Konzepte Arnold Schönberg, p. 95f.
62. At first Schönberg wanted to show his atonal compositions only to his closest friends. cf. Schönberg, Wie man einsam wird, p. 355. He was even more shy with his paintings. "Whether I should exhibit at all is already a question", he wrote in a letter to Kandinsky from March 8, 1912. Zaunschirm p. 33.

The Fool as Paradigm:
Schönberg's *Pierrot lunaire* and the Modern Artist[1]

REINHOLD BRINKMANN

So much, almost everything possible, has already been said or written about Pierrot and his long and prominent history – from Antoine Watteau's Gilles to Pablo Picasso's sad clown; from the old Italian Commedia dell'Arte, through the Théâtre des Funambules and Jean-Gaspard ('Baptiste') Debureau, to Vsevolod Meyerhold, the Berlin cabaret of the 1920s, and Jean-Louis Barrault in *Les Enfants du Paradis*; and, musically, from early Italian opera through Robert Schumann's *Carnaval* to Arnold Schönberg's twenty-one melodramas – critics and scholars from all fields have dealt with the European dimensions of this humble puppet figure. As always in 'late' positions, I find myself in the melancholic state of presenting you with many well known facts, more summarizing old than originating new ideas, and without always being able to add spoken footnotes referring to the many authors whose findings or thoughts might be behind my own presentation today. I acknowledge my debts to a variety of generous "Pierrot" scholars here in advance and in general, I will list as many of them as possible in the bibliography at the end.

My presentation today will focus on Schönberg's *Pierrot lunaire* of 1912 and its historical position. I will begin with reflections on two statements by Schönberg himself: the long and precisely designed title of the work and programmatic text about it. I will proceed to remarks on the general history of the puppet mask *Pierrot*, with special emphasis on 19th- and early 20th-century representations. I will then turn to other "Pierrots" from around 1900. An attempt to characterize Schönberg's *Pierrot* music, its form, structure, and meaning, will follow. Finally, I will briefly assess the historical significance of Schönberg's Opus 21.

With this, I am responding to the task to which I have been assigned: to introduce to non-specialists a work of art that will be performed later today.

I

My first section includes philological commentaries on two verbal communications by Schönberg. The first statement of Schönberg's about his *Pierrot lunaire* is the title of the work. This title, in its early version presented in the program brochure to the first audiences of the 1912 Berlin premiere and the subsequent concert tour, reads as follows:

Dreimal sieben Gedichte
aus Albert Girauds
"Lieder des Pierrot Lunaire"

(deutsch von Otto Erich Hartleben)
für eine Sprechstimme, Klavier, Flöte (auch
Pikkolo), Klarinette (auch Baßklarinette), Violine
(auch Bratsche) und Violoncell
(Melodramen)
von
Arnold Schönberg
Op. 21
In drei Teilen

Quite obviously, this title is – from its content and form through its presentation in print – a thoughtfully designed composition. As a clamp or frame, there is the numerical aspect, with "three times seven" in the first and "twenty-one divided by three" in the last lines. The old magical numbers three and seven evoke an aura with religious connotations (and the numerical center of Opus 21 will be a *Rote Messe*), and they are also certainly a reflection of Stefan George's artificial play with numbers in his poetic cycles which Schönberg knew so well during these years (the '5' in his *Buch der Hängenden Gärten*, Schoenberg's 15 songs Op. 15, and the multiplications of '7' in *Der Siebente Ring* from which Schönberg took the two poems for his Opus 10). As an inner circle, surrounding the center in lines 2, 4 and 10, there are the names of the two poets and of the composer, and, connected with the title of the cycle, three designations of genres between poetry and music, in a progressive order toward the latter: *"Gedichte," "Lieder,"* and *"Melodramen"*. The center of the title, however, is formed by the musical instruments, the *Sprechstimme* together with five players and their eight instruments. Instrumentation as the core of the title points toward color and gesture as the central aspects in this work of chamber music.[2] In an unpublished letter of July 5, 1912, to Emil Hertzka, the *Direktor* of Universal Edition, Schönberg remarked pointedly, that *Pierrot lunaire* belongs to a group of works where "die Farbe alles, die Noten gar nichts bedeuten, wo also nur die Partitur über das Werk Aufschluß gibt." This refers to *Herzgewächse* and *Die glückliche Hand*, works from 1911 and 1912–13, and probably back to certain aspects of the *Fünf Orchesterstücke* of 1909, and, especially regarding *Pierrot*, is certainly an overstatement. But it highlights the crucial importance of the color parameter even within the confines of a chamber ensemble. "*Kammermusiklieder*" was the term Schönberg later claimed to have avoided [*Die Jugend und ich*, 1923, see Style and Idea, 92ff.].

It is interesting to note that the title includes the two terms "*Gedichte*" and "*Lieder*." This clearly points to the 19th-century tradition of naming songs and song collections as "*Gedichte*." Wagner's *Fünf Gedichte* by Mathilde Wesendonck or Brahms's *Gedichte von Daumer*, both for voice and piano, are examples. The dominance of poetry, indicated by labelling songs as "*Gedichte*," certainly goes back to the old aesthetics of the German *Lied* of the so-called *Goethezeit*, where the term "*Lied*" oscillated between poetical and musical components. "*Lied*" was then a literary term characterizing a poem designated to be sung. But there is more behind the use of the term "*Lieder*" within the title of Schönberg's work. It places *Pierrot lunaire* within the tradition of the German song cycle. Indeed, *Pierrot* is very much a song cycle, even stronger: a "*Liederkreis*," as defined by Beethoven, Schubert, and particularly Schumann: There is a narrative, a story; selected poems are ordered according to a plot – as Schumann did with Heine or Eichendorff. In this case, Schönberg selected his twenty-one poems from among a collection of more than fifty, following a certain leading idea and forming a plot by grouping the poems in an order that was not pretended by the poets, neither by Giraud nor by Hartleben (their's was just a collection, not a cycle).

There are the traditional musical means by which a composer tries to achieve cyclic unity. A few examples regarding three major parameters may suffice:

(a) Thematic references at key moments, points of attraction, the beginning and the end in particular, are one element. Compare the melodic beginnings for the Sprechstimme of the first and the last melodramas:

Figure 1

(b) Identical rhythmic patterns related to a melodic cell and forming a
    quasi-motive are another unifying means. Compare the recurrence of
    the 16th-note figuration with its seven digits from the very beginning
    throughout the work.

Figure 2

(c) A harmonic orientation, or even gravitation toward a center E, or
    chords built upon E, is obvious in many pieces and gets stronger at
    the end of the cycle, with its strictest realization at the cadential
    confirmation of E minor/major in no. 21, bars 28/29.

Figure 3

(d) In addition, Schönberg composed direct connections between several
    songs (from no. 5 to 6, or 20 to 21, for example), as Schumann did in
    Dichterliebe (nos. 1 through 3, for example).

(e) And, Schönberg wrote instrumental transitions between several of the melodramas, including cross-references that function as musical commentaries. Schönberg's interlude between nos. 13 and 14, for example, refers back to no. 5, *Der kranke Mond*, and is such an instrumental commentary. (And again, one remembers Schumann: the postlude to *Dichterliebe* with its quote and expansion of the piano texture from song no. 12, *Am leuchtenden Sommermorgen.*)

(f) Certainly, the instrumentation has its function for the cyclic ordering. The central piece, no. 11, *Rote Messe*, the quasi-'negative' pole of the piece, uses the 'reversed' instrumentation, with piccolo, bass clarinet, and viola instead of flute, clarinet, and violin; and the very end has the 'heaviest' load: all eight instruments, primary as well as secondary ones, participate.

(g) Certain numbers are designed for their specific place and function within the cycle. Thus no. 14, *Die Kreuze*, was composed as a "*Schluß-stück*" (Albertine Zehme's term in a letter to Schönberg of July 16, 1912); the beginning of no. 15, *Heimweh*, has an introductory gesture; nos 20 through 21 are clearly consecutive pieces to end a section or a cycle.

It seems pertinent at this point, to remember that, throughout the 19th century, the *Lied* and the lyrical piano piece have an almost identical history; *Liederkreis* and *Klavierzyklus* follow the same aesthetic principles. (A comparison of Schumann's *Carnaval* and Schönberg's *Pierrot* could prove such a statement.[3]) As individual lyrical moments, these 'character pieces' can represent different states of a subjective mind; ordered sequences of such miniatures are able to form a process, designed and directed by a lyrical plot.

The last line of Schönberg's title arrangement refers to the specific 'plotting' of *Pierrot*. And it can well be that the work's three-part form with seven melodramas for each segment was found in connection with the assignment of the opus number, that is '21'. Most likely, Schönberg's earliest *Pierrot* plan was not "*In drei Teilen*". The form of the first *Pierrot* manuscript **A**, the complete first draft of the entire cycle, suggests a two-part form. The preparation of the manuscript in two separate gatherings – with each piece already assigned to a specific place – indicates this. (From this manuscript Schönberg made single Reinschriften for each piece immediately after he had drafted them.) We do not know the exact order within the first cyclical plan, nor do we know the number of pre-selected poems. But we do know from a letter of July 13, 1912, by Albertine Zehme that she had his 'preliminary plan'. At some point in

June/July 1912, Schönberg must have re-grouped the poems/melo-
dramas, now following a final plot. At the same time, or as a consequence
of this re-grouping, he designed instrumental transitions and other cyclical strategies. It seems that a plan pasted on to an empty page of manuscript **A** marks exactly this point within the compositional process (see
Figure 4).

As to the plot and its three-part division, it structures a reflection on the
state of the modern artist.[4] SECTION I, that is nos. 1–7, begins with the
intoxication of the artistic fantasy through the moon, the romantic symbol
of inspiration. Then mind and creative fantasy grow more and more
disturbed and disordered. In no. 7, the moon is pronounced sick. In
SECTION II, nos. 8–14, darkness descends; terror, destruction and artistic
martyrdom close in, with no. 11, the blasphemous *Rote Messe*, the numerically exact center of the 21 melodramas, as the deepest point of self-
sacrifice (Baudelaire's "absolute grotesque", displaying a mental split of
metaphysical dimensions!). In SECTION III, nos. 15–21, strong elements
of sentimentality, but also of parody and ironic reflection, are coming to
the fore. Pierrot abandons the moon (that is: backs away from his
advanced modernist standards); he returns home to his beloved Bergamo,
the town of all Zannis, Arlecchinos, Pierrots, and Kaspars – reconciliation
between artist and 'world' seems to take place, and at the end Pierrot is
bathing in sunlight from the small window of his bourgeois home peace-
fully looking at the world, as if everything were in order again: "*O alter
Duft aus Märchenzeit...*"

"*In drei Teilen*", Ferruccio Busoni's early description of Schönberg's
work refers to this three-part form and its meaning. In his letter to Egon
Petri of June 19, 1913, Busoni writes:

> "*Die Form des Pierrot lunaire ist sehr befriedigend. Sie besteht aus dreimal sieben
> Gedichten, also drei Sätzen. Die Anzahl und Anordnung dieser Gedichte scheint erst
> 'chemin faisant' festgesetzt und gefunden worden zu sein. Es formte sich alles unter der
> Hand. Trotzdem sie alle grotesk sind, so kann man die drei Theile (nach einigen
> überwiegenden Nuancen) immerhin mit lyrisch, tragisch und humoristisch überschrei-
> ben. – Zwischen einigen der Lieder scheinen kurze verbindende Übergänge nachkompon-
> iert zu sein, welches mir als 'Naht' auffiel. Im zweiten Theile ist ein ganzes
> instrumentales Intermezzo (ohne Text) eingefügt, die dreistimmige Paraphrasierung
> eines früheren Flöten-Monologs (der übrigens ein Kind von der traurigen Weise aus
> Tristan ist).*"

Indeed, all the motifs and images for Schönberg's plotting of his narrative
existed in Giraud/Hartleben's collection of *Pierrot* poems, but unordered,
scattered among the fifty poems. Schönberg's selection and ordering
followed an intention to create meaning, to narrate a paradigmatic

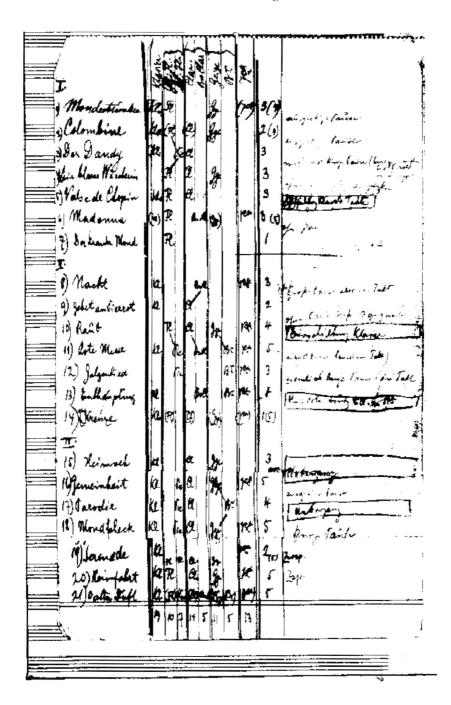

Figure 4

story. How do we understand this plot, especially the open ending, and what, in particular, is the role of the music?

I turn to a second statement by Schönberg and to my second commentary. In December 1916, Schönberg sent the printed score of *Pierrot lunaire* to Alexander von Zemlinsky, his former teacher, then composer colleague, brother- in-law and friend, and he included the following dedicatory text:

> *"Liebster Freund, meine herzlichsten Wünsche für Weihnachten 1916. Es ist banal zu sagen, daß wir alle solche mondsüchtigen Wursteln sind; das meint ja der Dichter, daß wir eingebildete Mondflecke von unseren Kleidern abzuwischen uns bemühen und aber unsere Kreuze anbeten. Seien wir froh, daß wir Wunden haben: wir haben damit etwas, das uns hilft, die Materie gering zu schätzen. Von der Verachtung für unsere Wunden stammt die Verachtung für unsere Feinde, stammt unsere Kraft, unsere Leben einem Mondstrahl zu opfern. Man wird leicht pathetisch, wenn man an die Pierrot-Dichtung denkt. Aber zum Kuckuck, gibt es denn nur mehr Getreidepreise? Viele Grüße. Dein Arnold Schönberg."*

Schönberg's statement sees Pierrot as a representational figure. He is the paradigmatic artist of the early 20th century – an alienated fellow, despised by society, suffering from wounds of hostility and isolation, but proud of these wounds, because they attest and prove to him that he lives and expresses the truth about world and society. At times when the price of grain means everything to his countrymen, the artist Pierrot, sentenced by society to a fool's existence, dares to live out of nothing but the strength of a moonbeam, the moonbeam 'fantasy', his artistic imagination. Yes, he seems to be the fool, but – as in Shakespeare's dramas – it is the fool, the comic outsider, who sees through outer appearances and, in fact, conveys the truth, laughing at the world that condemned him to accept this role. Within the contemporary context of the year 1910, this certainly is the position of decadence as a counterstrategy, aestheticism as an opposition to reality and its dominating forces. With its self-elevation of the 'absolute' artist it is a position of tragic hubris.

But Schönberg's *Pierrot* is more than the author's self-interpretation reveals. The score already contains an internal commentary, a critique. Thus, *Pierrot* represents an historical state of mind and its critical reflection. Both are evident in the music, evident as musical form, structure, and 'tone'.

Schönberg always stressed the 'light' tone of the work, referring to distancing as an artistic principle. In his letter to Schönberg of February 28, 1921, Erwin Stein wrote about his rehearsing *Pierrot* with Erika Wagner-Stiedry, quoting Schönberg himself:

> *"Ich finde, daß die Wagner gut ist . . . was sie bringt ist echt, ohne Sentimentalität und Pathos und Singsang. Vielleicht mitunter zu vornehm, der Ernst nicht kalt genug, die Tragik nicht überwältigend groß. Aber da ist beides, und ich glaubte Sie so zu verstehen, daß das nicht allzuviel ausmacht, als Sie schrieben, daß alles "Allegretto" bleiben müßte."*

And later, in a letter to Fritz Stiedry of August 31, 1940, Schönberg was even more precise:

> *" . . . denn ich beabsichtige diesmal zu versuchen, ob ich nicht vollkommen diesen leichten, ironisch-satirischen Ton herausbekommen kann, in welchem das Stück eigentlich konzipiert war. Dazu kommt, daß sich die Zeiten und mit ihnen die Auffassungen sehr geändert haben, so daß, was uns damals vielleicht als Wagnerisch, oder schlimmstenfalls als Tschaykowskysch erschienen wäre, heute bestimmt Puccini, Lehar oder darunter ist."*

This means irony, satire in a twofold manner.

Pierrot's mask of laughter covers a face that is full of tears. The modern Pierrot is defined by the paradox that Lord Byron had already stated: "And if I laugh at any mortal thing, 'Tis that I may not weep." The state of world and society (Schönberg's "price of grain") is experienced as such that the sensitive contemporary (Schönberg's artist, struck by the moonbeam), feels condemned to alienation and even self-destruction. Pierrot belongs to the tradition of the sad clown; as such his irony is a mask. And the artistic utterance of such a state of mind uses the form of the satirical, the burlesque, the grotesque. It indeed is the split of mind that Charles Baudelaire, in his important essay "On the Essence of Laughing", described as the "absolute comedy". Baudelaire uses the figure of Pierrot to exemplify that, at times, the comical spirit is forced to reach a metaphysical dimension. The contrast between things themselves, the split between the I and the whole (of which the relation between artist and society can form a model), the originating split within the sensitive Ego itself, becomes so fundamental that it can only be expressed through ironical means. Robert Schumann in his famous review of Berlioz's *Symphonie Fantastique* addressed exactly this problem when he commented upon the blasphemous superimposition of the "*Dies Irae*" with the dance from the Witches's Sabbath in the finale of the symphony:

> *" . . . if we could combat the spirit of the day, which tolerates a burlesque 'Dies Irae' we should only repeat what has been said and written against Grabbe, Heine, Byron, Hugo, and others. At certain moments in an eternity poetry may put on the masque of irony to cover her sorrowful face. Perhaps the friendly hand of a genius may also one day remove it."*

It seems that around 1912, and in the view of Schönberg, this friendly genius could not have appeared. Schönberg's Pierrot is a sad clown, the work's "light, ironic-satirical tone" is its modern masque of irony, a cover that veils the concerns about (to quote Schönberg's famous letter to Kandinsky from about ten years later) "the overturning of everything one has believed in."

The second aspect of irony as an aesthetic principle is its compositional perspective. Schönberg's letter to Stiedry already names the play with historical models, using the historicity of musical idioms as a central compositional means of realizing the tone of a constant 'Allegretto.' I will come back to this musical aspect at a later point. As a next step I need to take a look at the Pierrot figure itself, its history and its changes of character. The question I pose is why just Pierrot, why a puppet, the mask of the fool, could become the paradigmatic representation of the modern artist. Here are a few highlights of Pierrot's remarkable European history.

II

In the lecture presentation, this section dealt with the appearance of Pierrot in the different arts over several centuries. The intention was to elevate Pierrot to the range and recognition of other major characters in European intellectual history: Spain's Don Quixote and Don Juan, England's Hamlet, Germany's Faust. Pierrot was seen as the contribution of French culture to this quintet of great fictive characters. But the term 'character' points at some difficulties for Pierrot. As a figure of primary transitory genres like pantomime, cabaret, circus, and improvised theatre, there is no chance for a puppet to easily advance to the heights of the Parnassus. One may rightly assume that the main body of Pierrot's active theatre carrier is lost, just because a decisive part of his specific qualities was embodied in the actual performances on stage, and could not be kept in books or in scores. And it was not the literary quality but the specific 'pantomimic quality' of his actual presence that defined Pierrot's success. But what nevertheless survived in quite different artistic fields – theatre, lyric poetry, the visual arts, music, cabaret, film, and essays – is unexpectedly rich, both in quantity and in quality. And only recent research has discovered, or better: re-discovered, the importance of Pierrot as a topical figure between Watteau on the one end, and Daumier or Picasso, Lipchitz or Klee on the other, between the Commedia dell'Arte and Molière, Baudelaire, Verlaine, T.S. Eliot, Wallace

Stevens, Alexander Blok, and Robert Musil, not forgetting the acting geniuses of Meyerhold and Jean-Louis Barrault. Somewhere in between there, more towards the end, appears the trio of Giraud, Hartleben and Schönberg.

My sketch of this history began, at some length and illustrated by many slides, with the old Italian Commedia dell'Arte (represented by the 1621 title page of the play *La Gran Vittoria del Pedrolino* with its depiction of a typical scene), then proceeded to the French adaption of the Italian mask creating the typological figure of the stupid and clumsy Pierrot opposite, or as a complement, to the clever and agile Harlequin (with the addition of Pierrot to the casting of French drama finalized by Molière; culminating then in Watteau's famous *Comédiens Italiens* from 1719–20 and his *Gilles*, with its openness to romantic interpretations as the sad clown). However, the chapter centered on 19th-century Paris, the revival of the Pierrot figure in the theatre (after the French Revolution had abruptly ended the first half of the figure's history), with the Théâtre des Funambules and one actor in particular: Jean-Gaspard Debureau, called Baptiste, a native from Bohemia, who lived from 1796 through 1846 and created as well as established the 'nouveau Pierrot' on the theatre stages of Paris and, subsequently, stored this figure permanently into the memory of European intellectual history. (Jean-Louis Barrault in *Les Enfants du Paradis* is Baptiste's most eloquent monument.) And both the creation of the modern Pierrot itself and the way it was carried out, are significant.

Baptiste's Pierrot was no longer the prankish buffoon, no longer naive, fearful, coarse, and stupid, but detached, ironic, clever, and arrogant. And: Baptiste already added elements of perversion, of the macabre and violent actions to the repertory of the figure. (It was, by the way, during the time of Victor Hugo and Hector Berlioz, both of whom added the grotesque to the arsenal of European aesthetic values; also, Rosenkranz's *Ästhetik des Häßlichen* was about to appear.) However, Pierrot remained the sufferer. Here the fundament was laid for the development of the sad clown. Baudelaire described Baptiste's Pierrot as "pale as the moon – supple and mute as a serpent." And it was this change of its typological orientation that enabled Pierrot to become an allegorical figure: the paradigmatic mask for the modern artist. It is similarly significant that, from its very beginnings, Baptiste's creation of the modern Pierrot was accompanied by and reflected in the thoughts, aesthetics, and writings of the Paris intelligentsia since the 1830s. In 1832 the most up-to-date of all Paris critics, Jules Janin, wrote a glorifying book on Debureau, culminating in sentences such as these:

There is no longer a Théâtre Français; only the Funambules...Let us write the history of art as it is, filthy, beggarly and drunken, inspiring a filthy, beggarly and drunken audience. Since Debureau has become the king of this world, let us celebrate Debureau!

Such fanfares established Debureau's theatre as the cult place of modernist artists, as the Mecca of the Paris intellectual avant-garde: Charles Nodier, Gérard de Nerval, Théophile Gautier, Théodore de Banville, Charles Baudelaire, Jules Champfleury...Francis Haskell has correctly described this interplay:

"Debureau's talent attracted the intellectuals to a virtually forgotten and unexplored theatrical genre; and the intellectuals then proceeded to change the nature of that genre."

The intellectuals became attracted to Debureau's performances because they could mirror their own self-interpretation in this figure of 'Pierrot nouveau.' Gautier's definition is revealing:

"Pierrot – pallid, slender, dressed in sad colors, always hungry and always beaten, is the ancient slave, the modern proletarian, the pariah, the passive and disinherited being, who, glum and shy, witnesses the orgies and follies of his masters."

Baudelaire's important theory of the grotesque as the "absolute comic" – I already referred to it earlier – is informed exactly by the "metaphysical sadness" of Debureau's reinterpretation of the old Pierrot.

Here began Pierrot's importance as an allegorical image for the decadent spirit of the European fin-de-siècle, and here also began, as the reverse side of the medal, the marketing of the sad clown as an object of commerce. And the success was immense, on all fronts. The process may be summarized as follows. A theatre figure of popular culture, reinvented in the 1820s in Paris, gets intellectualized as a paradigm of a modernist counter-mythology against the official culture of the 'juste milieu' and its institutions. The publicized success of this adaption initiates commercialization; within the new realm of public mass media, the initial counter-image gets lost, and the original modernist intent remains a minor thread only.

The success also created actors. Baptiste, who died in 1846, was followed by other famous impersonations for the Pierrot figure: his son Charles Debureau, then Paul Legrande (who played in Champfleurie's pantomimes, for example in *Pierrot, Valet de la Mort* to which Baudelaire reacted with enthusiasm). Later it was the Paris caricaturist Adolphe

Willette (1857–1926), one of the founders of the "Chat Noir" on Mont-martre and editor of the journal *Pierrot*. Willette was one of the most successful agents, marketing Pierrot in newspapers, journals, bro-chures, cartoons, lyrics, photographs, sketches, the pantomime theatre, the music hall... His cartoon-sketch *Au Clair de la Lune* from about 1882 [see Storey, plate 2] is an example of the trivial 'serialization' of the figure. (At the beginning, the cartoon could be "*Der Wein, den man mit Augen trinkt*"; many of the ingredients are there, but it is turned into a trivial every-day story of an erotic fantasy that gets alcoholized and deceived.) At this time, Pierrot was all over the place. A popular Pierrot industry had emerged, and the serious metaphysical grotesque was only a small elitist branch within this massive production. Yet its imaginative power was unbroken, and that is what interests us here today. But certainly, as Schönberg's letter to Zemlinsky states, it is the 'power' of the moonbeam only, an aesthetic opposition, that defines Pierrot's mod-ernist physiognomy. And this is the historical position also of Schönberg's *Pierrot lunaire*. But before returning to it, let me briefly sketch its neigh-borhood.

The paradigmatic change of the Pierrot figure can be demonstrated with two examples. The first, still portraying the old Pierrot – the heavy, clumsy, naive comrade of Harlequin – is to be found in Robert Schumann's *Carnaval*, op. 9, from the late 1830s, the romantic cycle of poetic piano miniatures that obviously inspired Schönberg. *Car-naval*, just to point this out, includes twenty-one such character pieces, if one counts the silent *Sphinxes*; its titles name *Chopin, Colombine*, and – as the first piece after the introduction – *Pierrot*, followed by *Arlequin*. In Schumann's view of the two zannis, Pierrot is the slow, clumsy character, heavily tumbling in octaves, whereas Harlequin is the fast and witty one. That is still the old constellation. The second example, written in 1868, decades after the appearance of Baptiste Debureau, thematicizes the change. It is Verlaine's early poem "Pierrot," the sonnet with its meticulously constructed correspondences of pale and white images, and inner rhymes.

Pierrot

Ce n'est plus le rêveur lunaire du vieil air
Qui riait aux aïeux dans les dessus de portes;
Sa gaîté, comme sa chandelle, hélas! est morte,
Et son spectre aujourd'hui nous hante, mince et clair.

Et voici que parmi l'éroi d'un long éclair
Sa pâle blouse a l'air, au vent froid qui l'emporte,

D'un linceul, et sa bouche est béante, de sorte
Qu'il semble hurler sous les morsures du ver.

Avec le bruit d'un vol d'oiseaux de nuit qui passe,
Ses manches blanches font vaguement par l'espace
Des signes fous auxquels personne ne répond.

Ses yeux sont deux grands trous au rampe du phosphore
Et la farine rend plus éroyable encore
Sa face exsangue au nez pointu de moribond.

And the first line "You are no longer the lunar dreamer of the past" immediately points to the new view of Pierrot. The poem deals with the horrifying experience of the metaphysical split between the I and the world, the dimension now attached to Pierrot. Images of alienation, isolation, sadness, destruction, and death, of terror, pain, and suffering prevail. Examples for the 'sad clown' from the visual arts add similar images and thoughts: Daumier's *Pierrot with the Guitar*, the isolated figure from 1873, or the realism of his 1866 *Déplacement des Saltimbanques*, the homelessness of a group of artists, driven out of the city. And it is within this iconography of the lonely artist that Pierrot finds his most significant realization. Pablo Picasso's depictions of Saltimbanques and Harlequins from the beginning of the 20th century are the prominent examples, the series culminates in his "Sad Pierrot" of 1918.

This 'nouveau Pierrot' and its connotations name the environment in which the Belgian decadent Albert Giraud placed his 'Pierrot lunaire', from which then Otto Erich Hartleben created Pierrot's most important German versification. This is where Schönberg started, as far as poetry is concerned. But within the same context of public market and artistic representation there are musical realizations of Pierrot as well. Some of them may have shaped Schönberg's sensibility toward this specific subject.

III

How did music participate in portraying or using the Pierrot figure? A fuller picture of Pierrot in music is still missing. As indicated above, there are, and will always remain, severe problems for the historian. The nature of Pierrot's primary genre, extemporized theatre, does not favor the survival of sources, especially for music; even if librettos survive, the music is often lost.

For the early history, Nino Pirrotta can be called as a witness. His enlightening general account of the manifold connections between the Commedia dell'Arte and early Italian opera ends with a resignative statement. Certainly, we know works such as Orazio Vecchi's madrigal comedy *L'Anfiparnasso*, an attempt "to emphasize the unity of the Parnassus both of music and of comic poetry." But we will have to live with Pirrotta's negative summary:

> "Of Pantaleone, of Arlecchino, of Isabella, of Pulcinella – only thin shadows remain, for their life was embodied in the flesh, in the appearance, in the breath of their interpreters."

The same is true of 'Pierrot nouveau'. Theatrical genres such as pantomime are transitional by definition, and even if a score of some sort survived, it would only be a skeleton of the actual performance, and it would be almost impossible to reconstruct the real theatrical presence of the figures. Nevertheless, more could be done. To my knowledge, no one has so far conducted a systematic investigation into the remaining musical sources that include Pierrot.

To get a basic (though limited) and somewhat representative picture of what might have survived from Pierrot music circa 1900, I prepared a list of 'Pierrot' settings of all kinds in the holdings of two major libraries with printed title/subject catalogues, the British Library and the Boston Public Library – the addition of the Bibliothèque Nationale and the Library of Congress would certainly give a much broader and more representative account – and I added some compositions I happened to know from other sources. My compilation, ordered roughly according to three genres (stage, instrumental, song), and complemented by a list of *Pierrot lunaire* settings after Giraud/Hartleben, is given as a supplement [see appendix pp. 163–66]. Though this list is quite preliminary it allows a few general conclusions:

(a) The majority of 'Pierrot' scores from about 1880 to 1920 belong to theatrical genres, such as pantomime, ballet, or the so-called "opera comique," a term that, at the time, covered all kinds of musical comedies.

(b) The majority of composers are unfamiliar names; centers are Paris, Brussels, London. (And one remembers that already Baudelaire talks about French and English Pierrots.)

(c) After 1900 more and more songs are listed among the compositions. Poems by Sarah Teasdale especially received a variety of settings; they display a light conversational tone, and do not participate in the paradigm of the sad clown. The songs and their arrangements for various instruments by Hutchinson show the commercial aspect of popular culture.

(d) After 1900 the number of instrumental 'Pierrot' pieces is growing; the figure has become so popular that no identifying text is needed any more.

(e) I could locate eight composers (besides Schönberg) who set Giraud/ Hartlebens texts to music; one of them used Giraud's French original, the others used Hartleben's transformations. All compositions are songs in the traditional sense; seven select a smaller number of poems; one composer (Vrieslander) sets the complete collection.

[This section ended with brief commentaries on a few examples from among these songs.]

IV

What distinguishes Schönberg's *Pierrot lunaire* from the Pierrot settings of his contemporaries? What is the specific signature, the artistic and historical signification of his cycle of twenty-one melodramas?

This is not so much a question of artistic quality. Certainly, there is no doubt about the artistic superiority of Schönberg's cycle, truly a work "*auf höchstem Formniveau*," to use Adorno's term. Several of the other Pierrot songs display solid craftsmanship, though *in toto* they remain epigonic. A few of them are really fine songs, worth performing in recitals, especially Kowalski's twelve songs from 1912, which achieve an original tone, a sphere of their own between *Lied* and cabaret song. But this is not the difference in which I am interested.

All the other Pierrots hide the problematical and – in a historical sense – the significant and representational aspects of the texts behind the norms of the private Lied genre; they all domesticate the horrifying and blasphemous images through the moderating limits of *Hausmusik*. There is no indication of any historically paradigmatic perspective at all. Only Schönberg aims at constituting a paradigm. In other words: in the realm of 'Pierrot' music it is only Schönberg's cycle that elevates the puppet Pierrot to the level of an allegorical figure, to a model of identification for the late artist of modernity, for the problematic state of subjectivity, for the crisis of identity and cohesion of the I. And Schönberg aims at this historicalness not only by constructing a narrative plot from among the poems, but through form, structure and tone of his music. The music thus comments on the narrative of the texts, on the plot 'Pierrot lunaire', and only this self-reflection of the work of art defines its historical position.

As a work of the highest artistic degree, Schönberg's *Pierrot lunaire* offers a historical diagnosis. It presents the puppet Pierrot as an allegorical image for the modern artist, embodying contemporary concerns about the state of subjectivity, that is, the problematic relation between the I (not the 'We'!) and the world – again I am using this idealistic dichotomy. But it is also a critical commentary on itself, on its own representational intent. In an extreme state of self-reflection *Pierrot lunaire* is music about its own presence, that is, music about history. And the compositional means to achieve this is to construct a work as music about music, music about a specific musical tradition. Let me finally illustrate this with a few examples.

The basic compositional attitude was pronounced by Schönberg himself when he pointed to the "light ironic-satirical tone" of the work's original conception, the "Allegretto" throughout, and when he remarked that, what then, in 1912, might have been perceived as "Wagnerisch" or "Tschaykowskysch," was now to sound like "Puccini, Lehar, or even below."

Irony in music as compositional principle means distancing the composition from its own musical material. This enables a work to become a commentary in and on itself. Schönberg's and Webern's very fundamental theoretical distinction between 'laws of the material' ('*Materialgesetze*') and 'laws of presentation' or 'representation' ('*Darstellungsgesetze*') is crucial in this respect. The compositional strategies for *Pierrot lunaire* are *not* grounded in the 'laws of the material' used in the work, but are following the 'laws of presentation'. The musical material is being *used* for the purpose of presenting an idea, is being used in an almost Brechtian sense.

It is well known and much commented upon that many (most of the twenty-one) pieces in *Pierrot lunaire* are based upon traditional models: dances, old forms, old techniques, etcetera. No. 2, *Colombine*, truly is a waltz; no. 5, *Valse de Chopin*, is a slow waltz; no. 17, *Parodie*, is a polka; no. 8, *Nacht*, is a passacaglia; nos. 12 and 15, *Galgenlied* and *Heimweh*, are compositions based upon the technique of developing variation; nos. 17 and 18, *Parodie* and *Der Mondfleck*, proceed according to rules of imitative counterpoint, such as canon and fugue; no. 19, *Serenade*, is again, a slow waltz, but also a *Dramolett* designed as a miniature cello concerto, with a veritable cadenza; no. 20, *Heimfahrt*, is a barcarole. These models, traditional types, are being used (as, a few years later, Stravinsky will use waltz, march, and ragtime in a neo-classicist manner in his *Soldier's Tale*); they are being played with; they are presented as if the composition were playing with them. They are musical material for the purpose of presenting, for making a statement.

But beyond this, there are other types of references to tradition, allusions to specific styles, specific works and passages, that are clearly identifiable, even in the sense of quotations. A few examples again may suffice:

- no. 16, 'Gemeinheit', is (as Christian M. Schmidt has pointed out) evidently modeled after the classical design of recitative and aria,
- no. 6, 'Madonna', clearly quotes a specific Bach model, a three-part setting without *basso continuo*, and the precise point of departure is either the 'Adagio' from J. S. Bach's *Sonata for Flute and Violin*, BWV 1038 (the source for the section 'Gute Nacht' from the motet *Jesu meine Freude*, BWV 227, as Rudolf Stephan suggested) or, more likely, the 'Preludio' no. 24 in b minor from *Das Wohltemperierte Klavier I*, BWV 869.

More specific references include

- in no. 9, 'Gebet an Pierrot', at the word 'Lachen', an allusion to Kundry's famous outcry 'lachte' from m. 1182 of act II in Wagner's *Parsifal*, leaping there from the high b3 two octaves down to c#1; Christian M. Schmidt rightly identified this quotation. By the way, this was a passage Schönberg had already quoted elsewhere. Sieghart Döhring has pointed out that the 'Frau' at the singular climax of Schönberg's *Erwartung* (m. 189) uses exactly, and only there, the same pitches for her cry 'Hilfe'. And David Lewin reminds me that already the climactic 'Liebe' in Schönberg's Second String Quartet op. 10 uses the same reference (though not exactly the same pitches);
- in no. 3, 'Der Dandy', the emphatic upward passage almost certainly recalls the 'Schwung' of Richard Strauss's opening melodic gestures. I hear a clear reference to the opening of *Ein Heldenleben*, a title that could well be applied to Pierrot, appropriately in an ironic sense (while the 'Dandy' signature might have particularly appealed to Schönberg in connection with Richard Strauss...) And when in mm. 28/29 the *Heldenleben* theme appears on its original pitch Eb in the piano bass, appropriately illustrating the words "im erhabenen Stil," the quotation is unmistakably realized.

I could easily continue pointing out many more traditional patterns, techniques of thematic and motivic construction, textures, gestures. There is not a single piece in *Pierrot lunaire* that is not based upon pre-existing material. The entire cycle indeed is music about music. But as important as the use of such models, is the way in which they are being used. It was again Busoni, the great musician, who described this intention in an unsurpassed manner after he had heard a performance of *Pierrot* arranged for himself in June 1913 in his Berlin home. I quote again from his letter of June 19, 1913, to Egon Petri:

> *"Es ist als ob es* [the work] *aus zerbröckelten Bestandteilen eines großen Musikmecha-nismus zusammengestellt wäre, und als ob einige dieser Bestandteile zu einer andern Function angewendet würden als der zu der sie ursprünglich bestimmt waren."*

Busoni is perfectly true in all respects. Indeed, the musical material for *Pierrot lunaire* is "assembled from crumbled ingredients"; indeed, it is assembled to create a feeling of a music machine (the mechanical, puppet aspect of the piece!); indeed, the material is being used in other ways (and to other ends) than "those for which it was originally designed"; and, indeed, Busoni's 'as if', the subjunctive, is the mode of Schönberg's Pierrot music itself.

The 'as if'. The subjunctive. Consider the parodical use of double fugue, canon, and mirror retrograde in nos. 17 and 18, the most serious techniques just for the dullest and most comical texts. We have to understand that Schönberg was very well aware of the problem of strict counterpoint in free atonality, with no systematic control of the vertical dimension. Thus the superimposition of canon and fugue, together with the mechanical retrograde motion from the exact middle of the piece, might lead to exactly the opposite of strict order, to a loose texture, close to being chaotic, where the actual pitches do not matter any more, but line, contour, gesture and instrumental tone are the dominating forces. Or consider another moment, the Kundry quote, where not the voice with its text 'mein Lachen' is referring back to the Wagner heroine (how could poor Columbine do that at all...), but the clarinet. It is 'as if' the clarinet remembered what the *Sprechstimme* protagonist forgot or never knew. Just the opposite perspective of commenting is to be found in the recitative-aria relation of no. 16, *Gemeinheit*. The instrumental recitative ends with the colon, anticipating the *Sprechstimme* to continue. But, instead, the cello takes off, 'sings' the aria, so to speak, and the *Sprechstimme*, the drama's protagonist, is degraded to a secondary, accompanying voice. Now it is 'as if' the *Sprechstimme* were narrating a commentary on what is going on in the instrumental parts. And in no. 4, *Eine blasse Wäscherin*, Schönberg in fact demands that this reversed relationship should be observed – music 'as if'.

Consider, just for a moment only, who in fact might be the narrator of *Pierrot lunaire*. Pierrot certainly is a male character, the *Sprechstimme* is designated for a female singer. (Though the preface could raise some doubts with the 'er' for the reciter.) The first 'ich' is Columbine's in no. 2. In no. 3 Pierrot is introduced by an unidentified narrator. (Who is that? Could it be Columbine? Most likely not, since she was the object of the narration in no. 2.) The 'mich' in no. 5, *Valse de Chopin*, is not defined; it could be Pierrot, but here, indeed, it could also be Columbine. The 'mich' in no. 6, *Madonna*, is the poet – one would assume Pierrot (would one?). The 'mich' in no. 9, *Gebet an Pierrot*, is certainly not Pierrot but could well be female, again Columbine, for example. Nos. 10 to 20 have no 'I' but a narrator talking about Pierrot and others in the third person. No. 21 is, again, an 'I' poem. Clearly the poet (the poet Pierrot?) who has returned to Bergamo (it must be Pierrot) speaks, and there is the melodic reference to no. 1, where this poet was introduced by a narrator and did not speak.

Seeing this jigsaw puzzle together with the compositional strategies analyzed above, one might conclude that it seems 'as if' the work were narrating itself. Thus, its comments on the state of the modernist artist are a commentary from within, a modernist verdict about the ending of modernism. This highly artificial self-referencing would then define *Pierrot lunaire* as the 'absolute' work of art in which all theories of modernism culminate.

Let me add one final appendix: the very end. This ending showing a happy Pierrot, now domesticated, sitting in the bright sun of Bergamo, has always been interpreted as a positive homecoming for the artist, as a moment of peaceful reconciliation. I believe that is wrong. I already see Hartleben's text (not Giraud's with its reference to Watteau), his window image in an iconographical tradition. In my view, it refers back to E.T.A. Hoffmann's 1822 novel *Des Vetters Eckfenster*. This is a novel about a sick artist, a lame man, depending on a disabled servant's assistance, unable to move, unable to go from his apartment down to the street, but who looks at real life from his small window high above the market place (the Berlin *Gendarmenmarkt*) where the normal people live and interact, using his binoculars and imagining only what people down there might intend, think, and talk about. It is, apparently, a make-believe existence of pure fantasy, peaceful only as unreal imagery, but behind the facade lies a tragic life. ''Poor cousin'' are the last words of the novel. I see Hartleben's window image as a reference to Hoffmann's novel. And Schönberg's commentary on Hartleben's adaptation given in the harmonic language of his last melodrama, which seems more and more saturated with thirds and gravitates toward a key of E – Schönberg's commentary reveals the "aus meinem sonnumrahmten Fenster beschau ich frei die liebe Welt" as a nostalgic looking back, as a self-deceptive error. Not only is the proper cadence of the piano in mm. 28/29 (A minor – B major with 5# – E minor/major – quite ordinary, IV–V–I, though the notation of the dominant chord with G instead of F double sharp typically hides the actual function) not confirmed by the *Sprechstimme*, the tonal language itself is understood as an 'as if' only. It alludes to the past and its beauty as a world that is lost and can only be remembered (in the sense of Schönberg's letter to Busoni of 24 August 1909 where he talks about the necessary loss of beauties accompanying artistic progress). But at the same time the 'as if' does not allow a peaceful return. The spirit of fin-de-siècle, and of 'Fin-de-siècle Vienna' in particular, is gone. The catastrophe of World War I, anticipated by so many artists and foreshadowed in their works, would soon fulfill this projection. Schönberg, in his letter to Kandinsky from 1921 quoted already above, would later speak of "the overturning of everything one has believed in" as the actual background for the statement of no return. Walter R. Heymann's chanson *Abschied von der Bohème* on a text by G. von Wangenheim, written around 1920 for Friedrich Hollaender's Berlin cabaret *Schall und Rauch*, gives the quasi capitalist trivialization of this sentiment. In a sense, it also has an element of self-referencing. The chanson ends with the following refrain, a poet's commentary about a farewell to Pierrot, now in the first person,

> *Wir leben nicht mehr im Atelier*
> *Wir leben nicht mehr in der Nacht.*
> *Wir haben ein bürgerliches Metier*
> *Und den Tag zum Tage gemacht.*
> *Wenn ich verdiene bin ich froh.*
> *Ich singe wenn sichs lohnt.*
> *Ich bin der lebnde Leichnam Pierrot,*
> *Was weiß ich noch vom Mond.*
> *Wer zahlt mir das meiste für dies Poème,*
> *Für mein Abschiedslied von der toten Bohème?*

A very last twist, a codetta within the coda. There is a special 'couleur locale' in Schönberg's perception of the Pierrot figure. Let me call it the 'Hanswurst', or the 'Wurstel' perspective. In Alban Berg's library the

Viennese musicologist Regina Busch found an annotated copy of Peter Altenberg's *Vita Ipsa*. One of Berg's remarks reads as follows: "Schönberg sagte, als Busoni ihm vorwarf, daß das eine der Pierrot-Stücke nicht Italien vorstelle, wie der Text besage: Für mich ist der Prater Italien." And indeed, *Pierrot lunaire* is music about the Viennese tradition of music, about a modern artist participating in and growing out of this tradition. And it is not surprising at all that Schönberg wanted to locate Pierrot in Vienna. Extemporized theatre always had, and even continues to have, its place in Vienna, the great city of the Baroque. "Tschauner's Stegreif-Theater", the last surviving witness (rough and coarse as it is) of this wonderful tradition of popular culture will hopefully exist for many decades to come! (No one visiting Vienna should miss it!) But further: the puppet Pierrot has its Viennese brother.

Regina Busch is currently researching the many facets of 'Italy in Vienna', and has reported about the huge entertainment area in the Viennese Prater, a park called "Venedig in Wien", that apparently existed from the late 19th century through the 1930s, occupying about 50,000 square meters (in an area where today the famous Ferris wheel is located), with eight meter wide canals, gondolas, bars, restaurants, entertainment theatres, music groups, orchestras, singers, pantomimes, etcetera, etcetera. And it was only a few blocks away from the *Prater*, in the *Birkenau* of the *Leopoldstadt*, that Schönberg was born. Also, consulting Viennese journals and program brochures from around 1900, it is easy to recognize that any human being interested in Viennese cultural activities during these decades would constantly meet Pierrot. From Richard Spechts's *Pierrot Bossu* of 1896 through the 1897 ballet *Pierrot als Schild-wache* at the Vienna State Opera (repeated 1901), the Überbrettl performances of 1901 of *Pierrots Fastnacht* (text: Leo Feld, music: Oscar Straus), *Die beiden Pierrot* (text: Levetzow, music: Wendland), the 1901 Ronacher ballet pantomime *Pierrots Neujahrstraum* (music: Josef Hellmesberger/Josef Bayer) to Franz Schreker's two pantomimes of 1909 and Franz Lehar's *Faschingswalzer* of 1911 with the title *Pierrot und Pierrette* – year after year Vienna produced one Pierrot piece after the other.[5] Indeed, the young Viennese Arnold Schönberg could not have escaped this puppet.

However, it has escaped notice that the *Pierrot lunaire* score includes two explicit references that define the sad clown as a Viennese character. Both moments are musically designed as structural licenses, and both are quite unusual within their context as well as within the *Pierrot* music and its compositional principles.

The first Viennese identification happens at the very point where Pierrot is mentioned for the first time in the cycle. This is m. 21 of no. 3, *Der Dandy*, with the text "Pierrot, mit wächsernem Antlitz." At this moment, the piano plays a melodic formula, marked *Hauptstimme*.

Figure 5

Strangely enough, this melodic formula is set in octaves – the only time in the entire work that the piano part has octaves, a very unusual design, indeed, obviously pointing toward something. And the motive sounds somewhat familiar; it could also look more normal if notated this way

Figure 6

and, indeed, one commentator (Jonathan Dunsby) believes it to be a quote of unknown or hidden origin. To me, it seems not to be a direct quote from a specific work (though someone, at some point in the future, might find its source), but an allusion: it is a waltz fragment. It is not

Figure 7

[Johann Strauß, *G'schichten aus dem Wienerwald*], and it is not quite but almost

Figure 8

[Johann Strauß, *Künstlerleben*] – though "life of an artist" would be quite appropriate. But certainly, it is an idiomatic pattern, a quasi Viennese motto, that defines Pierrot when he is first identified by his name. Schönberg's Pierrot is a Viennese puppet.

The other moment of Viennese identification happens at the very beginning, in the third stanza of no. 1, *Mondestrunken*, where 'Der Dichter', the artist is mentioned for the first time. And here we find another strange compositional strategy: within a carefully designed placement of the participating instruments in the sequence of the three stanzas, the Violoncello is introduced only to double the tenor melody of the piano. The manuscript reveals that the cello was added later to an already existing instrumental texture. The veiled message of this strategy is obvious: the cello was Schoenberg's own instrument, the 'license' of doubling an existing voice–again unique within the entire work–is used to identify the 'poet', who will later be named as Pierrot. He is secretly identified as the composer himself.

I do not suggest understanding *Pierrot lunaire* as sounding biography, at least not primarily. But I take these two Viennese identifications, two musical definitions of *this* Pierrot as indicative for his heritage. In light of this, the first phrase of Schoenberg's 1916 letter to Zemlinsky, part of one of his most powerful artistic creeds, becomes a very distinct quality: 'Mondsüchtige Wursteln' called Schoenberg the truly modern Viennese artist. Schoenberg's allegorical Pierrot is the Viennese *Hanswurst*. Pierrot, the French puppet character added to the cast of the Italian *Commedia dell'Arte*, revitalized and intellectualized in 19th century Paris, a figure of popular as well as high culture, as such able to represent the endangered subject of European modernism, the modern artist, is musically interpreted as the representative figure of the Viennese new music. But Schoenberg's sense for history at the same time comments on, and questions, the quest of modernism to present the truth. And even if Schoenberg's self-reflection in the figure of Pierrot is again executed with modernist strategies, besides and beyond all its aesthetic qualities, it is this historical signification that makes *Pierrot lunaire* one of the great human documents of our century.

Appendix: Musical Pierrots around 1900

Stage

Vercken de Vreuschmen, Leon	Pierrot Fantôme	opera comique	Paris 1873 vocal score
Lagaye, Alexandre	La Pierrot d'à Côté	opera comique	Bruxelles 1879
Mariette, Georges Bletry Paul	Pierrot mendiant	opera	(?) 1898 vocal score
Cieutat, Henri	Pierrot puni	opera	Paris 1899
Rostand, Alexis	Pierrot qui pleure et Pierrot qui rit	comedie en musique	Paris 1899
Holbrook, Joseph Charles	Pierrot and Pierette. A Lyrical Music Drama, op. 36	opera	London 1909
	Pierrot. Ballet Suite or pianoforte solo, op. 36b	pf	London 1916, 1919
dell'Aqua, Eva	Pierrot Menteur	opera comique	Bruxelles 1918 vocal score
Renieu, Lionel	La chimère, ou Pierrot alchimiste	opera comique	Bruxelles 1926 vocal score
Lanciani, Pietro	Pierrot macabre	ballet-pantomime	
Hamburg 1886, pf	Pierrot macabre. Morceaux détachés	pf	Hamburg 1886
Vidal, Paul Antonin	Pierrot assassin de sa femme	pantomime	ca. 1888, pf
David, Adolphe	Pierrot surpris	pantomime	Nantes 1890
Palicot, Georges	Pierrot-poète	pantomime	Bruxelles 189?
Corta, Pasquale Mario	Histoire d'un Pierrot	pantomime	Paris 1893, pf London 1893, pf
	Pierrot's Serenade (words by W.A.), 2 nos.	v, pf (?)	London 1897
	Entr'acte Serenade for mandolin and pianoforte	mand, pf	London 1898
Schreker, Franz	Die blaue Blume oder das Herz des Pierrot	pantomime	1909 (plot in: Schreker, Dichtungen II, music not known)
	Der Vogel oder Pierrots Wahn	pantomime	1909? (plot: same as above)
Reger, Max	Eine Balletsuite für Orchester, op. 130 (1. Entree, 2. Columbine, 3. Harlequin, 4. Pierrot und Pierette, 5. Valse d'amour, 6. Finale)	ballet	Leipzig 1913
Korngold, Erich Wolfgang	Die tote Stadt (Fritz/Pierrot)	opera	premiered 1920
Noetzel, Hermann	Pierrots Sommernacht	ballet	Wien 1924, pf
Rathaus, Karol	Der letzte Pierrot, op. 19	ballet	[Berlin] 1927

Instrumental

Bantock, Granville	The Pierrot of the Minute. Overture to a dramatic fantasy of E. Dowson	orchestra	Leipzig 1909
	Arr. pianoforte	pf	Leipzig 1913
Ricordi, Giulio (J. Burgmein, pseud.)	Le Roman de Pierrot et de Pierettes. Histoirettes musicales	pf	Milano 1881
Foote, Arthur W.	Pierrot	pf	unpub.
	Pierette	pf	unpub.
Scott, Cyrill	2 Pierrot Pieces, op. 35	pf	London, New York 1904
	Pierette	pf	London 1912
	Pierrot amoureux	vc, pf	Mainz 1912
Lehar, Franz	Pierrot und Pierette. Waltz	orchestra	Vienna 1911 (?)
Kaun, Hugo	Pierette und Colombine. 4 Episoden, op. 71	pf	Berlin 1907
Debussy, Claude	Sonate pour Violoncelle et Pianoforte ("Pierrot fache avec la lune")	vc, pf	Paris 1915

Songs

Debussy, Claude	Pierrot (Th. de Banville)	v, pf	1881, pub. 1926
	Pantomime (P. Verlaine)	v, pf	1881 (1882), pub. 1926
Hutchison, William M.	Pierrot (F. E. Weatherly)	v, pf	London 1883
	Pierrot. Valse on W.M. Hutchison's song (pf solo with coronet; and pf duet) by J. Meissler, pseud. for W.M.H.	pf	London 1883
	Arr. pf by W. Smallwood	pf	London 1884
	Arr. vl + pf by J. Meissler,	vl, pf	London 1888
Reeve, Norman	The Pierrot and the Maid (N.R.)	v, pf	Chetham 1890
Andrews, John Charles Bond	Pierrot Coster (A. Chevalier)	v, pf	London 1895
MacDermott, Robert	Pierrots. Humorous Song (J.A. Muir)	v, pf	London 1902
Barritt, Clifton	The Pierrot's Song (H. Walther)	v, pf	London 1903
Lockname, Clement	Pierrot! Poor Fool! (Pierette's Birthday) (N.C. Rose)	v, pf	London 1908
Johnston, Jessie	Pierrot (S. Teasdale)	v, pf	New York 1911
	Pierrot, Trio for women's voices	3v, pf	New York 1911
	Pierrot and the Moon Maiden (E. Dowson)	v, pf	New York 1912
Buchanan, George	Pierrot Land (B. Salisbury)	v, pf	London 1912
Meyrowitz, Walter	Pierrot (S. Teasdale)	v, pf	London 1912
Livingstone, Helen	Pierrot (S. Teasdale) (Songs, No. 2)	v, pf	Minneapolis 1913

Kroeger, Ernst R.	Pierrot (S. Teasdale)	v, pf	New York 1914	
Bonner, Eugene M.	Pierrot Stands in the Garden (S. Teasdale)	v, pf	London 1914	
Goetzl, Anselm	Pierrot's Serenade (F. H. Martens), op. 28	v, pf	New York 1915	
Gaynor, Jessie L.	Pierrot (S. Teasdale)	v, pf	Boston 1919	
Reubner, Dagmar de Corval	Pierrot (S. Teasdale)	v, pf	New York 1921	
Heymann, W.R.	He! Halloh! + Abschied von der Bohème [chansons for Friedr. Hollaender's Berlin cabaret "Schall und Rauch"]	v, pf	(1919)	
	Und Pierrot lachte	v, pf	(after 1914)	Read, Gardner
	Pierrot (S. Teasdale)	v, pf	New York 1943	Tosti, Sir Francesco Paolo
	Pierrot's Lament	v, pf	(?)	*Giraud*
Prohaska, Carl	*Pierrot lunaire* 6 Gedichte aus Rondels bergamasques von A. Giraud, op. 14.	v, pf	Zürich 1920	

Giraud/Hartleben

Pohl, Ferdinand	Mondrondels. Phantastische Szenen aus *Pierrot lunaire* von A. Giraud, deutsch von O. E. Hartleben, op. 4.	v, pf	Leipzig 1891
Marschalk, Max	5 Lieder aus dem *Pierrot lunaire* von Giraud-Hartleben, op. 14.	v, pf	Berlin 1901
Vrieslander, Otto	*Pierrot lunaire.* Dichtungen von A. Giraud, ins Deutsche übertragen von O.E. Hartleben	v, pf	München 1905
	(4 additional songs) in: Giraud/Hartleben, *Pierrot lunaire*, ed. Fr. Blei,	v, pf	München 1911
	Pierrot lunaire...Neue Ausgabe	v, pf	Leipzig 1934
Gräner, Paul	Gesänge aus dem *Pierrot lunaire* v. O.E. Hartleben op. 25: Gebet an Pierrot, Störche, Moquerie	v, pf	ca. 1908
Marx, Joseph	Lieder und Gesänge 1. Folge, No. 7: Die Violine (1909) 20: Pierrot Dandy (1909) 25: Valse de Chopin (1909) 2. Folge, No. 9: Kolombine (1909)	v, pf	Wien 1910–1911
	Valse de Chopin	v, pf, str qu	Wien 1917

Kowalski, Max	12 Gedichte aus *Pierrot lunaire*	v, pf	Berlin 1913
	von A. Giraud, deutsch von		
	O.E. Hartleben, op. 4.		
Lothar, Mark	3 heitere Lieder op. 4 No. 1:	v, pf	Berlin (1921)
	Mondfleck		

BIBLIOGRAPHY

Binhorn, Gabriele. *Das Groteske in der Musik: Arnold Schönbergs "Pierrot lunaire."* Pfaffen-
  weiler, 1989.
Brinkmann, Reinhold. "Was uns die Quellen erzählen . . . Ein Kapitel Werk-Philologie," in:
  Hermann Danuser et al. (eds.), *Das musikalische Kunstwerk. Festschrift Carl Dahlhaus.*
  Laaber, 1988.
Busch, Regina. "Venedig in Wien." Unpublished lecture.
Dick, Kay. *Pierrot.* London, 1960.
Döhring, Sieghart. "Schönbergs *Erwartung,*" in: *Arnold Schönberg.* Publikation des Archivs
  der Akademie der Künste Berlin. Berlin, 1974.
Dunsby, Jonathan. *Schoenberg: "Pierrot lunaire."* Cambridge, 1992.
Green, Martin and John Swan. *The Triumph of Pierrot. The Commedia dell'Arte and the Modern
  Imagination.* New York, 1986.
Haskell, Francis. "The Sad Clown," in: Ulrich Finke (ed.), *French 19th-Century Painting and
  Literature.* Manchester, 1972.
Kirchmeyer, Helmut. *Die zeitgeschichtliche Symbolik des "Pierrot lunaire."* booklet for the LP-
  reording Wergo 60001.
Lehmann, A.G. "Pierrot and Fin-de-Siècle," in: Ian Fletcher, (ed.) *Romantic Mythologies.*
  London, 1967.
Pirrotta, Nino. "*Commedia dell'Arte* and Opera," in: *Music and Culture in Italy from the
  Middle Ages to the Baroque.* Cambridge, MA, and London 1984.
Schmidt, Christian, M. "Analytical Remarks on Schoenberg's *Pierrot lunaire,*" unpublished
  lecture at the Conference "From Pierrot to Marteau." Los Angeles, 1987.
Stein, Leonard, ed. *Style and Idea. Selected Writings of Arnold Schoenberg.* London: Faber &
  Faber, 1975.
Storey, Robert E. *Pierrot. A Critical History of a Mask.* Princeton, 1978.
Wechsler, Judith. *A Human Comedy.* Chicago, 1982.
Youens, Susan. "Excavating an Allegory: The Texts of *Pierrot lunaire,*" in: *Journal of the
  Arnold Schoenberg Institute.* VIII, 2. November, 1984.

NOTES

1. Designed as a sequence of commentaries, the actual lecture was given with a rather
   large series of slides. These illustrations cannot be reproduced in the printed version.
   The style of an extemporized oral presentation, however, has been preserved, as
   much as possible. Thanks go to Carol DeFeciani for her taking care of my manuscript.
2. Schönberg insisted that the score should be printed like a score of chamber music
   with piano, that is, in this case, with the piano and the *Sprechstimme* part in normal,
   the other instruments in smaller print. The appearance in the printed score reveals the
   genre: '*Kammermusiklieder*'.

3. The American musicologist Evan Bonds is preparing such a study.
4. As far as the texts and their order are concerned, Susan Youens was the first to describe this from a literary point of view.
5. And Ernst von Wolzogen who engaged Schönberg for his Berlin cabaret *Das Über-brettl* tells us that on the large poster for the first *Überbrettl* season 'the grinning Pierrot' was looking down from every *Litfaßsäule* (advertising pillar). See E. von Wolzogen, *Verse zu meinem Leben*, Berlin 1907, p. 134.

Expressionism and Rationality

KONRAD BOEHMER

One of the ineradicable misconceptions which throng the history of music is the notion that music is divided into two halves: a rational half whose products can be analysed numerically and not really amounting to much more than that analysis, and a purely emotional – indeed irrational – half which is amenable to a little philosophizing but defies any closer examination. Among the darlings of the "rationalists" (number fetishists to a man) are sundry examples of medieval and Renaissance music, J.S. Bach and then – after a deplorable historical gap – dodecaphonic and serial works. The music of the classical and romantic composers and above all that of the impressionists and expressionists is best left to the musical belletrists. However, no grass can grow where number fetishism has once encroached, and certainly no music can thrive. There is a simple reason for this: every number is an abstraction of reality, and reducing two apples to the number "2" says nothing about the quality of either apple. When every aspect of musical sound or structure can be formulated in numbers, the formulation degenerates into sheer tautology. Conversely, when it is generally believed that purely numerical constructs guarantee musical coherence, composition becomes mere handicraft. By that token, much of what is called "computer music" today is nothing more than arty-crafty kitsch; the music founders in the numerical construct in the same way that the very worst painting founders in its subject-matter. Even when music of quality – like Ockeghem, Bach or the early Stockhausen – imparts something of its rational premises, it always resists the tautological moment inherent in the number as a means of musical construction. Important works *always* have a surplus, an added value incongruent with its constructive rationality, and that is perfectly logical: if music were to cling exclusively to its rational components, musical *discourse* would have a hard time of it. Without this discourse music is simply sonic book-keeping. A great deal of this century's musical products are not much more than just that; when we listen to them our yearnings for an obscene tango or the voice of Edith Piaf becomes a legitimate affair of the heart...

The misconception that there is a dichotomy of rationality and emotion (that is: irrationality) has its historical roots in a growing need to explain music, a need which is itself an expression of the chasm which began to yawn between the bourgeois public and progressive serious music at the beginning of the 19th century. The entire "historicism" which has been spreading wider and wider since the 1820s, qualifies as one of the many reactions to the progressive music of that period: it resurrected the bones of composers long since decomposed and, to the accompaniment of vociferous verbality, rattled them against the modernists of the day. However appealing the retro-expansion of our historical consciousness may be, it has been catastrophic for every generation of contemporary music. The reason for this is that composers suffered increasingly under the psychic pressure of that "historical consciousness" and felt they had to achieve something "historical" instead of living music. What is more, they were sucked into the maelstrom of a compulsion to verbalize induced by historicism, a compulsion which generated the 19th century phenomenon of a "description of music" tending towards the philosophical and the 20th century reduction of music to its numerical "substrates". Two abortive attempts, then, to evade the musical issue. The shocking thing is the extent to which music subjects itself to its "explanation models". No sooner has a composer failed yet again to have an idea than he is already working on a lecture about what he has in mind. I have actually heard twenty-year-olds – in Darmstadt, for instance – expounding on the historical dimensions of works they had not even written yet, claiming that without an understanding of these unwritten works it would be impossible to grasp that already existing little piece for oboe and piano...

Please don't get me wrong. A composer as verbally active as myself, and who moreover regards the *construction* of the musical discourse as vital to the development of musical ideas today, is well aware of the relationship between musical expression and the desire for verbal expression. Nobody can ignore *that* contradiction today; but composers should beware of becoming willing victims of the latest variant of musical "historicism", which I would briefly term the musical "explanation industry" in order to indicate an industry with *Golem*-like pretensions, becoming increasingly bogged down in musical creation. Even today's popular music is infected with the disease, having assumed truly industrial dimensions.

If musical production – with its inherent risk of being produced into the void – and musical verbalization have made a marriage of convenience whose two partners were originally deadly enemies, their union is based on a totally false notion of rationality versus emotion. Without subjecting the history of the two concepts to an analysis which would go back to the primeval history of musical articulation, I do wish to point out that the contradiction between "reason" and "discourse" is a complete fiction, a historical artefact, caused by the "compulsion to verbalize" that is generated by historicism. Under that compulsion, music which cannot be *described* in words or numbers has skidded off the historical track. This notion is so very dubious because of proceeding from the unfounded premiss that rationality is only expressed in two forms of language: verbal and mathematical. To assume that thinking in pure sound or color, thinking in gesture or movement, is less "rational" than thinking in words or numbers is conventional nonsense which we repeat parrot-fashion without summoning up the necessary will-power to confute it. A bare three generations after the expressionist phase of the Vienna School, the thing behind the concept of musical rationale has finally turned against musical rationality. Today this kind of misunderstood rationale is celebrated entirely beyond the true musical issue, and even claims to act as a corrective of musical production, but – in my opinion – as a corrective which is even more of a constraint than the most constricting forms of musical bookkeeping of neo-classical provenance. It seems a good idea to look back from this situation to that of musical expressionism in an endeavor to trace the rational core of that seemingly so irrational epoch of music.

People have usually tried to describe expressionism as a period in which an old order (so-called "tonality") was definitively abandoned and a new one (serial) had not yet crystallized. According to this view, expressionist music is thus "a music of transition", a phenomenon existing only in theory, but certainly not in reality. Music theory's difficulties with expressionist music lie chiefly in music theory's traditional incapacity to take the object of its considerations for what that object really is, instead of judging it by the very standards it has been making the most strenuous compositional efforts to discard. To be sure, it is easy to observe, in the case of, say, Schönberg the expressionist, the moment of boundless subjectivity that defies all rationalization. However, the premiss of such observations is fundamentally false. Things are quite the other way round: Schönberg, seeking the constraint of a musical logic which was unable to develop any further within the convention of musical language, was forced to resort to a subjectivity which was the *necessary point of departure* for making musical decisions which actually *enriched the rationality content* of music. This is first apparent in his handling of the material, a compositional act down to the tiniest detail. There is no question of vaguely wandering chords in Schönberg the expressionist, simply because they are *composed* with regard to one another and not – as reactions suggest to this very day – selected from the established arsenal and concocted into a "modern" artefact. The intent to *compose* even the most sublime details of the musical process, presupposes a degree of rational control over the musical material that was unprecedented prior to Schönberg. What people call "subjectivity" is simply the loneliness in which the necessary compositional decisions had to be taken. By no means whatsoever may this loneliness be equated with musical anarchy (which would be a poor freedom); it is rather the price to be paid for a cogent musical logic. The nature of this logic – and hence of expressionist music – is that it jettisons all heterogony, working only with the material contexts which it has produced itself.

Schönberg, then, in the most intensive and expressive works of that epoch, mistrusted not only all given material constellations whose expressive content had become obsolete, and not only to himself. He also mistrusted every traditional concept of form, very likely realizing that the concept of "closed form" about which Wagner had already had his doubts was inconsistent with the extension of the composer's right of disposal and hence with all further development of the logic of musical language (which as we all know has nothing to do with formal logic). Schönberg's expressionist works succeed in resolving the contradiction between material and form – a contradiction inherent in serious western music since its earliest beginnings – into an all-embracing *composition*. The fact that this aspect was not developed further in the course of musical history (not even by Schönberg) is due, I think, to social factors. Their nature is complex, and together they heralded the refunctionalization that has become increasingly apparent in serious music since Stravinsky's neo-classicism. This refunctionality has long since degraded the composers of commercial music to the status of feudal subalternity that forces them into musically heterogeneous behavior patterns (the feudal lords are no princelings today, incidentally, but captains of the culture and media industry!). It has also left its mark on the conception of serious music, although there seems to have been an unprecedented thrust towards rationalization since expressionism. Let me clarify this a little, for this contradiction leads us back to that selfsame area of false musical rationality that I mentioned before. From an aesthetic viewpoint too, functionality, whose external aspect insidiously invades our ears from every point of "civilization", can present itself as pure internalization. When it does, it is a mimicry of administered society and becomes a kind of *self-administering music*. This internalization is particularly apparent in a few forms

of extremely rudimentary "serial" music and its most deplorable deriva-
tives. While the "driving force of the sounds" and compositional logic
were identical to Schönberg the expressionist, they separated again after-
wards, to behave as if the eternal bickerings of ancient Greek acousmati-
cians and mathematicians had to start all over again. The more the
conviction grew that the sound's inner life – the compositional penetration of which was an extraordinarily courageous act – could only be
mastered by administrative means – by which I mean the devising of
totally incongruent series for the various dimensions of the sound, something which the Cologne School consistently denied from the very beginning – the sonic process was invaded by an "internalized" functionality,
mercilessly exposed – on a social level – by people like Adorno, Horkhei-
mer and Habermas. The sound, divided into its various "parameters"
and henceforth "administered" on a variety of levels, rapidly became a
prime example of functional "internalization". Not only the pseudo-serial
organization of its individual aspects but also the individual rows'
mutual indifference meant a lapse into scholastic mental patterns inherent
to feudalism as a primitive system of rule. There, too, the interdependency of different social groups was only technically administered, without any thought for balancing their inherent potential. No wonder that a
conception like Peter Schat's "Tone Clock" is more like the construction
of a mechanical timepiece from the Middle Ages than a sensitive, post-
Cartesian logic of connected sounds...

It seems to me that in their continued resistance towards the forms of
false, merely mechanical "rationalization", Schönberg's expressionist
works are the writing on the wall, in that they make us wonder what
musical rationality really means. Seeing that musical "rationale" has
deteriorated into a ritual which is hostile to art, one might reflect upon
on how inalienable, compositional rationality must not only reconstitute
the musical elements which "harsh world-use has rent apart", but also on
how to derive compositional logic from them instead of continuing to
force upon them the forms of an established, long since untenable logic
which is completely alien to them.

Assuming the increase of compositional intervention in the musical
material stems from a more urgent need for expression, *its sole artistic
legitimacy*, Schönberg's expressionist work reveals the extent to which the
opening up of the sound's inner world depends on dramaturgical considerations and not in the slightest on pure calculus. The latter would not
make compositional sense anyhow: only the already existing, known
sound can be (re-) constructed numerically, but not the sound which
only exists in the composer's mind and cannot yet be formulated. There

are good reasons for the long periods of research and experiment that invariably preceded the most radical pieces of electronic music. The sole purpose was to find, for a product dwelling entirely in the mind, a formulation that would lead to composition, so as to prevent that composition from becoming an experiment itself. It is interesting to see how Schönberg tackled the contradiction of pure imagination and necessary formalization. The orchestral piece "Farben" from opus 16, all 44 bars of it, demonstrates, the extent to which Schönberg transfers what used to be called motivic work into the coloristic sphere, thus linking the musical texture and its constituent elements as never before. The first signs of this procedure could be observed in Debussy (the last movement of "La Mer", for example), but here the tectonics contrast sharply with the sediments. In composing a continuous relationship between the two levels, Schönberg created a completely new musical morphology. He stripped the sound of its *object-like* character and conceived it as a *process*. In "Farben" the development of this process is identical with the macro-form. Here, and not in so-called "atonality" as such, lies the break with the past. Even in earlier epochs, differentiation in motivic work often conflicted with the standard means of composition; indeed, perhaps this conflict is the driving force in the development of western serious music. All differentiation on the motivic level was followed by a refinement of the musical "material". One might also say that through every act of composition which boosted that motivic differentiation, the material itself acquired motivic qualities. What we see in this respect in Ockeghem, Bach, Mozart or Wagner culminates in Schönberg's expressionist phase, which constituted both the fulfillment of tradition and the break with it. It was a break inasmuch as motivic work was no longer confronted by the material as something objective, but enveloped it entirely. Music had found itself.

Exactly at this point in Schönberg's work begins what might be termed "functional rationalism" in music. The means are prepared for an aesthetic end, for the purpose of serving it. The means of the classicals and romantics were still isolated from that end and could consequently serve various purposes. A certain chord could perform different harmonic or formal functions. This was no longer the case with Schönberg for the simple reason that the *composition* of the sonic components embraces their goal. Motivic work had always been intended to produce musical *meaning*. In that respect it differs fundamentally from the "meaning" which some people claim to hear in "tonal" chord progressions. More precisely, such progressions could themselves be called a compositional act, vertically conceived motivic work. Only ideological soyabean eaters still envisage tonality as a natural product, and their pieces sound accordingly macroidiotic. In a composition class Pousseur once played us a dominant seventh chord on the piano, walked away and remarked sardonically: "Let's wait and see whether it *resolves* into the tonic." It didn't. Every musical construct, all products of serious music, are products of a rationalization process in which, to paraphrase Norbert Elias, the composer's dreams must be converted into a precise code. The same applies to even the simplest Mozart minuet. The important thing, however, is how this rationalization is accomplished, and I cannot help suspecting that in a lot of contemporary music – especially that which so vociferously insists on its rational foundations and procedures – it has led to a mésalliance of *misunderstood* rationalism and handicraft. I say this because such music is a bad analogy, an acoustic servant of science, naively assuming that its mathematical formulas *per se* guarantee some meaningful musical context or other. The fact that such music is invariably composed by people without the slightest idea of the nature of musical context – to a growing extent by studio engineers or computer specialists with barely a smattering of what it's all about – renders the entire rationalization strategy dubious: a mountain of expensive and sophisticated technical gadgetry brings forth a tiny musical Mickey Mouse which the simplest imaginable artefact of, say, the Mannheim School could put to flight in a trice. This misunderstood rationality boils down to the fact that you can add apples and pears with impunity as long as the books balance.

To reflect on Schönberg's compositional rationality also means seeing such naive fallacies for what they are: an attempt to upgrade unabashed amateurism into a new theology of composition. The functional rationalism of Schönberg's method is quite the opposite, because it places the smallest particles of the musical structure in a *direct relationship to one another*. Stuckenschmidt, in his biography of Schönberg, cites "Erwartung", op. 17, as an example of this. For a long time the piece was regarded as impossible to analyse, because nobody was prepared to examine this subcutaneous relationship. It exists not only – as Stuckenschmidt pointed out – on the level of a quite extraordinarily stringent motivic conception, but also on the level below – the level of the conception of the sound as the *vehicle for all musical processuality*. Let me elaborate on what I was saying about the third piece of opus 16, taking "Erwartung" as an example. On the very first pages of the score we notice how finely woven the fabric of the parts is; listening to them, it is hard to tell whether they are pursuing contrapuntal-motivic or coloristic goals. Closer scrutiny reveals that neither is the case, but that they eliminate the difference between the two established dimensions. Because the sound is composed as a process, thus banishing heterogenous elements, new *sound-types* emerge. They draw sustenance from their development *in time* in the way that a thematic, harmonic or rhythmic development formerly did. What was still relatively monolithic in "Farben" is fully-fledged in "Erwartung". The specific thing about this work is that it is not a rationalization of a vision in the usual sense but its *direct materialization*. What *action* was in opera is a dream in "Erwartung". The place of action is not objectively stated; "the edge of a forest" suffices. The only figure is not endowed with any individual characteristics except for jewellery and a white garment, attributes which have no bearing on the course of the piece, however. We do not know whether the sketchily indicated events are enacted on the level of reality or merely in the woman's mind, as a dream. In search of "the man", of whom we are told nothing at all, the woman gets into a state of psychotic panic which topples her inner and outer world: the borderline between psyche and reality disappears. This inner panic is reflected in all "nature". A similar impulse can only be found in Edward Munch's "Cry". It seems natural to speak of intensified irrationality in connection with this composition of Schönberg's, which I regard as the sublimate of musical expressionism. In terms of music, however, the situation is quite the other way round. The nightmare's musical psychogramme develops into an acoustic Armageddon *because of* the efforts of extreme rationality. This intermingling of reality and imagination can only be achieved by the music, which itself thus becomes part of the dream. In translating these two fluctuating levels into a compositional strategy, Schönberg runs the gamut of all historically evolved musical dimensions: on the "reality" side are musical textures in which melodic, harmonic and rhythmic components can be clearly distinguished. On the side of the psychic projection are complex structures in which these historical dimensions are so closely entangled as to produce an extremely dense, virtually impenetrable coalescence of sound. In it, the organizational principles of all traditional music merge: the grounds for the events in the melodrama are to be found in the music, but not for a single moment is the music a mere duplicate, a pleonasm. In "Erwartung", the functional rationalism of Schönberg's composition aims at integrating the music into the dream-structure instead of deriving the former from the latter. The technical substratum of this functional rationalism is a highly sophisticated counterpoint – the most rational compositional method imaginable. A true harbinger of the most highly developed serial thought, it determines all the dimensions, ranging from the horizontal-melodic (where it appears as the finest motivic work) to the coloristic, even in the most complex cascades of sound. The counterpoint in "Erwartung" may be termed polyvalent, because it *links* the most disparate musical dimensions without forcing them into the same pleonastic straitjacket, as is so often the case with bad serial or computer music. The pseudo-rationalism of such false analogies is not to be found in Schönberg's music.

Nor can it be found in the conception of "Die Glückliche Hand", op. 15, whose dramaturgy adds to the dimensions of sound and gesture the dimension of multiply refracted light. This example – especially when compared with Scriabin's "Prometheus" (1911) – clearly shows how firmly Schönberg's polyvalent counterpoint resists such feeble, false analogies as those encountered in Scriabin's conception of a purely mechanical correspondence of light and sound values. Schönberg counters Scriabin's totally ridiculous pseudo-rationalism, which pedantically assigns to each tone "its own" color, with a conception in which the light-forms are not the *equivalent* of musical processes but become a *secondary parameter*, meaning only *one* of the components of a time-space conception embracing more than just sound. What is expressed on the aesthetic level here is also the work's utopian programme: the suspension of the division of labour, meaning the product of capitalist industrial civilization. In this respect "Die Glückliche Hand" may be regarded as an expressionistically compressed reflection on Wagner's "Ring of the Nibelungs". While Wagner's ring – the epitome of the precious object with added value in the capitalist sense – is fashioned from the natural substance of gold with a few hammer-strokes Schönberg's "man" (the counterpart of the "woman" in "Erwartung") enters the murky cave of capitalist manufacture in order to show the workers, with a single powerful stroke of the hammer on the anvil, how things can be done "better", that is more rationally. Lo and behold, from the depths of the cloven anvil (shades of Wagner's ring!) he retrieves a piece of diamond jewellery, not a pragmatic industrial product. While Wagner's ring – as an item of jewellery, an idealized object of value – embodies infinite power and, because of the quest for power it signifies, causes the catastrophe, Schönberg's jewellery, fashioned in an equally rational way, generates nothing but impotence. This is because in Schönberg's concept the jewel is used as a direct means to an end: like today's pompous managers, Schönberg's "man" intends to buy his beloved with it, failing to notice that she has already transferred her affections to a dandy. It takes a choir to bring him back to his senses. The key problem in "Die Glückliche Hand" is frighteningly modern. The utmost rationality is sought for the purpose of a seemingly quite irrational goal: sensual satisfaction. If I had had to compose Schönberg's closing chorus, I would have at least pointed out this paradox in the text: the rationality of the capitalist production process aims at satisfying emotions whose foundations have long since been destroyed by that selfsame capitalism. It would perhaps have been better if Schönberg, an idealistic socialist at that time, had consulted Marx about the *antinomy* that is inherent to every capitalistic economical and social order, for Marx had formulated it concisely back in 1848. But that is not our concern right now. Our concern is the rationality of the aesthetic design.

Studying the score of "Die Glückliche Hand", we shall not find any mechanical analogy of sound, word and light. As in "Erwartung", the heterogenous elements behave in a dialectic-contrapuntal manner towards one another. This means that their diverse *qualities* are not squeezed into a corset of pseudo-rational analogues but played off against each other in a highly sophisticated game of counterpoint, only thus merging into dialectic unity. In his "Breslau Speech" (1928) on "Die Glückliche Hand", in which he dwelt on "the art of representing inner processes"[1], Schönberg opposed a conception of non-musical parameters in analogy to musical ones: "...it would be completely arbitrary to construct, say, a scale of facial expressions or a rhythm of light". This is a firm rejection of purely mechanical rationalism, long before it got its disastrous hold on the technical arts. Schönberg demanded the same of the organizational principles for extra-musical parameters as for the musical ones: without negating their material meaning they ought to be combined into forms and figures *independently* of that meaning; indeed, it ought to be possible, after measuring them in terms of time, height, width, intensity and many other dimensions, to relate them in accordance with laws more profound than the laws of the material, laws of a world built by its creator on the basis of measure and number. Schönberg stated that in this respect he simply relied on his imagination, without a theory. These remarks should be scrutinized carefully, for on a first reading everything seems to be contradictory. How can a composition be organized without negating its material meaning *independently* of that meaning? The contradiction is resolved by the hypothesis that the artistic material can only be organized on a certain level of abstraction. Better than Schönberg's rather unfortunate formulation might be "qualities inherent to the material" and "the meaning" of its combination into forms and figures, for Schönberg was undoubtedly referring to two different levels of meaning; he was demanding that the material qualities be respected as the basis of artistic organization but not be made the *goal* of that organization. I regard Schönberg's evocation of a divine world order governed by "measure and number" as his own business. Personally, I have my doubts about that...

Applied to the score of "Die Glückliche Hand", Schönberg's observations mean that sound and light-color are connected by internally congruent plans, but that this connection does not imply any direct causality. As the monodrama unfolds between desire and renunciation, and the development of the music follows this "asymptotic" symmetry, we see how the color changes in cycles from green to blood-red and back again (not literally!) to a greenish hue (grey-blue with a slight addition of red). In these cycles their various phases of development are indeed associated "without theory", but by no means arbitrarily, for they derive their meaning from their interdependency. Sound, gesture, word and color become the attributes of something else; their interaction generates that "internal process", the content, whose articulation is made up of the various dimensions that follow. It sounds paradoxical, but it perfectly describes the reality of the process of artistic creation. Not only does the artist think *in* the categories of the material itself – his logic is based on *association*, there being no scientific law for the production of art.

I have endeavored to voice my thoughts about a few aesthetic and compositional premises in Arnold Schönberg's expressionist oeuvre here. It seems appropriate to close with a brief look at the historical situation in which he composed the works in question. It is not so very surprising that the decomposition of the syntactic-tonal foundations of the bourgeois era took place at a time when that era, which claimed to be an age of reason, was producing monsters at a rapidly increasing pace. Nor is it all that surprising, that the chief motives of the artists in whose works that process of decomposition was taking place were panic, isolation and the desire to "épater le bourgeois" that dated from the height of the Romantic period. What *is* surprising is the grovelling attitude of the post-expressionist generation of artists who, despite the hideous miens of the monsters produced by abortive bourgeois rationality, concealed their fickleness under a pseudo-rationalistic cloak called Neo-Classicism then and computer music today. They all seem to have had the same physics teacher, who did his bit for Auschwitz and Hiroshima too, for Chernobyl and the Gulf War – all those abortions of human existence which obey – to quote Schönberg's ugliest metaphor – "the law of measure and number". In "A Survivor from Warsaw" – to some extent an expressionist work – the most horrifying moment is arithmetically rational. It occurs when the Nazi corporal makes the ghetto-dwellers *count themselves*, telling them why with mathematical precision: "In five minutes' time I want to know how many to send to the gas chamber." The forms of artistic rationalism devised by Schönberg in his expressionist works firmly resist such a rationality of organized apocalypse. Once tonality, that syntax of musical illusion, had been stripped of its roots, Schönberg focused on two possibilities which he thought would safeguard meaning under the conditions of a socially determined, hypertrophic rationality aimed at attaining completely irrational goals. These two possibilities are *extension* (as expressed in the use of extra-musical means in "Die Glückliche Hand", for example) and motivic-contrapuntal *concentration*, which appeared to him to be a guarantee for meaning on the abstract-musical level. Having completely lost his faith in the (tonal) sympathy and antipathy of the harmonies once propounded by Descartes, he saw only one possibility of investing music with meaning and innovation. It was motivic, "durchbrochene" work, described by Adorno, a kind of tracery affecting the very last detail, no longer confined to the horizontal but applied to the vertical and all areas in between. When else is a "motif" but the aforementioned union of "material meaning" with the "forms and figures" which are "independent of this meaning"? What else – and this question applies to *all* serious western music – is the *motif* but the subjective introduction of musical meaning? In that respect all Schönberg did – and he often flirted with the idea – was think a tendency of European composing through to the final consequence, right into the historical situation which forced art to fall from the heaven of ideas onto horrible, mortally wounded human soil.

Just over a quarter of a century ago (in 1966), I addressed the curious dialectics of rationale and discourse in Schönberg's work. Surprisingly, the remarks I made on that occasion (in a late-night talk for West German Radio), remarks which caused all the pseudo-serial rationalists to declare me Public Enemy Number One, do not substantially differ from what I have been saying today about Schönberg's compositional dialectics.[2] I have a reason for not discussing Schönberg's "serial" phase today: I wanted to *explain* a new aesthetic logic, not to *formalize* it, with all the consequences entailed by what is certainly a problematic undertaking. Perhaps we could discuss it at a future "ratio" symposium addressing real problems instead of pseudo-intellectual "chinoiseries".... There is no doubt that Schönberg shed a new light on musical time and space. I think that it will take a little longer for his syntax and language to erase the appalling adaptation strategies of the generation that followed him from the pages of musical history. History must credit him with responding in his expressionist works to the chimera of bourgeois rationality with a completely new, *aesthetically justified rationality* prompted by the historical situation of the human subject itself. To immerse oneself in the human subject at a time when this subject is in danger of extinction at the hands of rationality is a typically Schönbergian tour-de-force. May it be a lesson to today's rationalists: when they resort to numerical tables, modes or parametrical book-keeping for the musical articulation of their inability to cope with the world, the only thing expressed in terms of music is handicraft. I have my problems with Schönberg. But faced with the algorithms, tone cuckoo clocks and other rational cop-outs so far below the standards even of advanced tonality, I still think that Schönberg's expressionist oeuvre has revolutionary potential as a signal of a new musical humanism for future generations fed up with all this neo-Biedermeier self-mutilation. We must keep this in mind, summoning up all the rational and intuitive powers of our spirit, which thank goodness has survived the slings and arrows of modern history. Schönberg's achievements in the field of composition *technique* are still a thorn in music's flesh. And so they should be.

NOTES

1. See: Arnold Schönberg – Wassily Kandinsky: Briefe, Bilder und Dokumente einer aussergewöhnlichen Begegnung, ed. Jelena Hahl-Koch, dtv-Kunst, Munich 1983.
2. The text "Schönberg lebt" – containing a polemic against Boulez' Schönberg reception of the fifties (Boulez, 1952: "Schoenberg est mort") has been published in Konrad Boehmer: "Das Böse Ohr", DuMont Verlag, Köln 1993, p. 51–68.

promised land – works 8 hours. "Und gäbe es überhaupt kein Ornament, – ein Zustand, der vielleicht in Jahrtausenden eintreten wird – brauchte der Mensch statt acht Stunden nur vier zu arbeiten, denn die Hälfte der Arbeit entfällt heute noch auf Ornamente"[18]. For Loos the evolution of culture is the same as the removal of the ornament from the objects for daily use. Above all by the lack of ornament, art has reached the great heights of today. The individuality of the artist is so strong, that he does not waste his time at the ornament. As Loos wrote: "Ornamentlosigkeit ist ein Zeichen Geistiger Kraft."[19] (In a postscript Loos mocks the artists of the Wiener Sezession: "Und ich sage dir, es wird die Zeit kommen, in der die Einrichtung einer Zelle vom Hoftapezierer Schulze oder Professor Van de Velde als Strafverschärfung gelten wird."[20])

As Schönberg wrote his *Harmonielehre*, so in 1912 did Kandinsky by writing his treatise "Über das Geistige in der Kunst".[21] This work contains not only his own poetics, but also a more general art-theoretical explanation. Like Schönberg and Loos, Kandinsky speaks of the "holy art"; of the artists as its prophets. He makes a stand against the principle of "l'art pour l'art". "Die Malerei ist eine Kunst und die Kunst im Ganzen ist nicht ein zweckloses Schaffen der Dinge, die im Leeren zerfliessen, sondern eine Macht, die zweckvoll ist, und muss der Entwicklung und Verfeinerung der menschlichen Seele dienen...."[22] From this sentence we learn, that art isn't an ornament of life anymore – as Kandinsky reproaches l'art pour l'art – but an absolute essence. Kandinsky formulates a claim for unity of form and content and with that a criticism on the ornament. "Der Künstler muss etwas zu sagen haben, da nicht die Beherrschung der Form seine Aufgabe ist, sondern das Anpassen dieser Form dem Inhalt."[23]

Thus the form is subordinate to the content. This he explained very clearly in his essay "Über die Formfrage".[24] In this he argues that the evolution of art is a constant development of forms. A form, which was revolutionary yesterday and subverted old principles, becomes common and becomes itself the principle which will be subverted by the forms of tomorrow. The driving-force behind this movement is the human spirit. Form is only a device in which the spirit reveals: "Die Form ist den äussere Ausdruck des inneren Inhaltes."[25]

This point of view is of revolutionary importance for painting art. In "Über das Geistige in der Kunst" Kandinsky describes the history of art as a development from the subject, the "what it is", towards the way in which the subject is reproduced, the "how it is done". By the "what it is" is meant the material subject, which was painted only for reason of the reproduction. As art developed, the "how it is done" came ever more to the foreground. Not anymore was the subject itself the main thing, but the way in which it was painted and the technique which was used. But in modern times we'll return to the "what it is"; not in a material meaning, but in the meaning of a pure artistic content. "Dieses Was ist der Inhalt, welchen nur die Kunst in sich fassen kann, und welchen nur die Kunst zum klaren Ausdruck bringen kann durch die nur ihr gehörenden Mittel."[26]

I recall from memory Schönberg's motto: "Die Musik soll nicht schmücken, sie soll wahr sein". When we compare this sentence with Kandinsky's thoughts, we can explain it in this way: the musical content – that is the typically musical which can only be expressed by its own devices – has to correspond with the musical structure. Only then can it be spoken of as true art, which answers to its holy call. It is quite understandable that Schönberg was a great inspiration for Kandinsky and vice versa. "Schönbergsche Musik führt uns in ein neues Reich ein, wo die musikalischen Erlebnisse keine akustischen sind, sondern rein seelische. Hier beginnt die 'Zukunftsmusik'."[27] The experience of the soul is the effect of the "inner sound" of an object, a word, a sound or a thought. The revelation of the inner sound is the aim of the modern painter. He liberates the object from its coincidental, external envelope, so that the inner sound is revealed. Thus the exterior is concidental, the inner is essential.

The satirist Karl Kraus (1874–1936) is regarded as one of the leading personalities in artistic and intellectual Vienna.[28] Above all Kraus became well-known by his periodical "Die Fackel", which he edited almost weekly from 1899 until his death in 1936. In this anti-paper Kraus polemized in sarcastic satires against what he called the hypocrisy of the Viennese society. Especially the press, namely the influential "Neue Freie Presse" had to suffer for this. Kraus held this newspaper responsible for the spiritual and moral decay of the society. His sharpest criticism concerned the so-called feuilleton; this is a column in which journalistic information was colored by a pseudo-artistic use of language. The fact was ornamented by the fantasy of the author in such a degree, that the difference between fiction and reality became obscured or even disappeared. Kraus' criticism on this way of using language, on this connection between journalism and literature, can be compared with Adolf Loos' criticism on the connection between design and art.

In 1910 Kraus wrote his polemic "Heine und die Folgen".[29] This essay startled the literary world, because he had attacked a famous poet like

Heinrich Heine. In a later justification Kraus wrote, that he had not in mind to do the popular poet unjustice, although he also did not mean to do him justice. He had in mind to criticize an attitude of life, which aimed at ease and comfort. But above all he wanted to return language the place it belongs: "Hier ist irgendwie die Sprache von allem, was sie einzu-wickeln verpflichtet wurde, gelöst, und ihr die Kraft, sich einen besseren Inhalt zu schaffen, zuerkannt."[30]

The heated reproaches apparently concern Heine himself, but in reality they concern the Viennese world of journalism and literature; they con-cern the separation of form and content, which is, according to Kraus, Heine's inheritance to journalism. Language was regarded only as a technical device to cover a lack of content. Language was treated as an ornament! Nowhere is Heine's language the natural expression of a thought; nowhere for instance is it obvious, why Heine's poems had necessarily to be poems and not prose. "... Diese Reime sind Papilloten, nicht Schmetterlinge."[31] According to Heine and his imitators an artist is the master of the word; according to Kraus it is just the opposite: in deep respect the artist's eyes fell in front of the language. It is not the word which obeys him, but it is the artist who obeys the word. Only such words answer to the highest, which haven't been written with the lan-guage, but from the language. Kraus regarded the language as the natural expression of the thought.

In *Heine und die Folgen* Kraus implicitly associated himself with the metaphysics of Schopenhauer. Kraus was convinced of the metaphysical nature of the thoughts. He was confident that thoughts have always existed and are only manifested by the medium of the thinker. In other words: "... dass die Gedanken und die Gedichte da waren vor den Dichtern und Denkern." Only by the language can these thoughts come through: "Und nur in der Wonne sprachlicher Zeugung wird aus dem Chaos eine Welt." The thought only belongs to the one who is really seeking. Not the primate of the thought is the main thing, but the think-er's integrity. "Der Gedanke ist ein Gefundenes, ein Wiedergefundenes. Und wer ihn sucht, ist ein ehrlicher Finder, ihm gehört er, auch wenn ihn vor ihm schon ein anderer gefunden hätte."[32]

In the *Harmonielehre* Schönberg associates with the latter. Kraus explained the phenomenon of the thought as something metaphysical, Schönberg sought an explanation in the theory of instincts. For the com-poser the main thing is the ability to hear himself, to look deep inside, Schönberg writes in the final chapter. In the unconscious he'll find the musical thoughts, preformed – to use the word of Karl Kraus – but not yet manifest. The artist of language, the poet, the author, forms his thoughts by the language; the composer does the same by the music. But the musical technique shows us a continuous evolution: the devices of today are not the same as those of yesterday, because: "Alles ist nur Vorbereitung zu einer höheren Stufe der Entwickelung."[33] It is the same evolution of art which was described by Kandinsky. The developing tendency of the musical material can be translated as a compository urge for the seeking for ever new possibilities of expression. Schönberg illustrates this by the example of the diminished seventh chord. In the time of Bach, Mozart and Beethoven, this chord had enormous expressivity: it was experienced as extremely dissonant and was always connected with the most violent emotions. But, in the 19th century the chord became ever more common and thus lost its expressive meaning. Even more, the chord became stereotyped and only of value in the sentimentality of the light music. Instead of the diminished seventh chord appeared other, more dissonant chords, which overtook the force of expression. These too became common in the long run and their expressivity faded away. New chords were introduced, ... etcetera, etcetera.[34]

The ever higher degree of dissonance stimulated Schönberg to his revolution of the emancipation of dissonance. Emancipation of the dissonance means: the liberation of the dissonance from its conventional preparation and solution. Emancipation of dissonance also means that the principal difference between consonance and dissonance has been abolished. On this matter Schönberg has been attacked most. His critics, not only the critics of the paper, but also famous theorists like Heinrich Schenker and later Paul Hindemith, appealed to the naturalness of the tonal system, by common consent; and for this reason Schönberg's atonal music had to be rejected. Schönberg agreed with his critics, that tonality starts from nature. But he relativated its naturalness by pointing out the tempered system as a compromise between naturalness and artistic usefulness. A little curious is Schönberg's apology of atonal music: he does not doubt of the necessity of a natural system, but – on the contrary – he tries to prove the naturalness of his own atonal music. Schönberg particularly reproaches Heinrich Schenker for ending with the first five overtones, by pointing out the relative difference between a consonance and a dissonance: the first reflecting the simpler vibration number and the latter reflecting the complexer one. According to Schönberg the evermore "exploitating" of the overtone series is responsible for the continuous movement of the musical material: "Diese Bewegung ... (kann) nicht aufhören ..., ehe sie den Willen der Natur erfüllt, ehe wir in der Nachahmung nicht die äusserste Vollendung erreicht haben."[35] This is the ultimate goal of the musical development. Schönberg regards this restless seeking of new possibilities, situated in nature, as a condition for artistic integrity.

Probably Schönberg's apology is in this case influenced by his critics, who accentuated the naturalness of tonality. But we have to take Schönberg very seriously on the case of the historical musical development. In this he is part of the long tradition of "Enlightenment", of the belief in a continuous improvement of mankind. For Schönberg there is no choice: the artists duty is to push humanity forward. This is his main reproach to the common aesthetics: they only looked for explanations of the phenomena which already existed, without looking for those of the future. "Hier die Wahrheit, das Suchen – dort die Ästhetik, das vermeintlich Gefundende, die Reduktion des Erstrebenswerten aufs Erreichbare."[36] Integrity, according to Schönberg, is the endeavor for the highest truth; in the same time he hopes, that this truth will never be attained, that the movement will never be attained that the movement will never end: "Dass die Wahrhaftigkeit nie zur Wahrheit wird; denn es wäre kaum zu ertragen, wenn wir die Wahrheit wüssten."[37]

The climax of musical expressionism is in the period 1908–1909. In these years Schönberg wrote a great number of works in the so-called free-atonal style. These works are: the Klavierstücke op. 11, the George Lieder op. 15, the Orchesterstücke op. 16 and the monodrama Erwartung op. 17. These works are generally mentioned in one breath, because in these works Schönberg renounced tonality for expressive aims. Of course there is no discussion about this; there is also no discussion about the smooth transition between the last tonal works and the first atonal works. At this time I would like to discuss the development within this period of atonality.

This development doesn't concern the abandoning of tonality, but the gradual renunciation of an emphatic form-conception. We experience this evolution immediately when we compare the first atonal compositions – the George Lieder and the first two piano pieces op. 11 – with Erwartung, which is an extreme work in all its aspects. The piano pieces numbers. 1 and 2 – like some of the George Lieder – can be strongly associated with the late romantic style. The piano pieces are written in the tradition of the later Liszt works, even of Brahms' Klavierstücke.

The second piece of op. 11 – Schönberg's "Lugubre Gondola"? – shows a kind of a closed rondo-"Lied" form. The structure is determined by thematic development. Thematic development – so characteristic for classical and romantic music – can also be found in the first piece of this opus and in the George Lieder. It is interesting that the last number of op. 11

doesn't show this kind of development; the piece was written later, at the time of the last orchestral piece of op. 16.

The monodrama Erwartung shows us almost the opposite of the earlier atonal compositions. It is of overwhelming complexity; there is no clear musical course, because of a collapse of musical continuity. There are no themes; there are even no motifs which determine the structure for more than a few bars. And last but not least, there are no main "characters", which could be described as, for instance allegretto grazioso or presto furioso. Also in its expression the music is extreme; for moderate emotions there is no space. Adorno interpreted this formal crisis as an abolition of the work of art itself. In Western culture the work of art always had a kind of unassailability; there was always a certain distance between man and work. According to Adorno, Erwartung is a psychoanalytical protocol of a nightmare. The music registrates – like a psychiatrist – the shocks; it reflects the discontinuous emotional course. This course is going to determine the musical structure. "Die seismographische Aufzeichnung traumatischer Schocks wird ... das technische Formgesetz der Musik."[38] Although Adorno's postulate of loss of the work of art, in an emphatic sense is partly debatable – in our time Erwartung was given its place in music history, in some way comparable with Beethoven's "ninth" – it is true that Erwartung seems to contradict perhaps the most important feature of Western music: the idea of a form, more or less presented as being consciously constructed. At least we experience the suggestion of a musical piece not being determined by structure but by emotion.

The bridge between the earlier atonal works and Erwartung is constituted by the orchestral pieces op. 16. This work can be regarded as a symphony in five movements. In these pieces Schönberg seems to say good-bye to the older forms and to the traditional music in general. The first piece, titled "Vorgefühle", is the opening "allegro" movement; the second, "Vergangenes", is an "andante" in a clear dacapo liedform; the third piece, "Farben", a kind of intermezzo in slow tempo; the fourth, "Peripetie", is a real scherzo; and the last piece, "Das obligate Rezitativ", is the symphony's "Finale".

The first piece is in some way comparable with a sonata form. It contains an exposition (bars 1–25), a development section in two parts (26–78; 79–103) and a rudimentary reprise and coda in one (103–128). But only by these outlines can the structure be associated with a classical sonata form. The exposition shows us several thematic gestures. There are no connections between the themes; and although some are more or less related, most of them are characterized by contrast. The result is a dis-

Figure 1

Figure 2a

Figure 2b

continuity which had hardly ever been heard before. The first part of the development section is mainly determined by two processes. The first one is the introduction and fugal development of a new pattern (Fig. 1) in the strings, resulting in a three to five part ostinato.

The second process is a development of the main theme of the exposition (Fig. 2a). The several phases of this development are not connected in a traditional melodic or harmonic way; on the contrary, it shows a discontinuous course comparable with the exposition. There is an increasing complexity, leading into a double canon (Fig. 2b). We experience, together with the ostinato of the first process, an emotional outburst, which is a superlative of all espressivo in Western music.

The second part of the development starts from this total "crisis" – of form and expression – and begins with the seeming chaos of a six part (!) counterpoint of the pattern shown in Figure 1. (This is a problematic aspect of this piece: by the immense quantity of not always audible musical "events" Schönberg seems to lose the control over the form.) The musical tension of the development is completely nullified by the following reprise and coda: after some reminiscences of the exposition a static closing ostinato is built up.

The third piece can be regarded as an example of the so-called "Klang-farbenmelodie". But the orchestral piece "Farben" is in no sense an impressionistic characterpiece: it is a fugue in five voices. There is a theme – though rudimental – there is even a counterpoint. After this fugue-exposition (Fig. 3a) there is a development of the three notes fugue-theme. The end is a final part including a stretto, "in motu contra-rio" (Fig. 3b).

Figure 3a

Figure 3b

It is a fugue; at the same time it has nothing to do with a fugue. As in the first piece, the outline remembers the old form, but the inner structure seems to contradict it: the moving voices have been fossilized into a static chord progression. It is a fugue in the same way that Ravel's "La Valse" is a waltz. La Valse is not a real waltz, it is about a waltz, it tells us the story of Viennese waltz. Schönberg here reflects the history of the fugue, he is burying the fugue after a last salute.

Behind this salute – to sonata form, to lied-form, to fugue and scherzo – the new world begins. In the fifth orchestral piece Schönberg definitely abandoned all form-conventions, to create a totally expressive and personal style. It is true, musical continuity is restored, regarding the Hauptstimme, indicated in the score by Schönberg himself (Fig. 4). But here the "thematische Arbeit" has been completely abolished. The piece shows a series of connected, but not clearly related musical ideas. Schönberg called this device "musical prose",[39] that is a free, irregular course of

Figure 4

musical thoughts; it is Schönberg's answer to Wagner's Unendliche Melo-
die. The last orchestra piece is not constructed anymore in a traditional
sense. It has lost the closed and rounded form of the traditional composition. It has no beginning, no "once upon a time" and no ending, happy or
not.

Whether this work is a result of the conscious or the unconscious –
when we look at the very complex and worked-out polyphony, as for
instance the double canon in the development section of the first piece or
the fugal techniques in the third, it is rather difficult to believe Schönberg
when proclamating the primate of the unconscious – this piece has
bridged over, by abolishing all outer conventions, the distance between
the work of art and the inner composer. Music has become emotion itself;
form and content are presented as a unity.

NOTES

1. Der Blaue Reiter, ed. by W. Kandinsky and F. Marc, 1912. Dokumentarische neuaus-
   gabe von K. Lankheit. München/Zürich 1984.
2. Ibid., p. 60.
3. Carl Dahlhaus draws this conclusion in: Schönberg's aesthetic theology (orig. Schönbergs ästhetische Theologie, 1984), in: Schönberg and the new music; essays by Carl
   Dahlhaus, transl. by D. Puffet and A. Clayton, New York 1987, p. 85.
4. Schönberg; Franz Liszt's Work and Being (orig. Franz Liszts Werk und Wesen, 1911).
   In: Style and Idea, selected writings of Arnold Schönberg, ed. by L. Stein, London
   1975, p. 442.
5. Schönberg: Problems of teaching art (orig. Probleme des Kunstunterrichtes, 1911), in:
   Style and Idea, p. 367.
6. Adorno: Philosophie der Neuen Musik (1949), Suhrkamp Frankfurt a. M. 1976, see the
   chapter Schönbergs Kritik an Schein und Spiel, pp. 42–46.
7. Quoted in: Adorno, p. 46.
8. Schönberg: Harmonielehre, Vienna 1911 (7th, new edition, 1966).
9. Ibid., p. 243.
10. Ibid., p. 325.
11. Ibid., p. 490.
12. Ibid., p. 6.
13. This has been described by Allan Janik and Stephen Toulmin in: Wittgenstein's
    Vienna, New York 1973.
14. Loos: Architektur, in: Trotzdem, Innsbruck, 1931, new edition Vienna 1982, p. 101. It
    is remarkable that Loos omits capitals in the substantives: without doubt this German
    use was for Loos nothing more than an ornament.
15. Ibid., p. 102.
16. Loos: Ornament und Verbrechen, in: Trotzdem.
17. Ibid., pp. 78–79.
18. Ibid., p. 83.
19. Ibid., p. 88.
20. Loos: An den Ulk, in: Trotzdem, p. 89.
21. Kandinsky: Über das Geistige in der Kunst, München 1912, new edition Bern 1959.

22. Ibid., p. 134.
23. Ibid., p. 135.
24. Kandinsky: Über die Formfrage, in: Der Blaue Reiter.
25. Ibid., p. 137.
26. Kandinsky: Über das Geistige in der Kunst, p. 34.
27. Ibid., p. 49.
28. Janik and Toulmin: Wittgenstein's Vienna.
29. Kraus: Heine und die Folgen (1910), Reclam, Stuttgart 1986.
30. Ibid., p. 66.
31. Ibid., p. 50.
32. Ibid., pp. 53–54.
33. Schönberg: Harmonielehre, p. 112.
34. The same explanation has been given by Adorno in the chapter Tendenz des Materials, pp. 38–42.
35. Schönberg: Harmonielehre, p. 288.
36. Ibid., p. 386.
37. Ibid., p. 394.
38. Adorno, p. 47.
39. Schönberg: Brahms the progressive (orig. Brahms der Fortschrittliche, 1947), in: Style and Idea.

The Dialectics of Artistic Creativity: Some Aspects of Theoretic Reflection in Arnold Schönberg and Wassily Kandinsky.

LAURENS VAN DER HEIJDEN

Introduction.

In the comparison between painting and music different levels of interpretation can be distinguished. The simultaneous developments in both arts that led to abstraction and atonality can also be approached in divergent ways.

The relation between both arts and their mutual influences have inspired many artists into making pictoral translations of musical concepts, as for example 'counterpoint', 'rhythm' and 'dissonance'. Theoretical reflections underlying artistic developments in abstraction and atonality, show a similar variety of approaches of comparable artistic phenomena in these two realms of aesthetic experience, in a decisive period of idiomatic transition.

In the interdisciplinary search for common characteristics in the arts, specific qualities belonging either to painting or to music became applicable to both areas of artistic expression. Time or temporality is thus connected to painting, whereas the aspect of space and spatiality is articulated in relation to music.

When attempting to relate painting and music on the basis of assumed common features it is important, however, to realize that commonly used terms do actually have their own specific significance in their own aesthetic realm. The same holds true for the inherent qualities of the artistic means themselves. The fact that in painting and music color and harmony are emancipated in the same span of time is in fact a remarkable phenomenon, but may all too easily lead to the assumption that identical aesthetic implications based these artistic developments. One should bear in mind, that the art-theoretic and formal motivation at the basis of this autonomization of sound and color in the works of Schönberg and Kandinsky, to a large extent do have their own unique artistic context.

A distinction between the level of art-theoretic considerations (historical, philosophical and ideological) and that of technical craftmanship has to be taken into account, in order not to interpret art in a gratuitous and too speculative way.

A more theoretical field of research studies the abstract-philosophic implications of the interdisciplinary discourse. Philosophic reflections on the relation between art and nature, objectivity and subjectivity, or the role of the rational and the unconscious in artistic creation belong to this more abstract category of approach.

Many publications, primarily based on philologic research, have already sketched out extensively the biographic history of the artistic kinship of Arnold Schönberg and Wassily Kandinsky and placed their artistic productivity and mutual influence against the historical background of contemporary developments in the arts. In this essay, I will primarily focus on a few theoretical and philosophical issues related to the paragon of abstraction and atonality. Central conceptions in the work and theoretic notions of Arnold Schönberg and Wassily Kandinsky will be my main references.

Objectivity and Subjectivity.

In *Über das Geistige in der Kunst* (1912) Kandinsky ponders on the 'Inner Necessity' of the creative spirit. The concept of Inner Necessity, understood as the inner urge to create, is a key-concept in Kandinsky's justification of abstract art. In his exposure on the Inner Necessity, Kandinsky uses a tripartite division. At first he distinguishes the duty of the artist to give shape to his personality. Next to this individual motive, the artist has to take into account that he is an exponent of his time and social milieu. As a third factor finally, the artist has the responsibility to make his art transcend time and space[1].

Also in Schönbeg's aesthetic theory of art there is a similar tripartite division. In the first place here, there is the compelling element of the individual expression. In the *Harmonielehre* (1911) Schönberg goes into this conviction:

> *"Ich entscheide beim Komponieren nur durch das Gefühl, durch das Formgefühl. Dieses sagt mir, was ich schreiben muss, alles andere ist ausgeschlossen. Jeder Akkord, den ich hinsetze, entspricht einem Zwang: einem Zwang meines Ausdrucksbedürfnisses."[2]*

In another passage in the *Harmonielehre* Schönberg notices that each period has a specific notion of form[3]. This "Formgefühl" however, is partly limited by the restrictions that time imposes on artistic freedom. The third element, Kandinsky calls it "pure and eternally artistic", can be discerned in Schönberg's conception of an absolute, abstract world of sounds.

Considering both the subjective element of the Inner Necessity and the third level of the 'pure and eternally artistic', one becomes aware of a paradox which characterizes artistic reflection in the art-theory of expressionism in general; On the one hand the work of art is looked upon as the result of a subjective expression of the artist, while on the other hand the individual expression has an objective and timeless value. Thus, there is the tendency to exclude the personal and to regard the origin of the work of art as a process that takes place outside the free will of the artist.

The relation between artistic subjectivity and objectivity takes different forms through partly divergent philosophic notions and influences. Along different paths the absolute – as objective dimension – is reached through the artist. In his explanation of the tripartite division of the Inner Necessity, Kandinsky reflects about the way through which the subjective and the objective level relate to one another. Point of departure is an interaction between both levels. The first two personal and time-related factors of the Inner Necessity are in Kandinsky's view, of a relative nature. The individual and temporal components of the creative process, constitute in this conception a subjective nature. Kandinsky explains the development of art from the ability of the artist to transcend these first two levels to reach the 'pure and eternally artistic':

> "The process of the development of art consists to a certain extent in the ability of the pure and eternally artistic to free itself from the elements of personality and temporal style."[4]

The dialectic relation between the subjective and objective is an ever-present factor. It is the dynamic character of the tension between both levels that determines the evolution in art. In this dialectic model, art obtains the significance of a synthesis between the subjective and the objective:

> "In short, then, the effect of inner necessity, and thus the development of art, is the advancing expression of the external–objective in terms of the temporal–subjective. Thus, again, the struggle of the objective against the subjective."[5]

With the notion of a cosmic mission of the artist, the idea is put forward that the work of art is not exclusively the result of a subjective expression. In this conception of the artist as a prophet, art is regarded as a reflection of an objective nature. As was pointed out by Klaus Lankheit, this idea – not uncommon with many other abstract painters – can be traced back to the early romantic philosophy of identity. According to this philosophic notion, nature – as an objective dimension – can be found within Man itself. Amongst others through Schelling's doctrine of the unity of Nature and Spirit, these philosophic notions have been one of the cornerstones of the theory of 20th century abstract painting[6].

Also in the art-theoretical and philosophical reflections of Schönberg there is the explicit awareness of a tension between subjective creativity and artistic objectivity. In this context, it is interesting to quote the philosopher Ernst Bloch. In his *Geist der Utopie* (1918) we find a passage describing the significance of the new harmonies in Schönberg's early atonal works. Bloch notices "selbständige harmonische Ausdruck-relatio-nen" and refers to Schönberg's dictum that the new sound in music is an "unconsciously found symbolic expression of a new man and his new world of feelings"[7]. Further on Bloch mentions "dieser Zusammenfall von Audruckwahrheit und Konstruktionswahrheit" and introduces in this context the concept of 'Expressionslogik'. In the concept of the 'Expressionslogik', subjective expression and the objective component of artistic logic are paradoxically related.

This coinciding of 'Ausdruckwahrheit' and 'Konstruktionswahrheit' seems to contradict or deny a tension between the subjective and objec-tive. In Schönberg's free atonality, subjective intentional content and artistic-constructive form coincide. Bloch refers to "the subjective musical genius" as justification and ultimate instance. The harmonic system constitutes no restrictions by which the genius can be limited. Bloch mentions "das subjektiv Irrationele...das sich über Regeln, letzthin auch über Taktstrich, Dissonanz, Harmonie und Tonalität hinwegsetzen darf."[8]

In Kandinsky's theoretical foundation of abstraction, form and color had likewise been absolute. Against this background, the new relation between emancipated forms and colors in the early abstract work of Kandinsky, can be considered as the pictorial counterpart of what Bloch indicated in music as "selbständige Audruckrelationen".

In Schönberg's philosophic notions and artistic argumentations, theo-retical concepts are closely related. As regard to the issue of the subjective and objective, it is relevant here to shed a light on the concept of 'Idea' with Schönberg. In his interpretation of the Idea, as with the Inner Necessity, three levels can be discerned. The musical technical Idea con-sists of two levels. The totality of a musical composition reveals itself with the composer in a vision. During this moment of artistic inspiration, the composer surveys the totality of tonal relations that he wants to fix. In the next stage of compositional creation Schönberg works at what he indicates as the "reconstruction" of his vision. At this stage, themes, motives and tone-rows are invented. Here, inspiration does not play a decisive role.

The second level of Schönberg's division of the compositional process refers to the issue of self-expression. Schönberg adopts Schopenhauer's notion that the artistic genius – as musical medium – has the ability to intermediate between the 'essence of the cosmos' and the domain of human experience. This revelation of the 'cosmic' or 'absolute', is the third level of meaning in the concept of Idea in the process of compositional construction[9].

Overviewing the three levels of Schönberg's Idea, we become aware that, although through divergent philosophic perspectives, a connection has been made between the levels of subjectivity and objectivity. As in Schopenhauer's philosophy, the subjective mind objectivates itself through its acts. With Schönberg, the artist is the vessel between the absolute and human experience.

Also in Kandinsky's theoretical speculations, the artist has a visionary prophetic power, even a cosmic mission. Through this train of thought self-expression transcends the exclusive individual. The coinciding of Bloch's 'Ausdruckwahrheit' and 'Konstruktionswahrheit' can thus be achieved by this art-theoretic framework. These concepts, refering on the one hand to the intentional artistic, and on the other hand to the logic as an objective rational component, can coincide, because through this speculation expression is connected to the absolute. The act of creation is no longer exclusively expression-of-the-self. The artist is the ultimate instance for the justification of new sounds and new constellations of color and forms.

Rationality, Irrationality and Criticism.

In Thomas Mann's novel *Doktor Faustus* the artistic consciousness of the composer Adrian Leverkühn is projected against a broad cultural-historic background. As is commonly known, through mediation of Theodor Wiesengrund Adorno, Schönberg's music served as the model for the musical implications of the fictive oeuvre of Leverkühn. In *Doktor Faustus*, the dialectic relationship between the mathematic and the ultimate subjective is presented as a Faustian dilemma against the background of a broad cultural panorama. The paradoxical coinciding of rational organization and emotion is connected by Mann with the concepts of freedom, subjectivity and objectivity. In a discussion on creative freedom Adrian Leverkühn argues:

"Aber Freiheit ist ja ein anderes Wort für Subjektivität, und eines Tag hält die es nicht mehr mit sich aus, irgendwann verzweifelt sie an der Möglichkeit, von sich aus schöpferisch zu sein und sucht Schutz und Sicherheit beim Objektiven. Die Freiheit neigt immer zum dialektischen Umschlag. Sie erkennt sich selbst sehr bald in der Gebundenheit, erfüllt sich in der Unterordnung unter Gesetz, Regel, Zwang, System – erfüllt sich darin, das will sagen: hört darum nicht auf, Freiheit zu sein."[10]

Considering this interpretation of the concept of artistic freedom in relation to art in general, one meets problematic issues that clearly can be discerned in the succeeding stages of stylistic development with both Schönberg and Kandinsky.

Apart from simultaneous artistic developments, one notices within artistic thought of both artists an inner conflict stemming from a tension between rational creativity and emotional expression. In the justification of free atonality and dodecaphony as well as in Kandinsky's theoretical foundation of abstraction, there is from time to time a clear need to cope with that tension between intuition and calculation. Against this background, the appeal to the Inner Necessity can be explained as an intensified attempt to defend their achievements for critique from the outside. After the idiomatic evolution of subsequently the early abstract and early atonal works, a new explanation of the concept of freedom had become inevitable.

The conflict between rationality and irrationality in artistic creation was not an isolated personal issue, but can also be regarded in connection with objections that were raised against both abstraction and atonality. The disapproval of the cerebral is one of the most remarkable issues in this critique on the new artistic achievements. Notions related to the cerebral as opposed to the emotional are put in antagonistic terms. The topic of the 'cerebral' as opposed to the 'emotional' was also thematic in a discussion on two other assumed polarities namely that of the 'conscious' and the 'unconscious'. Before, this problematic notion had already been explored extensively by the artists themselves. In his first letter to Schönberg, Kandinsky gives his vision on the future of painting:

"Ich finde eben, dass unsere heutige Harmonie nicht auf dem 'geometrischen' Wege zu finden ist, sondern auf dem direkt antigeometrischen, antilogischen. Und dieser Weg ist der der 'Dissonanzen in der Kunst', also auch in der Malerei ebenso wie in der Musik."[11]

Schönberg's answer to this letter indicates a similar perspective. He writes:

"Ich verstehe das volkommen und bin sicher, dass wir uns da begegnen. Und zwar in dem wichtigsten. In dem, was Sie das 'Unlogische' nennen, und das ich 'Ausschaltung des bewussten Willens in der Kunst' nenne. Auch was Sie über das konstruktive Element schreiben, glaube ich. Jede Formung, die traditionelle Wirkungen anstrebt, ist nicht ganz frei von Bewusstseins-Akten. Und die Kunst gehört aber dem Unbewussten!"[12]

Artistic expression is not determined by craftmanship and rationality. Schönberg recapitulates:

"Das unbewusste Formen aber, das die Gleichung: 'Form=Erscheinungsform' setzt, das allein schafft wirklich Formen."[13]

In Kandinsky's remarks on the origination of abstraction, a comparable relation between the unconscious and the origination of artistic forms is stipulated. In his essay "Reminiscences" (1913) Kandinsky explains:

"Every form I ever used arrived 'of its own accord', presenting itself fully fledged before my eyes, so that I had only to copy it, or else constituting itself actually in the course of work, often to my own suprise."[14]

Kandinsky continuously expresses his mistrust of the rational component in art. Here, the concept of logic – as objective category – is opposed against the emotional. Also in the essay "The value of a concrete work", dated 1938, Kandinsky emphasizes:

"Art forms are not found 'on purpose', by willpower, and nothing is more dangerous in art than to arrive at a 'manner of expression' by logical conclusions. My advice, then, is to mistrust logic in art. And perhaps elsewhere too!"[15]

In a retrospect of his own artistic career, Kandinsky characterizes his artistic development as a gradual process starting with a conscious use of form and color[16]. Already in *Über das Geistige in der Kunst* Kandinsky had mentioned three sources and results of artistic creation in progressing stages of rational organization. At first there are "the direct impressions of 'external nature' expressed in linear-painterly form". Kandinsky denotes these pictures as "Impressions". The second category are the "Improvisations". Kandinsky explains that they are "chiefly unconscious, for the most part suddenly arising expressions of events of an 'inner character', hence impressions of 'internal nature'". The third category Kandinsky mentions are the "Compositions". Kandinsky clarifies at this point:

"The expression of feelings that have been forming within me in a similar way (but over a very long period of time), which, after the first preliminary sketches, I have slowly and almost pendantically examined and worked out."[17]

Kandinsky proceeds:

> *"Here, reason, the conscious, the deliberate, and the purposeful play a dominant role. Except that I always decide in favor of feeling rather than calculation."*[18]

In one of the final passages of *Über das Geistige in der Kunst*, Kandinsky prophesizes that in the near future a conscious system of composition will be achieved. According to this view, painters will be proud to be able to explain their work in terms of 'construction'. It is typical for the issue we are dealing with now, that Kandinsky concludes his book placing these remarks in a mystical context:

> *"We see already before us an age of purposeful creation, and this spirit in painting stands in a direct relation to the creation of a new spiritual realm that is already beginning, for the spirit is the soul of the epoch of the great spiritual."*[19]

In an article, written for *Kroniek van de Hedendaagse Kunst* dated 1936, Kandinsky sums up the most frequently used critical oppositions against abstract art[20]. At first, he mentions the fact that most critics assert that criteria for a quality-estimation of abstract art are lacking. Secondly, the assumed unlimited freedom of morphology is used as an argument for a negative assessment of the abstract idiom.

Finally, Kandinsky mentions the cliché that abstract painting is a cerebral art par excellence[21]. This criticism is based on the conviction that the intuitive capacities of the artist can only be evoked by a material environment. According to this theory, the artist excludes himself from the outer world and hence can only produce a rational art. Kandinsky, defending himself against these arguments, contends that the abstract working artist receives his stimuli from nature not in a "fragmented manner", but that the artist is inspired by "the totality of natural appearances". The current subdivision in the arts is, in the view of Kandinsky, the result of a process of specialization dating from the nineteenth century within artistic as well as in cultural fields. Kandinsky asserts that the exaggerated interest in the outer qualities of artistic form can be understood as the negative output of a cultural and artistic process. The choice of artistic form, Kandinsky mentions at several places, is primarily a concern of the artist.

Also Schönberg's succeeding artistic stages of artistic development – from the late romantic idiom, to free-atonality and, later, dodecaphony – are connected with distinct stages of intellectual involvement and increasing rationalization.

As in Kandinsky's artistic development, in Schönberg's artistic career, one can discern the problematic issue of an increasing rationalization in the use of artistic means. As had been the case in early atonality, also dodecaphony endured critical comments labelling it as being orderless and without form. It is understandable that notably dodecaphony suffered most from these accusations.

Also Schönberg defends himself firmly against the cliché that the dodecaphonal composition is the result of "uninspired construction."[22] In the article "Komposition mit zwölf Tönen", he refers to the "unfailing imagination of the composer" and denies that dodecaphony is a one-sided cerebral method of composition.[23]

Schönberg explains this critique on the cerebral as a "sentimental" and "pre-Wagnerian" aversion against the dissonant. Categories such as 'sharpness' or 'mildness' cannot be criteria for aesthetic evaluation. In *Die formbildende Tendenze der Harmonie* Schönberg clarifies:

> *"Schönheit, ein unerklärter Begriff, ist als Grundlage für ästhetische Unterscheidungen ganz nutzlos, und dasselbe gilt für Gefühl. Solch eine 'Gefühlsästhetik' würde uns zur Unzulänglichkeit einer veralteten Ästhetik zurückbringen."*[24]

Schönberg clearly rejects a 'Gefühlästhetik' that is based on a naïve, hedonistic conception of art.

It is remarkable how Schönberg and Kandinsky, in relation to their later constructivistic and dodecaphonic work, explicitly point to the fact that the origin of a picture or musical composition is a balance of rational and irrational forces. This seems to be not only a defense-system against art-criticism, but may also indicate the presence of an inner conflict. The continuous accentuation of the purely emotional origin of artistic creation may also reveal the artist seeking to hide the rational component of artistic reality.

In his second theoretical treatise *Punkt und Linie zur Fläche* (1926), Kandinsky contemplates the necessity of a 'science of art'. The need for such a new branch of study can, according to Kandinsky, be explained from the need of the painter to achieve a balance between intuitive and calculative forces. In 1935, in the article "Art Today", Kandinsky emphasizes the fact that the painter is guided by his inspiration. The stress on the irrational and unconscious origin of the creative process is opposed here to the constructivistic view on the origination of art.

In an indirect way, Kandinsky refers to a controversy that 10 years before had also played a role at the Bauhaus. Artists such as Kandinsky, Paul Klee and Johannes Itten emphasized the intuitive qualities in art as

opposed to a utilitarian conception of art. Artists like El Lissitzky, Vladimir Tatlin and Aleksandr Rodchenko on the other hand, represented a
group who argued that emotionality and intuition were the remains of a
'bourgeois-sentimentality' that soon had to be replaced by calculative
methods of construction. Kandinsky replied:

> *"Finally, art is never produced by the head alone. We know of great paintings that came
> solely from the heart. In general, the ideal balance between the head (conscious moment)
> and the heart (unconscious moment–intuition) is a law of creation, a law as old as
> humanity."*[25]

Kandinsky thus stresses the fact that this balance is important for
abstraction as well as for figuration:

> *"Neither reason nor logic can be excluded from any consideration of art, but perpetual
> corrections are necessary from the angle of the irrational. The feeling must correct the
> brain. This assertion applies to art in general, without distinction between representa-
> tional and concrete art. From this point of view the two kinds are alike."*[26]

In an interview with the Berlin art-dealer Karl Nierendorf, Kandinsky
defends himself against the accusation that abstract art is of an exclusively rational nature. Asked whether abstract painting is the product of
rational considerations Kandinsky replies:

> *"Man's 'head' is a necessary and important 'organ', but only if organically linked to the
> 'heart' or the 'feeling' – call it what you will. Without this link, one's 'head' is the source
> of all kinds of dangers and disasters. In all realms. Hence in art too. In art even more so:
> there have been great artists without heads. But never without 'hearts'. During great
> periods, and in the case of great artists, there has always been this organic link between
> head and heart (feeling)."*[27]

As has been indicated here before in relation to Schönberg's Idea, inspiration and rational elaboration are distinguishable stages in the creation of
the musical composition. Both aspects are involved in the creation of the
work of art and are not mutually exclusive. Intuition as well as calculation
are essential aspects in the scenario of the musical Idea. In the article
"Brahms, der Fortschrittliche", Schönberg emphasizes this opinion: "Die
Trunkenheit der Phantasie eines Künstlers, sei sie dionysisch oder apolli-
nisch, erhöht die Klarheit seiner Vision."[28]

As with Kandinsky, the emotional and the rational do co-exist harmoniously in the process of artistic creation. In Kandinsky's essay "Thesis–
Antithesis–Synthesis" the dialetic relationship between emotionality and
rationality is brought to the fore. The painter accentuates that both factors

play an equal role in the conception as well as reception of the work of art. There is however, it cannot be denied, a programmatic emphasis on the aspect of feeling:

> *"In conclusion, I would cordially like to advise the transmitter (the artist) and the receiver (the admirer of art) to keep thought and feeling separate from another... One's head is not a bad device. But an 'unfeeling' head is worse than a 'headless' feeling, at least in art."*[29]

In 1937, in the French art journal *Cahiers d'Arts*, we find a summing up of the most frequent objections against abstract art. According to some criticism 'plastic rationalism' deprives abstract art of every possibility of a real evolution. By ignoring physical nature, the artist bans his emotion and over-estimates his technical abilities in the manipulation of forms and colors. Looking at things from this angle, abstract art cannot be an expressive idiom. Kandinsky reports how he had tried several times to 'construct' a picture on a purely rational and mathematic basis. None of these experiments however, had enabled him to solve adequately any artistic problems. Once again Kandinsky mentions that intuition is the common origin of all arts.

Theoretical considerations however, should never play a dominant role in the act of painting. In this context, Kandinsky quotes his master Anton Azbè who had said to him "You must know your anatomy, but in front of your easel you must forget it."[30] In a catalogue of the exhibition "Abstracte Kunst" in the Stedelijk Museum in Amsterdam in 1938, Kandinsky again refers to the artistic process as a synthesis of rational and emotional influences:

> *"To my mind this creative path must be a synthetic one. That is to say, feeling ('intuition') and thought ('calculation') work under mutual 'supervision'. This can happen in various ways. As for me, I prefer not to 'think' while working. It is not entirely unknown that I once did some work on the theory of art. But: woe to the artist whose reason interferes with his 'inner dictates' while he is working."*[31]

Looking back at his musical development, Schönberg emphasizes that rational considerations do not interfere with musical ideas that enter the mind of the artist through his unconscious:

> *"Ich bin immermehr doch noch mehr Komponist als Theoretiker. Und wenn ich komponiere, trachte ich alle Theorien zu vergessen; und ich setze nur fort, wenn ich meinen Geist von solchen Einflüssen frei gemacht habe."*[32]

Schönberg warns for a dogmatic interpretation of his method of composing with twelve tones. He regards dodecaphonic composing in the first place as a method that provides a logical ordering and organization of tone-material. The composer has to trust his total control of the musical laws governing a balanced composition, nonwithstanding the idiom. According to the opinion of Schönberg, craftmanship and professional mastery over the musical material is developed with the true artist 'from within'.[33]

Schönberg and Kandinsky share the typical expressionistic conviction that individual expression searches for a form that suits the subjective intention. Or, in other words, artistic form is not a pre-fixed structure, but is the result of an unconscious process where form and content coalesce.

This view on form in art implies a relativation of style. But abstraction and atonality have been severly rejected by art criticism as being formalistic. In the Soviet–Russian campaign against atonal composers, as well as in later polemics against musical serialists, dodecaphony has been rejected for being formalistic. In painting, the emphasis on formal means has been regarded as the last stage of a process of formalization that had started with the Impressionists. According to this criticism, abstract art has lost all significance because of the fixation on the non-figurative form. The coinciding of form and content is in this rejection the negation of the 'objective' content. This so called 'objective content' can, according to these critics, only be based on optical, mimetic experience. Kandinsky's concept of a painting of 'purely pictorial means', where non-representational pictoral means coincide with the intentional content, is regarded from this viewpoint as a tautologic starting point.[34]

Theodor Wiesengrund Adorno situates the origin of the dodecaphonal method in the context of an increasing tendency of 'Naturbeherrschung' in Western civilization.[35] Pre-determination of tone-material may implicate the danger of 'system-fetish' that finally can be traced back to a fundamental doubt of the composer to make music 'from within'. Through an integral rationalization of musical parameters, the composer runs the risk of placing himself on the outside and thus becomes a slave of a cold and mechanical process where technical principles are goals in themselves.

This increased rationalization had resulted on the artistic level in an abstraction of musical means and concepts. Up to a certain degree, through dodecaphonical determination the relationship between composer and musical material had been revised. At the same time, it should however be emphasized that this development in musical history originated from the urge to intensify the expression of music-for-itself. Adorno describes Schönberg's oeuvre as a "dialectical process" between expression and construction, and characterizes the composer as a "dialectical composer" because by a far reaching rational organization Schönberg has paved the way to a new musical freedom.[36]

In the article "Über einige Relationen zwischen Musik und Malerei", Adorno puts forward a few critical remarks on the rationalization of the compositional process, but he points at the same time to the irrational subjective ideology which these artistic developments are actually based upon.[37]

Comparable critique concerning the coincidence of extreme subjectivism and 'rational compulsion' was also aimed against Kandinsky's painting. In this criticism on his abstract idiom the over-emphasis on formal means is rejected likewise. At the same time, the critique is pointed against the artistic rationalization that is regarded as being incompatible with intuitive artistic creation. According to this argumentation, the abstract-working artist cuts himself out of the assumed 'objective' and 'optic' world and looses himself in a far reaching determination and systematization of formal means.

From another angle, the gap between artistic–technical conception and the receptive capabilities, are interpreted as an alienation of the artist with his social environment.[38] This alienation is also interpreted as the result of social circumstances. In this train of thought the programmatic emphasis on the subjective–emotional can be regarded as a psychological and artistic reaction to the 'de-individualization' of Western Society. By withdrawing into his most individual experience, the artist defends himself against the threat the individual faces within a technological and bureaucratic society.[39]

In their later artistic career, both Schönberg and Kandinsky had arrived at a point where an equilibrium between emotionality and artistic constructivism had become increasingly problematic. This issue was reflected in their artistic productivity as well as in the art–theoretical writings supporting – and even defending – their artistic decisions.

One might conclude that an essential shift has taken place in the relation between art–technical decisions on the one hand and the emotional urge to expression on the other hand. It seems as if, with the gradual autonomization of artististic parameters, the distance between artist and artwork gradually has been increased and has become problematic. This development can be interpreted as an increased consciousness of the contrast between 'Gefühlsästhetik' and 'Materialästhetik'.

The issue of a tension between rationality and spontaneous expression presented here, points to more than the existence of an academic polemic. The appearance of an increased awareness of a problematic relation between the rational mind and emotion cannot be understood as an isolated or purely artistic phenomenon.

It is my view that advanced research into the simultaneousness of atonality and abstraction should not be based primarily on the level of traditional musicological or art–historical philology, but on a wider comprehension of contemporary socio-cultural developments. The concept of the work of art as a monad still has not lost its suggestive power.

NOTES

1. A comparable tri-division can be found in the art-theoretical debate of early Expressionism. Besides the element of the individual artistic vision, artistic vision is regarded as that what has been determined by external factors. The art-theorist Riegl mentions the "external" factors of milieu and time as "Kunstwollen". The artist has a "Weltgefühl" that is determined by the relation with his environment. Artistic form or style therefore, is more than the reflection of an inner state of mind. See for theoretical concepts in expressionism: G. Perkins *Contemporary theory of Expressionism*, Bern/Frankfurt.
2. *Harmonielehre*, Leipzig/Vienna 1911 p. 466.
3. Ibid., p. 144.
4. *Über das Geistige in der Kunst* (Translated as *On the Spiritual in Art* in: *Kandinsky. Complete writings on art.* ed. K.C. Lindsay and P. Vergo London 1982 p. 174. Quotations from Kandinsky's complete works are cited from this edition, abbreviated as *KCW*.
5. Ibid., (*KCW*. p. 175).
6. See K. Lankheit, "Die Frühromantik und die Grundlagen der 'gegenstandslosen' Malerei", in *Neue Heidelberger Jahrbücher*, 1951, par. III en IV, pp. 82–90.
7. *Harmonielehre*, p. 447.
8. *Geist der Utopie* Gesamtausgabe Vol. 3, second edition 1923, Frankfurt am Main 1964, pp. 162–163.
9. With regard to the different levels of meaning of the "Idea" with Schönberg see C.M. Cross in: "Three levels of Idea in Schoenberg's thought and writings", in *Current Musicology*, nr. 30 (1980) pp. 24–36.
10. *Thomas Mann. Doktor Faustus, das Leben des deutschen Tonsetzers Adrian Leverkühn, erzählt von einem Freunde*, Stockholmer Gesamtausgabe der Werke von Thomas Mann, 1947, p. 295. Thomas Mann describes the main motive of his book as "Die Nähe der Sterilität, die eingeborene und zum Teufelspakt prädisponierende Verzweiflung", see: *Die Entstehung Dr. Faustus*, Berlin 1949, p. 60.
11. *Arnold Schönberg. Wassily Kandinsky. Briefe, Bilder und Dokumente einer aussergewöhlichen Begegnung*, ed. J. Hahl-Koch, Salzburg/Vienna 1980, p. 19.
12. Ibid., p. 21.
13. Idem.
14. "Reminiscences" ("Rückblicke" in *Kandinsky, 1901–1913*, Berlin 1913 (*KCW*., p. 370).
15. "The value of a concrete work", in *XXe Siècle*, Paris 1938–39 (*KCW*., p. 827).
16. See "Cologne lecture" ("Kandinsky über seine Entwicklung"), in *Kandinsky und Gabriele Münter, von Ursprüngen moderner Kunst*, Munich, 1957 (*KCW*., p. 393).
17. *KCW*., pp. 218–219.
18. Idem.

19. Idem.
20. See "Abstract Painting" ("Abstrakte Malerei"), in *Kroniek van hedendaagsche kunst en kultuur*, Amsterdam 1936 (*KCW.*, p. 784–789).
21. See for a defense against this criticism "Two suggestions" ("Zwei Ratschläge" in *Berliner Tageblatt*; Berlin 1929. (*KCW.*, p. 735–743).
22. "Zeitwende" in *Aufsätze zur Musik. Gesammelte Schriften, Arnold Schönberg*, ed. I. Vojtech, Nördlingen 1976, p. 384. Schönberg's complete writings cited here from this edition are abbreviated as *AzM*.
23. "Komposition mit zwölf Tonen" in *AzM.*, p. 75.
24. *Die formbildenden Tendenzen der Harmonie*, New York 1954, p. 190.
25. "Art Today", in *Cahiers d'Art*, Paris 1935 (*KCW.*, p. 771).
26. "The value of a concrete work", in *XXe Siècle*, Paris 1938–39 (*KCW.*, p. 827).
27. "Interview with Karl Nierendorf" in *Essays über Kunst und Künstler*, Bern/Bümpliz 1963 (*KCW.*, p. 807).
28. "Brahms, der Fortschrittliche" in *Stil und Gedanke*, quoted here from *AzM* p. 49.
29. "Thesis–Antithesis–Synthesis", in *Exhibition catalogue "thèse–antithèse–synthèse"* Kunstmuseum Luzern 1935 (*KCW.*, pp. 772–773).
30. "Reflections on abstract art" ("Reflexions sur l'art abstrait"), in *Cahiers d'Art*, Paris 1931 (*KCW.*, p. 759).
31. "Abstract or concrete" ("Abstract of concreet?"), in *Tentoonstelling abstracte kunst*, Amsterdam 1938 (*KCW.*, p. 832). See for the idea of a synthesis between intuition and rational analytic thinking with Kandinsky "The value of theoretical instruction in painting ("Der Wert des theoretischen Unterrichts in der Malerei", in *Bauhaus*; Dessau 1926 (*KCW.*, pp. 701–705).
    A comparable explicit discussion on this thematical issue can be found with Schönberg in his article "Herz und Hirn in der Musik", in *StuG.*, pp. 104–122.
32. "Rückblicke" in *AzM.*, p. 40.
33. In "Probleme des Kunstunterrichts" Schönberg makes an explicit distinction between the craftsman and the artist: "Der Kunsthandwerker kann. Was ihm angeboren ist, hat er ausgebildet; und wenn er nur will, so kann er. . . . Aber der Künstler muss. Er hat keinen Einfluss darauf, von seinem Willen hängt es nicht ab." *AzM.*, p. 165.
34. A typical example of neo-marxistic criticism on Kandinsky's abstract painting is R. Korn's book *Kandinsky und die Theorie der abstrakten Malerei*, Berlin 1960. For a comparison relating to this criticism see "Arnold Schönberg im russischen Kulturkeis", in *Bericht über den 1. Kongress der Internationalen Schönberg-Gesellschaft*, Vienna 1974, pp. 187–195.
35. *Philosophie der neuen Musik*, Tübingen, in Philosophie der neuen Musik, Tübingen 1949, p. 88.
36. "Der dialektische Komponist" in *Musikalische Schriften IV*, Gesammelte Schriften vol. 17, Frankfurt am Main 1982 pp. 198–204. Compare Adorno in "Arnold Schönberg und der Fortschritt", in *Gesammelte Schriften*, vol. 16, Frankfurt am Main 1978, pp. 628–642.
    See for aesthetic controversies relating to artistic freedom and music–technical considerations J. H. Lederer "Pfitzner–Schönberg: Theorie und Gegensätze", in *Archiv für Musikwissenschaft*, Abl. 35 (1978) pp. 297–309.
    Compare H. Pfrogner "Das Inhalt-Form-Problem im Schaffen Arnold Schönberg", in *Österreichische Musikzeitschrift*, 2 (1947), pp. 266–269.
37. T. W. Adorno, "Über einige Relationen zwischen Musik und Malerei", in *Gesammelte Schriften*, vol. 16, Frankfurt am Main 1978, pp. 628–642.
38. The German art-critic Wilhelm Worringer opposes in 1908, in his book *Abstraktion und Einfühlung*, the tendency of abstraction against naturalism. "Abstraktionsdrang" is interpreted here as the reflection of a fundamental distortion in the relation between humanity and its physical environment.

39. See for the historical and sociological background R. Brinkmann, "Schönberg und das expressionistische Audruckskonzept", in *Bericht über den 1. Kongress der Internationalen Schönberg Gesellschaft*, Vienna 1974, pp. 13–19.

Notes on Contributors

Konrad Boehmer studied Composition, Musicology, Philosophy and Sociology in Cologne, where he completed his degree thesis "Zur Theorie der offenen Form in der neuen Musik" (published 1967 in Darmstadt). Professor at the Royal Conservatory, The Hague, since 1972, he has been director of the Institute of Sonology, the large studio for electroacoustic music within the Conservatory, since 1994. In 1993 his book *Das Böse Ohr* (*The Malicious Ear, Writings 1961–1991*) was published by DuMont.

Reinhold Brinkmann studied Music, Musicology, German Literature and Philosophy in Hamburg and Freiburg. He was professor of Musicology in Marburg 1972–80 and at the Academy of Fine Arts in Berlin 1980–85. From 1985 he has been professor of Music at Harvard University, where he has held the James Edward Ditson chair since 1990. His special field of research is Arnold Schönberg and the Second Viennese School.

Albrecht Dümling studied Music, Musicology, German Literature and Journalism in Essen and Berlin. In 1978 his "Öffentliche Einsamkeit. Untersuchungen zur Situation von Lied und Lyrik um 1900 am Beispiel des 'Buches der Hängenden Gärten' von Stefan George und Arnold Schönberg" was published as a book. He was co-organisor of the exhibition "Entartete Musik" shown in Germany, The Netherlands and the U.S.A. He is currently director of the Hanns Eisler Archiv in Berlin.

Frans Evers studied psychology with professor N. Frijda in Amsterdam. He is dean of the Interfaculty Sound and Image, an institute which links the Royal Academy of Fine Arts and the Royal Conservatory of Music in Den Haag (The Netherlands). He was one of the main initiators of the Schönberg–Kandinsky Symposium. He is editor-in-chief of a book on music psychology published by Van Gorcum, Assen, in 1995.

Bulat M. Galeyev is a Russian scholar currently working at the Prometheus Institute in Kazan. Mr Galeyev has done research in the field of kinetic art and is preparing a book on Scriabin.

Jelena Hahl was born in Riga and spent her school years in Germany. She took her degree in Heidelberg on "Marianne Werefkin and Russian Symbolism". From 1965 to 1971 she was a university lecturer in Russian language and literature at Erlangen. In 1976 and 1977 she lectured on

"Kandinsky in Tutzing" at Harvard, UCLA, Ann Arbor, Wayne State University and several other universities in the USA. Her book *Arnold Schönberg/Wassily Kandinsky, Briefe, Bilder und Dokumente einer außergewöhnlichen Begegnung* (dtv, 1983) has been published in England (Faber & Faber, 1984), France, Japan, Spain and Italy.

Job IJzerman studied piano in Utrecht and music theory at the Royal Conservatory, The Hague, where he is now professor of Music Theory. He also lectures at the Conservatories of Hilversum and Amsterdam. His specialisation is the music of the Second Viennese School. He has published "Die Symmetrie in Weberns Orchesterstück op. 10 Nr. 1" (*Musiktheorie*, Laaber, 1990/2).

Hans Janssen studied art and history in Groningen. He was curator of Modern Art at the Bonnefantenmuseum, Maastricht, from 1987 until 1991. Since 1991 he has been curator of Modern Art at the Municipal Museum, Den Haag (Haags Gemeentemuseum).

Klaus Kropfinger was until recently professor of Musicology at the Free University, Berlin. At present he holds the chair of the Music Department of Kassel University. He is a contributor to the complete editions of Beethoven's as well as of Hindemith's compositions. He has written widely on music history and aesthetics from the 18th to the 20th century (especially about the Second Viennese School, Busoni and Nono). Special aspects of his research are the perception of music and the relationship between music and painting – especially between Schönberg and Kandinsky. His book *Wagner and Beethoven* was recently published in a revised edition by Cambridge University Press.

Laurens van der Heijden completed doctoral degrees both in musicology and in art history at Utrecht University. After graduating he studied with Reinhold Brinkmann in the USA. He has specialised in the interrelationship between the arts, in particular between painting and music. At the moment he is preparing his dissertation on abstraction and atonality.

Irina L. Vanechkina is a Russian scholar currently working at the Prometheus Institute in Kazan. She has undertaken research in the field of kinetic art.

Index

As the names of Arnold Schönberg and Vassily Kandinsky appear on nearly all pages, they have not been included in this index. The spelling—especially of Russian names—corresponds to the orthography of the different articles. Alternative spellings are indicated by [ ].

217